Kayaking
Vancouver
Island

Kayaking Vancouver Island

Gary Backlund & Paul Grey

Harbour Publishing

Published by
Harbour Publishing Co. Ltd.,
P.O. Box 219, Madeira Park, BC V0N 2H0
www.harbourpublishing.com

Edited by Audrey McClellan, Nadine Pedersen and Craig Carpenter
Cover and page design by Roger Handling
Maps by Paul Grey and Gary Backlund
Front cover photograph of Poett Nook by Gary Backlund
Back cover photograph of islets off Vargas Island by Jacqueline Windh
All photographs by Paul Grey and Gary Backlund except on pages: 11, 15, 17, 25,
81, 105, 127, 135, 145, 149, 154, 191 by Jacqueline Windh; 118, 286 Keith
Thirkell; 86, 92, 102 Bob Milne; 56, 58, 59 Kelly Irving; 8, 12, 23, 65, 73 Michael
Levy; 268, 265 Celia Norris; 27 Jim Belfry; 151, 153 Nicole Roth; 181 Mark
Kaarremaa; 193 Brian Colleen; 229 Chantelle Tucker; title page Leo Hebert; 238
courtesy Campbell River Museum.

Printed and bound in Canada

Harbour Publishing acknowledges the financial support from the Government of
Canada through the Book Publishing Industry Development Program (BPIDP) and
the Canada Council for the Arts, and the Province of British Columbia through the
British Columbia Arts Council, for its publishing activities.

THE CANADA COUNCIL | LE CONSEIL DES ARTS
FOR THE ARTS | DU CANADA
SINCE 1957 | DEPUIS 1957

National Library of Canada Cataloguing in Publication Data

Grey, Paul, 1951-
  Kayaking Vancouver Island : great trips from Port Hardy to Victoria /
Paul Grey, Gary Backlund.

  Includes index.
  ISBN 1-55017-318-9

  1. Sea kayaking--British Columbia--Vancouver Island--Guidebooks. 2.
Vancouver Island (B.C.)--Guidebooks. I. Backlund, Gary, 1951- II.
Title.
GV776.15.B7G74 2003   797.1'224'097112   C2003-910505-9

Contents

Acknowledgements

Local information can be invaluable. The authors of *Kayaking Vancouver Island* are greatly indebted to the following people, who shared their time and knowledge in order to make your future paddling more enjoyable. Thanks to all of them.

Peter Harris of Vancouver Island Kayak and Canoe Centre in Victoria answered many questions about the latest paddling equipment and Sooke, Finlayson Arm and Clayoquot kayaking. **Scot Taylor** of The Ocean Kayak Institute and Rush Adventures gave us pointers on paddling Sooke Basin and Harbour.

We'd like to thank the many kayaking guides, outfitters and experts who donated their time to fact-check sections of this book. Among others they include: Joanna Streely, Jackie Windh, Penny Mullen of Hornby Ocean Kayaks, and Brian Cullen of Pacific Northwest Expeditions.

Tips and advice from **Jack Rosen** of Island Escapades and **Bill Elford** of Sea Otter Kayaking on Saltspring Island expanded our knowledge of Saltspring and neighbouring islands. **Sue Konen**, owner of Kayak Pender Island, provided us with detailed information about the Pender Islands.

John Waibel and **Christine Portmann** from Spirit of the West gave good advice for paddling Quadra Island. We have crossed **Liam Edwards'** (Geophilia Adventures) path a few times (though we haven't always seen him), and he has given us a wealth of information about Quadra Island, particularly Granite Bay.

We spent a couple of hours with **Pat Kervin** from Odyssey Kayaking of Port Hardy in a coffee shop perusing local charts and getting his suggestions for local kayaking routes. We would also like to thank **Debbie Erickson** from North Island Kayaks of Port Hardy for sharing her knowledge of local history.

Over a cappuccino at **Dan O'Conner'**s (Zeballos Expeditions) house in Zebellos, we learned about his town, and about Nutchatlitz and Catala Island. Thanks to **Leo Jack** of Kyoquot Water Taxi, who ferried us to Rugged Point from Fair Harbour and gave us a bit of a First Nations perspective of the area.

Many people, including the members of the **Nanaimo Paddlers Club**, gave advice for paddling Clayoquot Sound. A special thanks goes to **Dan Lewis** of Rainforest Kayak Adventures for helping us gain cultural and ecological sensitivity for this area.

Tracy Morben of Majestic Kayaking and **Randy Oliwa** of Coastal Knights took time from their busy schedules to highlight the best of Ucluelet for us. On the other side of Barkley Sound in Bamfield, **Liz Isaac** of Bamfield Kayak Centre and **John and Sheryl Mass** of Broken Island Adventures shared their intimate understanding of Bamfield and the Deer Group.

We thank both **Ian Race** and the people of Current Designs and **John Surtees** and the people of Seaward Kayaks for building great Vancouver Island-made kayaks.

A number of people made essential contributions including the **Canadian Coast Guard/Garde côtiere canadienne**; **Drew Chapman** of BC Parks; the **Clandening family** regarding Quadra Island; **Elida Peers** for information on Sooke's history; **Sandra Parrish,** the Exhibit/Collections Manager of the Campbell River Museum; and the **Webb family** (especially Kelsey) for their hospitality at the Peninsula Motor Inn.

We would like to give special thanks to our families as they saw us through the trials and tribulations of producing a second kayaking book. A very big thanks to **Teesh Backlund** for her many hours of editing and proofreading and her suggested improvements. Last of all, thanks to all the friendly folks we met and visited with while researching and paddling our way through this book.

Happy paddling,
Gary Backlund
Paul Grey

Paul's introduction

Paddlers are aware of the mystery and beauty of Vancouver Island long before they set foot on it. An enticing call to paddlers everywhere echoes well past the shores of this legendary island. Almost unparalleled beauty awaits the kayaker along its beaches, harbours, inlets and coastal islands. The magic of Vancouver Island waters is experienced in many ways—as you hike trails through old-growth forests, shower under cool waterfalls, watch bears scrounge for shellfish at low tide, paddle past sea otters floating idly on their backs, listen to the eerie call of loons in a lonely passage, or gaze at lichen hanging from trees overhanging the ocean's edge.

Vancouver Island, on the west coast of Canada, stretches parallel to the BC mainland. It is 460 km (285 mi) long and its width varies from 50 to 120 km (31 to 75 mi). The moderating influence of the Pacific Ocean gives Vancouver Island the mildest climate in Canada. The combination of mild climate and incredible beauty is perhaps the reason it's the most paddled place in the world.

For this book, Gary and I have chosen some spectacular paddling places that capture the heart and soul of Vancouver Island kayaking. The trips vary from serene inner-city day paddling to rugged West Coast kayaking and camping. Whether you wish to paddle Long Harbour on Saltspring Island or depart from Little Espinosa Inlet toward the Pacific Ocean and Nuchatlitz and Catala Island Provincial Parks, there are trips that fit your paddling desires.

The mystique of Vancouver Island is enhanced when the kayaker knows the local history that accompanies most of these paddling paradises. The island's First Nations people developed a rich culture with unsurpassed carvings, costumes, and legends. English and Spanish explorers later navigated the area's deep fjords and inside waterways looking for passages and riches. Their names mark many of the points, bays, harbours, straits and inlets of the island. Europeans came to Vancouver Island to harvest sea otter pelts, mine coal, log, fish for salmon and cod, and settle the land as pioneers. Some lost the battle with nature, but many won, and all were part of a vanishing breed of hardy souls that could live remotely and mainly off the abundance of the land. We sometimes see a glimpse of their stories as we float past an old farm or walk through the remnants of a log cabin amidst an over-grown orchard tucked away in some small, remote cove.

We have often been asked, "What's your favourite trip?" It's a really difficult question to answer. On the northeast tip of Vancouver Island we had a dreamlike paddle around Beaver Harbour. Our visit included sightings of porpoises and seal pups, and the chance of seeing a visiting grey, humpback or minke whale.

Tofino, a west coast tourist town near Pacific Rim Park, is the launching site to Clayoquot Sound, a timeless place where pad-dlers could spend a summer. In our book we describe a breath-taking paddle along the old-growth-covered shores of Meares Island and amazing sand beaches of Vargas Island Park. Few kayakers leave Clayoquot Sound unaffected by its magic.

We paddled a historic waterway called the Gorge that winds through the heart of Victoria. From the late 1800s through to the early 1900s the Gorge was a summertime paradise and play-ground. A scenic paddle past the Inner Harbour and its hustle and bustle revealed a completely different perspective of Victoria.

The Southern Gulf Islands in the Strait of Georgia are a unique marine environment from both a wilderness and a geological perspective. We describe several trips from Saltspring Island, a popular summer destination. For example, launch from Long Harbour, paddle past many luxury homes and journey to Prevost Island Protected Area Marine Park where you can camp in an old orchard above a small beach. Your reward may be the surprised look of a mink on the water's edge or simply a paddle past a new coastline.

Three and a half hours north of Victoria on the east coast of Vancouver Island lies Campbell River, with Quadra and Cortes islands, the Discovery Islands, nearby. I cherish the day we spent exploring Quadra's Granite Bay. It was late August and hot when we arrived in this cozy bay that boasts a population of 16 people. We soon found ourselves amidst a marine miracle—hundreds of thousands of moon jellyfish "belling" their way into nearby Small Inlet. Later in the day we hiked from Small Inlet to a view of Octopus Marine Park and witnessed ferns emitting thousands of spores into the air. Some days of kayaking are extraordinary. What else could one ask for?

There's a lot more to discover on Vancouver Island. The island has a lifetime of paddling adventures and magical spots that will call you back again and again. Rekindle friendships and family bonds by sharing the beauty of a wilderness beach and a setting sun. After supper experience a quiet, windless evening paddling along a rocky shore or walking a pristine beach. For those of you who have never set foot on a Vancouver Island wilderness beach or kayaked along its unique shorelines, a fantastic new experience awaits you. For the rest of you who know the joys I've just described, I hope this book helps you find some new special paddling places.

Happy paddling!

Paul Grey

Gary's Introduction

The soft song of a small bird marks the moment when dawn gently strikes. I lie comfortably in my tent listening as the next bird calls. Soon there's music all around me. Eventually another form of nature calls and I emerge from my tent.

The sun hasn't risen, or maybe it's just up. That's my time. No one is stirring but me. The stiffness from sleeping on the ground quickly disappears as I start my walk. There are fresh animal and bird tracks in the sand. The daytime hunters, seed gatherers and nectar feeders are all looking for breakfast.

I take a short walk, enjoying the peacefulness of the hour. If I'm lucky I find a handful of wild berries. Then it's back in the tent and my cozy sleeping bag for an hour of reading. The view from my tent is usually spectacular, either huge old-growth trees with massive trunks or beautiful British Columbia beach landscapes of rugged mountains and water.

The sky is usually trying to make up its mind. Sun or clouds, what will it be today? Patches of blue appear and disappear. I turn on the VHF weather channel and listen for the day's weather and marine forecasts.

The bird song is replaced by the quiet call of a male duck. Eagle cries echo in the distance. Soon gulls are screeching, joined by noisy crows and the occasional raven. My peace and serenity are gone for a moment. Then I hear the whooshing of heavy wings and I see branches bobbing at the edge of my view out the zippered screen entrance. Something large has landed. A deer walks within a few metres of my tent.

It's hard to read when the view is fantastic and wildlife keeps distracting me. Soon I hear Paul and our other paddling compan-

ions rising, and it's time for breakfast. As we gather to make our hot chocolate, tea, coffee, oatmeal, pancakes, etc., a woodpecker drums so noisily that we can hardly talk over it. Our next entertainment is an eagle flying by, with nine gulls in half-hearted pursuit. Breakfast always seems to taste just a little better outdoors.

This typical kayaking morning is simply the start of why I love paddling. If God's willing and the winds don't blow, the day only gets better. My hope in writing this book is to give you, the reader, an opportunity to experience some of the joy Vancouver Island paddling brings.

For those of you who have not yet started kayaking, I encourage you to give it a try. You might be 8 or 78, you needn't go far, but you should experience the feeling. It's not like being in a canoe or rowboat; you don't feel as if you're in a boat. It's more like the boat is part of you, as if you're wearing it. You feel as if you're in the water instead of on it. There are plenty of Vancouver Island companies that specialize in providing a gentle introduction to first-time kayaking. Try it. You might really like it!

Happy paddling!

Gary Backlund

Introduction

Getting Started

Vancouver Island is a kayaking paradise. It would take a lifetime to explore all its paddling areas, but we have travelled much of the island, taking to the water and also talking to outfitters, guides and kayakers about the best kayaking in their areas. From our own experience and the advice of others we have chosen some favourite paddling places for this book.

How did we choose them? We started with those narrow, pristine waterways and still lagoons with towering mountains and the echoing cry of eagles. Then we looked for interesting historical locations like Sooke Basin, Bamfield and Malaspina Galleries. We also added an urban paddle, Victoria's Gorge Waterway, which offers a change from the typical wilderness experience.

Our favourite kayaking is in serene water conditions, so we've looked for paddling areas that provide some shelter should the weather not fully co-operate with your plans. The whitecaps can be thrilling, but a day of exploring beautiful Vancouver Island coastline in idyllic conditions is unparalleled.

For the paddling areas and paddling trips described in this book we have included difficulty ratings and the approximate distance of the trip as well as the time it will take, plus the relevant references

for charts, tide tables and marine weather forecasts. We explain each of these headings below, but first a few words on safety.

Basic Safety

Before setting out on a kayaking trip you should know how to do a self- and assisted-rescue; how to read charts and tide and current tables; how to use a compass; and how to interpret a marine weather forecast. We also recommend that you file a float plan before every trip so that people know where to look for you if you don't return from a trip on time.

Always kayak with at least one other person. Stay within calling or whistle-blowing distance of each other. A two-person rescue is much easier than a self-rescue. Also, it's hard for boaters to see lone kayaks. If you are in a group of kayaks, other boats are less likely to run into you. You should be familiar with the water's "Rules of the Road," also known as "Collision Regulations." Check out the Government of Canada marine safety web site for the Pacific Region (*http://www.tc.gc.ca/pacific/faq/marine/boatingsafety.htm*) or the Canadian Coast Guard site (*www.ccg-gcc.gc.ca/obs-bsn/sbg- gsn/main_e.htm*). They have the rules of the road, plus a list of required safety equipment, details on how to obtain a "Safe Boating Guide" booklet, and other useful information.

Having the proper equipment is essential. According to the safe boating regulations for kayaks under 6 m (20 ft) you must have an approved personal flotation device (PFD) or lifejacket for each person on board, a bailer or pump, a whistle or other signalling device, navigation lights (if you're paddling at night), a paddle and a buoyant heaving line at least 15 m (50 ft) long.

Kayaks over 6 m (20 ft), which include many doubles, require the above-mentioned equipment plus at least three flares. Although not part of the regulations, a sprayskirt is also needed for safe kayaking. Carrying more than this basic equipment, such as a compass, chart and at least one spare paddle, will give added security. Expensive items such as a GPS locator can be helpful for navigation, and having a VHF radio could be a lifesaver. You can find information on these topics in our first kayaking book, *Easykayaker*, and in other "how-to" sea kayaking guides.

It is good practice to take a litre of drinking water for a day's kayaking—more for hot days. Have the water accessible. It's easy to get dehydrated. Take a snack to help maintain energy levels. We also carry a first aid kit, waterproof matches, toilet paper and a change of clothes in a waterproof bag.

Information on Paddling Areas

Trip Rating Guidelines

For the purpose of rating the difficulty of trips outlined in this book, we have broken kayaking skills into three categories. The following ratings assume you are travelling in normal summer marine conditions with moderate winds (less than 20 knots—see "Marine Winds and Weather" below) and moderate tide changes. When assigning ratings we took into consideration the length of the trip and of open-water crossings, the likelihood you'd face rough sea conditions and the availability of landing sites in case things got beyond your comfort level.

Although you should consider the length of your paddling experience when ranking your skill level, you also need to evaluate your navigational ability (i.e., your ability to read charts and use a compass), your overall comfort level for paddling in waves and tidal currents, and other factors such as strength, endurance, balance, speed of your reflexes and age.

The ratings only apply if paddlers heed the warnings listed for each paddling area.

All trips rated intermediate are suitable for novice paddlers if done with a guide or adventure outfitter.

Novice: Two years or less paddling experience, comfortable in small non-breaking waves and mild currents up to 2 knots, minimal navigational abilities.

Intermediate: Three to nine years of experience, comfortable in whitecap conditions and waves up to 1.5 m (5 ft) in height, experienced paddling in tidal currents, good navigational abilities and some experience with small-surf landings.

Advanced: Ten or more years' experience or have taken advanced guide training, comfortable in 3-m (10-ft) waves and breaking seas, experience paddling in tidal rapids with whirlpools, excellent navigational skills, very familiar with marine weather, capable of doing surf landings.

Trip Length Guidelines

We described trips included in this book as half-day, full-day or multi-day excursions. We assume a travel speed of 4 km/hr (2.5 mph) for fully loaded kayaks and 6 km/hr (3.75 mph) for relatively empty kayaks (day paddles). As above, this is based on normal summer marine conditions of moderate winds and tide changes.

Many of the places described are not so much trips as they are paddling areas that a kayaker could take an hour, a day or even a few days to explore fully.

Trip Distance

The trip distances shown are approximations, and we indicate whether they are one way or round trip. When we give the distance to a cove, it usually indicates how far it is to the head of the cove. The distance given is the most direct route. When planning a trip you can expect to paddle farther as most paddlers explore many of the ins and outs of the coastline and take short side trips to explore other points of interest.

Canadian Hydrographic Service Charts

For each paddling area described in this book we give the number(s) of the Canadian Hydrographic Service (CHS) chart or charts that cover that area. CHS charts are available at some magazine outlets and most kayak and marine shops. They are best kept in large ziplock bags or plastic marine chart bags. The charts can also be laminated, but most kayakers prefer using the chart bags instead because laminated charts are harder to fold.

Most of the marine charts for Vancouver Island waters are drawn at a scale of 1:40,000, although some are at 1:20,000 or 1:80,000. The 1:40,000 scale is ideal for kayaking because one inch equals one kilometre on these charts. As we normally travel between 4 and 6 km/hr (about 3 mph), it's easy to predict paddling times and crossing times—if winds and currents don't play too large a factor. Usually a chart of 1:40,000 scale can be folded to fit the chart bag so that the area covered by one day's paddling is visible without having to refold the chart halfway through the day.

CHS charts contain useful information about things like tidal flows, rapids, whirlpools, depths and even kelp beds. The federal government's Department of Fisheries and Oceans publishes a booklet called *Symbols, Abbreviations and Terms*, which sells for about $6. This booklet explains the symbols and notes you will see on marine charts, including the type of shoreline and beach.

The Canadian Hydrographic Services website, *www.charts. gc.ca*, contains information on CHS products, including price lists and contact information for some of the dealers. You can order charts directly from CHS by calling 250-363-6358. You can also write to *chartsales@pac.dfo-mpo.qc.ca* or:

Canadian Hydrographic Service
Pacific Coast Distribution Office
9860 Saanich Road
Sidney, BC V8L 4B2

Tide References

For each paddling area we list a tidal reference port. Tide predictions for Vancouver Island and the Gulf Islands are listed for these ports in *Tide and Current Tables*, Vol. 5 and 6. Tide times in the paddling area may vary slightly depending on its distance from the reference port. If the tide times vary by more than 15 minutes, we will mention it. (As well, from April to October you have to remember to add an hour to the times given in the tables to allow for Pacific Daylight Time.)

You can make more prudent plans and decisions if you know what the tides will be doing before you leave shore. Here are a few reasons for knowing tide levels and direction:

➤ Knowing the tidal flow will help you predict currents so that you can paddle with instead of against them.

➤ Knowing when slack tides or minor tide changes occur will make it safer to travel through areas, such as a narrows or a pass, that normally have currents.

➤ Waiting for a tide change might provide you with improved water conditions, as tide flowing in the same direction as the wind produces calmer water.

➤ Knowing how high the tide will come up overnight can be very important when you are choosing a tent site on the beach.

➤ Knowing when and how far the tide will ebb might save you from getting stranded on mud flats at low tide—sometimes requiring a portage up to a kilometre to reach deeper water.

The Canadian Hydrographic Service publishes *Tide and*

Current Tables annually, and they are available for the very affordable price of $6.50 per volume.

Local advertisers often produce tide booklets that are available for free or at very low cost. These predict tides in feet rather than in metres. The booklets are also corrected for Daylight Saving Time. Because they are small, it's handy to have one of these stashed in a ziplock bag in the back pocket of your PFD.

The Internet is also a great place to find tide information for the locations featured in this book. Check out the links under the "Reference Tables" section on our Easykayaker website at *www.easykayaker.com*. This site also lists the tidal reference points to use for looking up tides for each area.

Currents

Most kayakers paddle at a speed of about 3 to 3.5 knots, but Gary and I have travelled at speeds of up to 5 knots with a mild current in our favour. (Note that a knot, which means nautical mile per hour, equals 1.852 km/hour.) On the other hand, a combination of a headwind and a 1 to 3 knot current against you can turn the joy of gliding easily through the water into work. In several Gulf Islands passes the current can flow at more than 5 knots (Dodd Narrows, for example, can flow at close to 10 knots), making it impossible to paddle against and dangerous to paddle with—you can lose control or be drawn into a whirlpool or onto the rocks. For this reason, you will want to enter a pass during or near a slack water time, which is usually when the tide is changing directions.

Tide and Current Tables, Vol. 5 and 6, provide slack water times and maximum flow times for current reference stations and secondary stations in Vancouver Island waters. Current tables are provided for each of the current stations, which are located in areas that have substantial currents. A listing at the back of the book gives secondary station information for the weaker current areas. This list tells you which current station table to consult for the secondary station and what flow speed and time adjustments to make. (For example, if you want to look up current information for False Narrows, the secondary station list tells you to refer to the table for Dodd Narrows. The flow will be 50 or 55 percent of that at Dodd and you will need to add 10 or 25 minutes or subtract 35 minutes depending on the four factors listed.)

You can locate the more dangerous passes by referring to these tables and also by looking for current arrows on the marine charts. Look for the symbol ◆A on charts, for the location of current stations. Weaker currents are shown on the chart with current arrows and speeds. Beginning kayakers often miss the ◆A symbol and enter into dangerous water conditions unwittingly, assuming an area is safe because they don't see a current arrow on the chart.

The waters outside some of the fast-moving passes can be affected for quite a distance. You may be drawn into the passage or encounter a tidal rip if you are too close to the mouth. A tidal rip is a sideways flow of water caused when two streams of water moving in different directions meet. Normally the meeting happens as the streams converge at an islet, rock or point, which causes them to ricochet off in a new direction.

Although currents are related to tides, there isn't a direct correlation. The time of slack tide (i.e., the moment of either low or high tide) and the time of slack water (i.e., when the pressure from backed-up water is finally relieved and there is little or no water movement in the narrows or passage) often differ by 30 to 60 minutes and can differ by over 3 hours. One of the best ways to understand what the current is doing is to use the *Current*

Atlas: Juan de Fuca to Strait of Georgia, produced by the Canadian Hydrographic Service. The book consists of 94 charts showing tidal current flows for the area from Campbell River to Port Angeles. The *Atlas* costs about $25, but you can use it year after year if you have a set of Murray's tables (which cost about $8) for the present year. By looking up each hour you will be paddling, you can predict currents not just for the passes and narrows, but for your entire paddling route.

Marine Winds and Weather

There is a network of marine weather reporting stations spread over Vancouver Island. Using reports from these stations, the Canadian Coast Guard and Environment Canada provide round-the-clock marine forecasts. Forecasts are valid for 24 hours and include an outlook for the next 24 hours as well. You can hear forecasts over VHF radio weather channels and find them at the "Weather Office" on the Internet (*www.weatheroffice.com*). For each paddling area we have listed the closest reporting stations and the forecast area.

The forecasts are a synopsis of weather systems that will most likely influence local waters. It is useful to know the technical or common terms used on the broadcasts. For example, wind orientation is given according to the wind's direction. In other words, a southeast wind is blowing from the southeast toward the northwest. Wind speed is measured in knots and is described using the following terms:

➤ Light: 0 to 10 knots
➤ Moderate: 11 to 19 knots
➤ Strong: 20 to 33 knots (also known as Small Craft Warning)
➤ Gale Warning: 34 to 47 knots
➤ Storm Warning: 48 to 63 knots
➤ Hurricane Force Wind Warning: 64 knots or more

On the west coast of Vancouver Island, forecasts sometimes give swell heights, then wind-wave heights or the combined swell and wind-wave heights. On the east coast normally only wind-wave heights are given. The reporting stations are located in exposed areas and will usually have worse conditions than the paddling areas featured in this book.

Weather reports often speak about "high" and "low" pressure systems. The net difference between neighbouring high and low systems is called a pressure gradient. Winds travel from a high to a low.

Winds are generally predictable and conform to regular patterns with a few exceptions. Local knowledge can help with these exceptions. Talk to local kayakers and other boaters if the paddling area is new to you. Paying attention to observable effects, such as flags extending themselves or long unbreaking waves, can also help you assess weather conditions.

Sea breezes occur when bodies of land and water heat up and cool down at different rates. Sea breezes most often happen on warm sunny days during the spring and summer. In the morning the land and the water start out at similar temperatures. As the sun beats down on the land and sea, the land heats quickly while the sea or ocean stays at a more constant temperature because it can absorb a lot of heat without warming. Once a significant differential of temperature exists, the sea breeze begins blowing onto shore.

At night the wind often reverses direction and blows from the land to the sea. This is because the land cools faster in the evening while the sea retains more of its heat.

As most Vancouver Island paddling is at least partially sheltered, there is usually somewhere you can paddle in any area without exceeding your comfort level. An added benefit to being a kayaker is that you become much more attuned to winds, weather, tides and currents.

Other Vancouver Island Paddling Areas

In an effort not to duplicate trips covered in our first book, *Easykayaker: A guide to laid-back Vancouver Island paddling*, we have left some popular paddling areas out of this book. You can find information for such locations as the east coast of Vancouver Island from Duncan to Nanoose, the northern Gulf Islands, the Broken Group Islands, Nootka Sound and Jedediah Island in *Easykayaker*. There are many other exquisite paddling areas around Vancouver Island that we have not covered in either book as it will take many more volumes to cover all the fantastic paddling areas found here.

In both books we have taken the "Easykayaker" approach, adding a travelogue as well as technical information to provide some local flavour for the reader. We want you to find a paddle that is not only intriguing but also soothing to the spirit. We have covered dozens of areas and specific trips in the two books. We hope to see you on one of your journeys!

The beach was sublime this morning ... The air, the earth and the sea seemed to be holding some splendid wonderful secret, folding it up between them and saying to you, "Peep and guess. If you guess right you can have it." And you're almost scared to guess for fear of being wrong and not getting it.

—Emily Carr

Southern
Vancouver Island

Sooke Basin

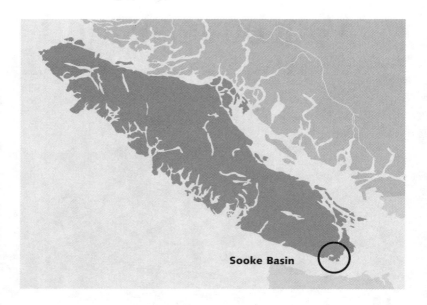

Sooke Basin

Only 34 km (21 mi) west of Victoria, Sooke Basin is a wonderful place to explore. The area is rich in history, offers sheltered paddling and has superb views across Juan de Fuca Strait.

If you look at CHS chart 3411 of Sooke Basin and Sooke Harbour, you will see that the marine area looks much like the Big Dipper constellation. Sooke Basin (the dipper) is an almost square body of water 4 km (2.5 mi) long by 3 km (1.9 mi) across. It's connected to an arm of water (the ladle) called Sooke Harbour, which is 4 km long. At the end of Sooke Harbour is Whiffin Spit. Past Whiffin Spit is Sooke Inlet and beyond that Juan de Fuca Strait. Across the strait is Washington's Olympic Peninsula.

The Strait of Georgia and Puget Sound form a massive body of water that floods and ebbs from as far north as Campbell River, west to Vancouver and south to Seattle. This water drains through Juan de Fuca Strait, creating very strong currents. On calm days strong and very experienced paddlers can harness the currents and explore some interesting shoreline and inlets southeast of Sooke Inlet.

Difficulty levels:
- ➤ Anderson Cove and Cooper Cove areas: Novice
- ➤ Sooke Harbour side of Whiffin Spit: Novice to intermediate
- ➤ Juan de Fuca Strait side of Whiffin Spit: Advanced

Approximate travel time: Half day or longer

Approximate distances (one way to head of coves):
- ➤ Whiffin Spit to Cooper Cove: 7.4 km (4.5 mi)
- ➤ Cooper Cove to Hutchinson Cove: 2.4 km (1.4 mi)
- ➤ Hutchinson Cove to Roche Cove: 3.0 km (1.9 mi)
- ➤ Roche Cove to Anderson Cove: 3.2 km (2 mi)
- ➤ Anderson Cove to Hill Head: 4.0 km (2.5 mi)
- ➤ Hill Head to Whiffin Spit: 3.7 km (2.3 mi)

CHS charts:
- ➤ 3411—Sooke Basin, Sooke Harbour and some of Juan de Fuca Strait
- ➤ 3410—Sooke Harbour and the coast from Sooke Inlet to Parry Bay

Tidal reference port: Sooke

Weather and sea conditions reference:
- ➤ Race Rocks
- ➤ Sheringham Point
- ➤ Juan de Fuca Strait

Sooke area

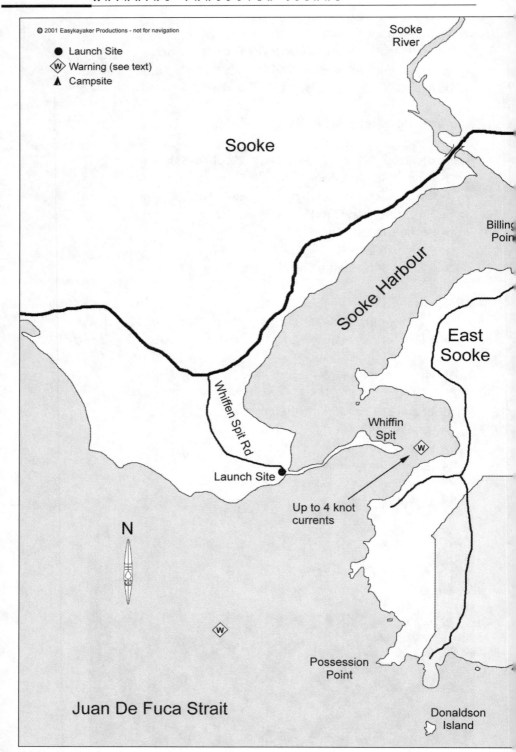

© 2001 Easykayaker Productions - not for navigation

● Launch Site
W Warning (see text)
▲ Campsite

Sooke River

Sooke

Billing Poin

Sooke Harbour

East Sooke

Whiffen Spit Rd

Whiffin Spit

W

Launch Site

Up to 4 knot currents

N

W

Possession Point

Juan De Fuca Strait

Donaldson Island

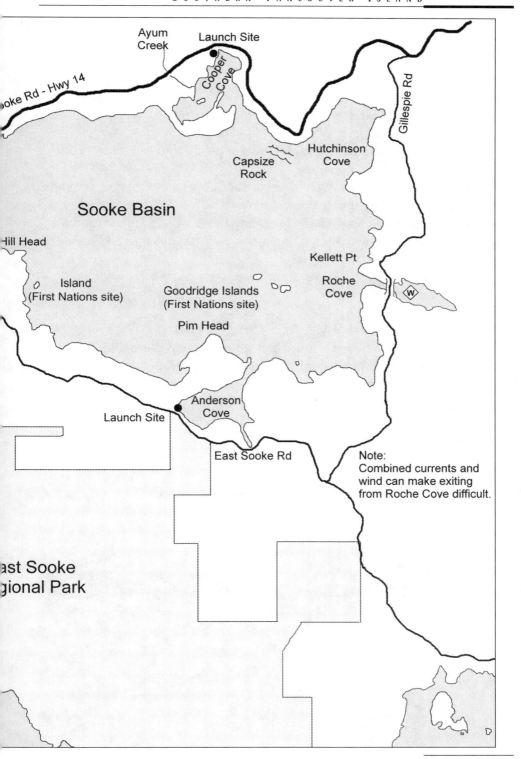

Ayum Creek

Launch Site

Sooke Rd - Hwy 14

Cooper Cove

Gillespie Rd

Capsize Rock

Hutchinson Cove

Sooke Basin

Hill Head

Kellett Pt

Island
(First Nations site)

Goodridge Islands
(First Nations site)

Roche Cove

Pim Head

Anderson Cove

Launch Site

East Sooke Rd

Note:
Combined currents and wind can make exiting from Roche Cove difficult.

East Sooke
Regional Park

Prevailing winds: West or southwest, often windy in afternoon during the summer.

Warnings:
> Juan de Fuca Strait is often windy and has strong tidal flows.
> Strong currents near Whiffin Spit (4 knots).
> Roche Cove can be difficult for weaker paddlers to exit if wind combines with a strong flood tide.
> Avoid the mouth of Ayum Creek, near Cooper Cove, during nesting season, from early spring to midsummer.
> Most islands in Sooke Basin (including the Goodridge Islands and the unnamed island by Hill Head) are sacred First Nations sites and should not be landed on.
> Just outside Cooper Cove, strong winds can cause turbulence along the shore near Capsize Rock.

Getting there: From Highway 1 (Trans-Canada Highway) look for the Sooke turnoff signs near View Royal. The road to Sooke is called Old Island Highway. It starts out as Highway 1A and becomes Highway 14 and then Sooke Road. From the Trans-Canada turnoff, it's about 23 km (14 mi) to the closest launch site at Cooper Cove.

Recommended launch sites:
> **Anderson Cove**: Our favourite launch site. Located near East Sooke Park, Anderson Cove offers the most scenic and sheltered paddling with little exposure to prevailing summer winds. The launch site is easy to use

Anderson Cove is our preferred launch site. Its narrow mouth shelters against wind.

but muddy at tides lower than 1.2 m (4 ft). To reach Anderson Cove, turn off Highway 14 onto Gillespie Road (near 17 Mile House). You will pass the Grouse Nest and Roche Cove Regional Park. Turn right on East Sooke Road. The small boat launch area is about 7.6 km (4.7 mi) from Highway 14 and is located just before Anderson Cove Road. Boats can be off-loaded near the water. Parking is available along East Sooke Road or at the parking lot for East Sooke Park, just a short distance away.

➤ **Cooper Cove**: The Ocean Kayak Institute (TO'KI), a.k.a. Rush Adventures, is located on the left side of Highway 14 at **Cooper Cove**. Cooper Cove is an easy launch site, but a bit muddy when the tide is very low. Parking is available next to the launch site and there is other parking nearby. Cooper Cove is very sheltered and offers some exploring. When you launch from Cooper Cove, a recommended paddling route is to travel clockwise around the Basin so that you can paddle east along the south shore, which is protected from the wind. Once you reach Hill Head it's a short crossing and then you can let the wind take you back along the north shore to Cooper Cove.

There are launching areas on both sides of Whiffin Spit. The area offers great views of Washington's Olympic mountain range.

Other launch sites:

➤ **Whiffin Spit Park**: The turnoff for Whiffen Spit Road is on the left, 10 km (6.2 mi) west of Cooper Cove on Highway 14. Whiffen Spit Road takes you to Whiffin Spit Park. Be prepared to carry kayaks 100 m (300 ft) or so. You can launch from either side of the spit and paddle Juan de Fuca Strait or Sooke Harbour and Basin. Parking is plentiful but could fill up quickly in summer. The views here are spectacular. Those wishing to explore the shoreline and inlets to the southeast of Sooke Inlet should head toward Possession Point and then on to Iron Mine Bay.

➤ **Sooke Harbour**

Accommodations: Luxury resorts, inns, hotels, motels and many B&Bs. Call the Sooke Visitor Information Centre at 250-642-6351 or 1-866-888-4748. Reservations can be made through Tourism BC, 1-800-435-5622.

Camping:

➤ Sooke River Flats Campground: Maintained by the Sooke Community Association at Sooke Flats, 1 km (0.6 mi) off Highway 14 on Phillips Road, 250-642-6076.

➤ Sunny Shores: Just off Highway 14, about 5 km (3 mi) east of Sooke, 250-642-5731 or 1-888-805-3932.

➤ French Beach Provincial Park: 20 km (12.4 mi) west of Sooke. To reserve a site call 1-800-689-9025 or book on-line at *www.discovercamping.ca.*

Capsize Rock at the entrance to Cooper Cove. When winds pick up in the cove it's not hard to figure out how this rock got its name.

Travel notes (Gary)

As we started our paddle from Cooper Cove, we enjoyed a wonderful view of the snow-capped mountains on the Olympic Peninsula. On our right were Ayum Creek's large estuary and mud flats. The tide was too low to explore the flats, but we would have stayed away from Ayum Creek anyway because it was late spring and waterfowl were nesting. (At the time of writing, a small lagoon near the mouth of Ayum Creek was under consideration as a bird sanctuary.)

As we paddled out of Cooper Cove toward Hutchinson Cove we passed some rocks and a rock shelf that Scot Taylor from TO'KI refers to as Capsize Rock. This area gets the full effect of

the afternoon westerlies and the rock shelf creates larger waves. We paddled past Hutchinson Cove and headed into Roche Cove.

Roche Cove is a magical place. A small inlet leads you under a trestle bridge into the cove. Unless you arrive here at slack current, which may differ from slack tide by 30 minutes or more, you'll get a thrill going either against or with the current under the bridge. I went hands-free with the current, taking photos as I passed between bridge pilings.

Roche Cove appears pristine with glass-like water and a towering forest. Since it is protected as part of a large regional park,

Roche Cove is part of a large regional park. A current gently swept us under a trestle bridge into the cove's calm waters.

it should remain unspoiled. After a slow paddle around this jewel of a cove we challenged the current under the bridge on our way out.

Farther along is Anderson Cove, a beautiful cove with a narrow opening and our favourite launch site for this area. By launching at Anderson Cove, you can paddle Sooke Basin's most scenic coastline from Roche Cove to Hill Head. It is a sheltered paddling place with sandy beaches, rugged cliffs, narrow inlets, coves and large tracts of uninhabited forest. Although not completely protected from wind, this area seldom gets hit with rough seas.

On a different trip we launched from Anderson Cove. Paddling out of the cove, we experienced a strong southeast wind. We went along the sheltered coast past Hill Head, following the shoreline partway back and then riding the wind over to the Goodridge Islands. The wind was blowing about 15 knots so we reached the islands quickly. The marine life, clear water and little inlets made the visit worthwhile. The paddle back to Anderson Cove was a bit of a workout, with the spray hitting us, but the body of water is not wide enough for the waves to build very high.

During our paddle we saw several mother ducks with very young ducklings. Occasionally we'd see one of the ducklings riding on mom's back, with the rest swimming after. We didn't want to disturb them so we kept our distance. Paul noted that the ducklings would be easy pickings for the eagles we had seen on our last paddle here.

On the way back we passed the driveway and sign for the Grouse Nest. This Sooke Basin resort has had a checkered history and many of its luxurious buildings have often sat idle since the mid-1960s. According to *Sooke Story*, edited by Elida Peers, the property was first settled in 1910 as the Gillespie farm. It was at the end of the road until the Roche Cove Bridge was built in 1929. In 1930 the Knight family bought the property, and in 1939 their son built a resort. I've heard from several people who grew up in Victoria that the Grouse Nest was the playground of the city's elite.

Grouse Nest circa 1981. Replete with jade-inlaid bar, dance floor, and bidets in all of its numerous bathrooms, this resort once played host to the rich and famous.

A spark from a sawdust burner was blamed for the fire that destroyed the resort in 1950. Rebuilding took three years. In 1963 Mr. Knight decided to retire and the property was sold to a European named Hassam Kamil, who lived there with his family until the late 1970s. Kamil employed European craftsmen to extensively renovate the resort. Temporary living accommodations were built for the craftsmen's families, and a school was even set up for their children.

Seeing the resort took me back about 20 years to when Bob, my then-girlfriend's uncle, was its caretaker. Bob invited us over to visit and gave us a tour of the property and buildings. The blackboards were still in the temporary school. Several luxury chalets looked out over the water. The crown jewel was the lodge building. Every post and beam was ornately hand carved. A 9-metre-long bar lined the dining room and dance floor. The entire length of the top of the bar was inlaid with a wide strip of jade.

The front of the bar was covered in sealskin. The dance floor had a dome gilded with gold leaf. There were three wine cellars so wines could be kept at their proper temperatures. Each of the bedrooms had a full luxury bathroom with a bidet. There were many other bathrooms throughout the building—so many, in fact, as to seem unusual. All in all, the level of luxury and extravagance in this building, combined with the superb craftsmanship, was overwhelming.

Sooke Basin is well worth visiting and I'm sure we'll return again and again. The town of Sooke is also a fun place to explore. There are some great outdoor shops, including Eagle-Eye Wilderness Company and Juan's Wharfside. Sooke Potholes Provincial Park is a famous swimming spot of incredible beauty, and don't miss the Sooke Region Museum while you're in the area.

Local History

In 1849 the Sooke Basin became the location of Vancouver Island's first European settlement that was not dependent on coal mining or the Hudson's Bay Company. It was the site of BC's first successfully operated, steam-powered sawmill and its first water-powered sawmill. In 1864 a short-lived gold rush drew prospectors to the nearby Leech River. Later, the Sooke area was home to Lady Emily Walken, an early love of England's King George V.

With a little imagination one can visualize scenes from the area's past while exploring its many coves, inlets and bays. The following bits of historical information cover a paddler's journey around the harbour and basin, starting at the mouth of the harbour and proceeding clockwise around the shoreline.

Whiffin Spit. The spit is named after John George Whiffin, clerk on HMS *Herald*, a ship that surveyed the area in 1846. Whiffin Spit is now a park with fantastic views of the harbour, straits and Washington's Olympic mountain range. Salmon fishing was a major industry here. The fish were caught using an extensive system of fish traps on the outside of Whiffin Spit in Juan de Fuca Strait. The traps were used until the late 1950s. The wharf for handling the fish was in Sooke Harbour.

Billings Point. This is where Sooke Harbour ends and Sooke Basin begins. The head of the oxen road to Leechtown was located east of Billings Point where Lannan and Saseenos creeks enter Sooke Basin. First constructed in 1864, the road serviced the gold rush to Leechtown. Parts of this road are now part of the Galloping Goose Trail. Emily Carr, one of BC's most famous artists, camped in her caravan at Saseenos, near where the gravel pit is now located, and sketched the area by the mouth of Lannan Creek.

Goodridge Peninsula. A sawmill was constructed at this site around 1950 and a land bridge was built to a nearby island, creating Goodridge Peninsula. The mill was initially called Goodridge Sawmill, later became Sooke Forest Products and eventually Lamford Forest Products.

Cooper Cove. Cooper Cove is the name shown on the chart, but many still refer to it by its original name, Cooper's Cove. Between 1911 and 1915 this cove hummed with activity. More than 400 men were employed in constructing a water flow-line from Sooke Lake to the Goldstream Reservoir to supply Victoria with water. Large, steam-powered concrete mixers were set up at this site to build components for the flow-line. A 60-centimetre-wide rail line was built along the route and removed as each section of flow-line was installed on the rail bed.

The west side of Cooper Cove used to be an oyster farm. On the east side of the inlet into Cooper Cove a bit of the road marks the location of a former log dump. In the late 1980s a group of people brought in the body of a young dead grey whale and sank it between here and the Goodridge Islands. The whale was found offshore from East Sooke Park and was sunk to allow the crabs to clean the bones. The recovered skeleton was reassembled as part of an Edward Milne Community School project in the mid-1990s.

Lorimer Point. Around the corner toward Hutchinson Cove is Lorimer Point, named after George Lorimer, one of five brothers who grew up near the intersection of Sooke Road and Gillespie Road. George was killed while in the service during World War II and the family applied to have this point named after him.

Hutchinson Cove. Veitch Creek at the head of Hutchinson Cove was the site of the first water-powered sawmill in BC, started in 1849 by Walter Colquhoun Grant. Grant is considered the first independent deeded settler in the Colony of Vancouver Island (i.e., he was not here with the Hudson's Bay Company or any other company). He paid 100 pounds sterling for a 40-hectare deed.

Because it has warmer water than most of Sooke Basin, Hutchinson Cove is a favourite swimming spot. It is also a traditional First Nations clamming area.

Hutchinson Cove is home to the Grouse Nest.

Anderson Cove. Anderson Cove was formerly known as Caffery Bay and for three generations was the home of the Caffery family. The tiny inlet off Anderson Cove was the location of the family oyster business and is worth exploring if the tide is high enough.

Hill Head. The small unnamed island that is shown on the chart to the east of Hill Head is known as Deadman's Island. It is believed to be a First Nations burial site. A careless visitor set the island on fire sometime around 1952, and the fire exposed many bones. Please do not land on this island.

Hill Head is where the basin ends and the harbour begins. Current, wind and boat traffic become more pronounced along this side of the harbour heading toward Whiffin Spit.

Whiffin Spit. Now a park, the spit is named after John George Whiffin, a clerk on HMS Herald, a ship that surveyed the area in 1846.

The Gorge Waterway and Victoria Harbour

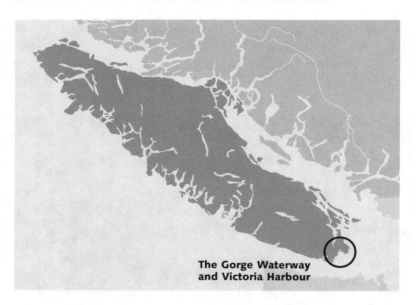

The Gorge Waterway and Victoria Harbour

The Gorge Waterway winds from the suburb of View Royal to Victoria's Upper Harbour. From here it's a short paddle to the city's popular Inner Harbour area. Along the way expect to see luxury homes and gardens, parks, industrial development and boats of all shapes and sizes. From the Inner Harbour and James Bay you can see landmarks like the Fairmont Empress Hotel and the BC Legislative Buildings. In warmer months there are often street performers entertaining along the Inner Harbour causeway.

Difficulty levels:
➤ Portage Inlet: Novice
➤ The Gorge: Novice
➤ Tillicum Narrows: Novice to advanced (depending on current and tide conditions)
➤ Victoria Harbour: Intermediate (due to high levels of traffic)

Approximate travel time: Give yourself half a day to explore Portage Inlet, the Gorge or Victoria Harbour, and a full day if you plan to combine all of these areas.

Approximate distances (round trip):
- ➤ Portage Inlet from Kinsmen Gorge Park: 5.5 km (3.4 mi)
- ➤ Kinsmen Gorge Park to the Upper Harbour: 6 km (3.75 mi)
- ➤ Kinsmen Gorge Park to Victoria Harbour: 10 km (6.3 mi)
- ➤ Portage Inlet, the Gorge, Victoria Harbour and James Bay: 16 km (10 mi)

CHS chart: 3415 Victoria Harbour (or a good road map of Victoria)

Tidal reference port: Victoria

Secondary current station: Gorge–Tillicum Bridge

Weather and sea conditions reference: Victoria

Winds: Reports available 24 hours per day from Environment Canada, 250-363-6717 or VHF weather frequencies.

Warnings:
- ➤ Strong currents (7 knots) and, depending on the tide, a possible waterfall near Tillicum Bridge. Many years ago a member of the Victoria Canoe & Kayak Club told us a hair-raising story about the waterfall. He

Views of the BC Legislative Buildings in Victoria's Inner Harbour are part of the urban paddling experience.

was unaware of the hazard until he faced the 75-cm (2.5-ft) foaming waterfall. His canoe capsized as he attempted to navigate the falls head-on.

➤ Currents in areas between the Upper Harbour and Portage Inlet.

➤ Heavy boat traffic south of Tillicum Bridge, especially in the harbour area.

➤ Seaplane traffic in Victoria Harbour and James Bay.

➤ Swimming and rowing races north of James Bay.

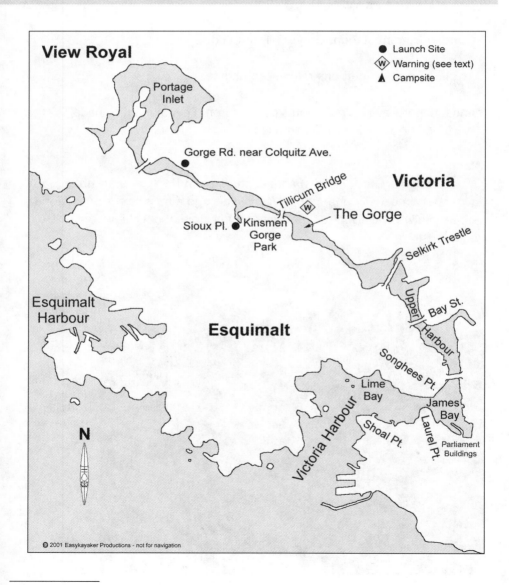

Getting there/launching:

➤ **Kinsmen Gorge Park**: Our recommended launch site. From Highway 1 (Trans-Canada Highway) in Victoria, turn west onto Tillicum Road, cross the Tillicum Bridge, continue past the park, turn right onto Craigflower Road and right again onto Sioux Place. Sioux Place ends in a large parking area at the water. The decommissioned wading area is a good launch spot, though you have to navigate a concrete channel and slip under a concrete beam.

➤ **Gorge Road near Colquitz Avenue**: From Highway 1 turn west on Admirals Road. At Gorge Road turn left.

Accommodations: Hotels, motels, luxury resorts and B&Bs. Call the Visitor Information Centre, 250-953-2033.

Camping:

➤ Thetis Lake Campground & Trailer Park: 1938 West Park Lane, Victoria, 250-478-3845

➤ Victoria West KOA: 230 Trans-Canada Highway, Victoria, 250-478-3332

➤ All Fun Recreation Park: 2207 Millstream Road, Victoria, 250-474-4546

➤ Fort Victoria RV Park: 340 Island Highway, Victoria, 250-479-8112

Travel notes (Gary)

When planning which paddles to include in this book, we hesitated to include the Gorge because it's in the middle of a large city and hardly the kind of wild, pristine environment we normally love to paddle. Nonetheless, we figured it would probably be sheltered and scenic, so we decided to give it a try.

Before paddling an area it's wise to learn as much as you can about it, so we read an article by Alan Wilson in *WaveLength* magazine and talked to the good people at Ocean River Sports and Vancouver Island Canoe & Kayak. From them we learned about the Gorge's current and the narrows at Tillicum Bridge.

Figuring out when it's safe to pass under the bridge can be a challenge. The slack water time here can vary from the slack low tide by as much as 3 hours 15 minutes on a turn to flood tide and 1 hour 15 minutes on a turn to ebb tide.

Think of the end of the waterway, Portage Inlet, as the body of a large bottle and the narrows as the neck. When the tide falls

rapidly it can take more than three hours to empty the excess water out of Portage Inlet. The good news is that Victoria is the only area of southern Vancouver Island with mostly diurnal tides, meaning there is usually only one high and one low tide per day. The other low and high tides are very minor, creating a long period of slack tide, especially during the first and third quarter phases of the moon.

It is best to paddle this area on a day with as little tidal variation as possible. The day we chose for our outing had a minimal tide change—the tide was expected to rise from a low of 1.8m (5.9 ft) to a high of 2.5m (8.2 ft) over a six-and-a-half-hour period.

Don't be fooled! Though calm when we were there, conditions on a different day can create strong currents near Tillicum Bridge.

Paul and I arrived early and decided to paddle over to check out the current under the bridge. We paddled across the decommissioned wading area, through the concrete channel and under the concrete beam. The launch site is on the inland side of the bridge, and if my theory was correct, a minor current would be flowing out toward the harbour. We paddled under the bridge and although the surface indicated currents at work, they were hardly noticeable. Paul and I paddled a little farther into the Gorge and then had an easy paddle back to meet our friends, Dave and Celia, as they paddled under the concrete beam to join us.

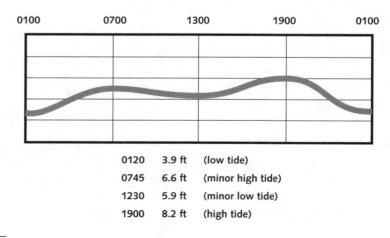

0100	0700	1300	1900	0100

0120	3.9 ft	(low tide)
0745	6.6 ft	(minor high tide)
1230	5.9 ft	(minor low tide)
1900	8.2 ft	(high tide)

Across from the launch site we saw an assortment of paddling and rowing craft and many people in PFDs standing on a float, the home of the Victoria Canoe & Kayak Club. One boat that caught my attention was a narrow 22-person canoe. We saw many members of this club out paddling and rowing throughout the day.

I turned on my GPS to track our paddling distance. We decided to go with the mild current to the Upper Harbour and maybe even as far as James Bay. Along the way we passed small old boats, beautiful homes and gardens, paddlers, harbour tour boats and even a Russian submarine! (This sub was a tourist attraction, but it broke free from its moorings during a storm and the owners have since moved it away from Victoria.)

After our imaginations ran wild thinking about life on this 86.5-metre-long vessel (264 ft) (with its crew of 78 people sharing three toilets, two showers and 27 bunks for 54 sailors), we paddled on, passing several kayak rental businesses, another park, and a recreation centre where a group of about 30 teens were starting a swimming race.

Code name Cobra. It is rumoured this Russian submarine once patrolled the west coast of North America to spy on us.

It was a wonderful warm Saturday and the waterfront was busy with people biking and walking. We read the drawbridge contact instructions on the old Selkirk railway trestle as we paddled by. This trestle is part of the Galloping Goose Trail, used by hundreds of people to walk and bike to work every day.

Boat traffic increased as we entered the Upper Harbour, and we noticed that several large fishing boats, a ferry and a navy ship were tied up at the shipyards. We decided to stay close to the right shore and before we knew it were in Victoria Harbour. A loud roar filled the air as a float plane approached, landing about 30 m (100 ft) away from Paul.

Travelling with the current made 5 km go by quickly. Everyone was enjoying the trip so we decided to travel farther out. We headed toward Lime Bay, hugging Songhees Point until we saw the outside waters and crossed the harbour to Shoal Point. The weather channel on my VHF radio stated that Victoria Harbour had 8-knot winds. The water was bumpy, we could feel the wind, and boat and ship traffic was constant.

At Laurel Point we tucked in and paddled from the marina to the causeway, then headed toward James Bay. The Empress Hotel and Parliament Buildings were quite a sight from our vantage point. We dodged one boat after another and bobbed in the wake left by the Victoria–Washington State ferries crossing our path. As the four of us live in the countryside outside a small town, this paddle was quite a contrast to what we were used to.

We were happy to get past the ferry terminal and over to the Undersea Gardens, an underwater aquarium with a popular dive show. The diver was getting ready to perform and a friendly seal kept bobbing up next to us as if to see if the diver had all his gear on yet. Later we saw another "tame" seal and a

A "citified" blue heron is a common site in Victoria's Inner Harbour.

great blue heron that seemed to have no fear of people. The wildlife here is obviously not too wild.

Bagpipes, fire breathers, a unicyclist, buskers, rock bands and other entertainment made paddling along Victoria's Inner Harbour a bit surreal, but very entertaining. A steady stream of whale-watching boats headed in and out of the harbour.

The current had changed and once again we had it flowing with us as we headed back to the Gorge, looking for a lunch spot. We decided to land near our launch site and enjoy the park, its restrooms and food stand. After lunch we filled up water bottles and headed to Portage Inlet about 2.5 km (1.5 mi) away. It was a very easy paddle as the current was still moving with us. Much of this area is shallow, and the paddle wouldn't be as nice at a 1.5-m (5-ft) or lower tide, though we're told there are channels kayakers can navigate at lower tides.

Over the years the Gorge had become the dumping ground for many unwanted items. A big and successful push was made to clean it up. However, due to Portage Inlet's shallowness and limited flushing action, the water here has a lot of algae growth and wasn't as nice as on the rest of our paddle.

On our trip back to the launch site the water's surface and the eelgrass indicated a strong current, but our kayaks glided across the water easily and soon we completed our 16-km (10-mi) journey.

Local History

The site of the reversible falls, now located under the Tillicum Bridge, was a sacred place for the Lekwammen (Songhees) First Nation. A midden here has been estimated to be 4,120 years old—making it the oldest known archeological site on southern Vancouver Island.

In the late 1800s and early 1900s the Gorge was a summertime playground. Its shores were lined with mansions, rose gardens and lovely sprawling lawns. World-class swimming and rowing races were held and attracted huge crowds. People picnicked at Tramway Gorge Park and couples went for moonlit strolls by the water in this romantic setting.

Over time the mansions grew old and properties became subdivided. Industry and commercial enterprise began to dominate certain areas, the water became unclean and the Gorge lost its appeal. Thanks to the efforts of many people over the last few years, the Gorge has been cleaned up and is now a success story of urban renewal and a real joy once again to row, paddle and swim in.

Finlayson Arm

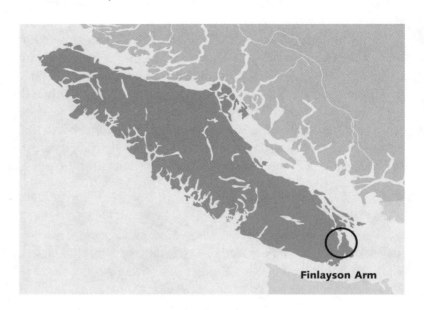

Finlayson Arm

Finlayson Arm is a long, narrow finger of water that extends from Saanich Inlet to Goldstream Provincial Park. Its steep, forested shoreline has several nooks and crannies to explore. Crossings here are no problem as Finlayson Arm is only 1.5 km (1 mi) at its widest point. Landing spots are few and far between, but there are places to pull out about every 3 to 4 km (2 to 2.5 mi).

Difficulty levels:
- ➤ South of Spectacle Creek: Novice to intermediate
- ➤ North of Spectacle Creek: Intermediate

Approximate travel times:
- ➤ Finlayson Arm to Spectacle Creek: Half day
- ➤ Exploring Finlayson Arm: Full day

Approximate distances:
- ➤ Goldstream Boathouse to Spectacle Creek: 15 km (9.3 mi) round trip if following the shore, 13 km (8.1 mi) direct
- ➤ Spectacle Creek to McKenzie Bight: 2.2 km (1.4 mi) one way

CHS chart: 3476—Approaches to Tsehum Harbour

Tidal reference port: Fulford Harbour

Weather and sea conditions reference: Juan de Fuca Strait

Prevailing winds: Southeast in the summer, northwest in the winter. The winds can be strong here, especially in the warmer months. The winds travel over fairly flat land from Juan de Fuca Strait and funnel into Saanich Inlet and Finlayson Arm. If they are blowing hard from the southeast it may be difficult to paddle back to Goldstream Boathouse Marina.

Warnings:
> ➤ Check the winds before setting out.
> ➤ Do not enter the estuary into Goldstream Provincial Park; it is an environmentally sensitive wildlife habitat.
> ➤ Do not paddle beneath the store at the marina.
> ➤ If venturing past Finlayson Arm into Saanich Inlet, watch for ferry traffic.

One of many amazing views of Finlayson Arm from the Malahat

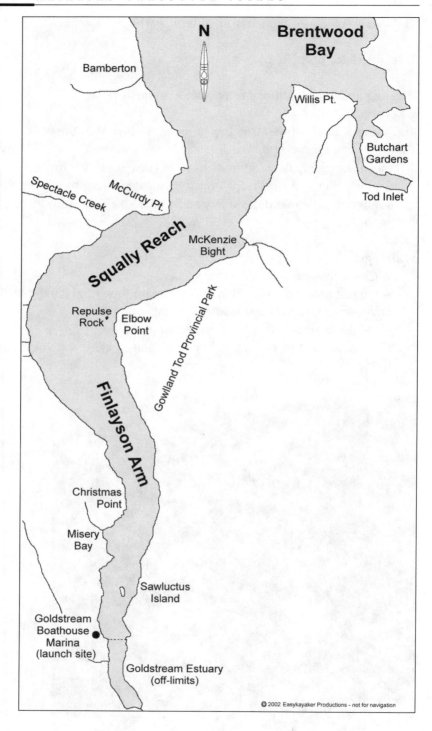

N

Brentwood
Bay

Bamberton

Willis Pt.

Butchart
Gardens

Spectacle Creek

McCurdy Pt.

Tod Inlet

Squally Reach

McKenzie
Bight

Repulse
Rock

Elbow
Point

Gowlland Tod Provincial Park

Finlayson Arm

Christmas
Point

Misery
Bay

Sawluctus
Island

Goldstream
Boathouse
Marina
(launch site)

Goldstream Estuary
(off-limits)

© 2002 Easykayaker Productions - not for navigation

A good place to get in the water. Goldstream Boathouse Marina charges a small launch and parking fee.

Getting there/launching:

➤ **Goldstream Boathouse Marina**: Our recommended launch site. Heading north on Highway 1 (Trans-Canada Highway) from Victoria, Goldstream Boathouse Marina is the first driveway after Goldstream Provincial Park. Look for a small Goldstream Boathouse Marina sign. There is an $8 launch and parking fee per vehicle.

➤ **Beside the Brentwood Bay ferry dock (on the Saanich Peninsula)**: This launch site is quite far north. To get there from Victoria go north on West Saanich Road and turn left onto Verdier Avenue.

Accommodations: Motels, hotels, resorts and B&Bs in Victoria, Duncan and points in between. Call the Victoria Visitor Information Centre, 250-953-2033; the Duncan/Cowichan Visitor Information Centre, 250-746-4636; or make reservations through Tourism BC, 1-800-435-5622.

Camping:

➤ Goldstream Provincial Park: Off Highway 1 south of the Malahat. To reserve a site call 1-800-689-9025 or book on-line at *www.discovercamping.ca*.

➤ Bamberton Provincial Park: Off Highway 1 north of the Malahat. Same reservation info as above.

Travel notes (Paul)

We paid a launch fee of $8 for our two kayaks and drove my truck to the boat launch. Our goal for the day was to check out the waterfall at the end of Spectacle Creek in Squally Reach. Gary and I quickly launched and crossed Finlayson Arm to a small bay at the foot of a steep hill. Gary immediately noticed a mussel-encrusted winch lying on a partially submerged wooden barge. A local later told us that years ago someone used the winch to lower logs into the inlet on a bet to prove that the hill could be logged—everyone considered it too steep.

More than mussels. This winch was once used to drag logs into the inlet.

A southeast wind of 10 to 15 knots was blowing as we paddled from the winch past Sawluctus Island and over to the west side of the arm. Across from us on the east side, the entire shoreline and much of the hillside forms part of Gowlland Tod Provincial Park. The park area runs from near Sawluctus Island to just north of McKenzie Bight.

Along the way we saw several jellyfish with dense yellow masses inside them. They were common sea blubber, a species that grows to half a metre or more across the bell. The tentacles on these large jellyfish, which are abundant in the late summer, pack enough sting to cause blisters. On another paddle, I saw one of them locked in mortal stinging combat with an equally large white jellyfish. Now that's one fight I really wouldn't want to get in the middle of!

We paddled slowly through Misery Bay to Christmas Point. Listening to Gary's VHF radio, we heard that the weather prediction had been upgraded to a small craft warning and decided to cut our trip short.

Across Finlayson Arm, on the east side near Elbow Point, you can see a narrow, steep-sided valley. This is the San Juan–Survey Mountain Fault, where two of the earth's tectonic plates collided about 100 million years ago. Gary and I have been told large boulders occasionally tumble down from this area. We are not sure how dangerous it is, but we wouldn't eat lunch here.

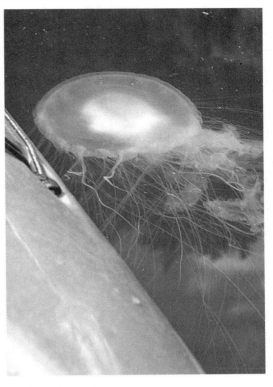

The tentacles of the common sea blubber, a species of jellyfish that can grow to half a metre across, pack enough sting to cause blisters.

Farther down the west side in Squally Reach, Spectacle Creek ends with a waterfall. Claude Harrison, a former Victoria mayor, owned a hunting lodge near here in the 1930s. The lodge has long since burned down but the foundation and steps are still there.

Spectacle Creek is called "Rough Creek" by the local boaters because this is where water conditions can start to get rough as you head toward Saanich Inlet. Names like Squally Reach and Misery Bay give you the impression the people who named these places didn't like the local weather very much. I wasn't too fond of it either when the wind whipped my special Zellers hat off my head and into the water, seriously upsetting me.

After struggling against the wind, we finally made it back to the marina. We paddled under the docks past the boat launch but were asked not to enter the area beneath the store. Some day when there is less wind we will return to this idyllic location for a round trip to Spectacle Creek and maybe over to McKenzie Bight and Gowlland Tod Provincial Park.

Local History

A step into BC's past is as simple as a drive down to the Goldstream Boathouse. In the 1920s the marina was the location of the BC Cement Company. The rock was hand mined from what is now the parking area and transported to the water in wheelbarrows, mostly by Chinese labourers. Poor-quality rock and amalgamation with another company caused the operations to be moved to the current site of Butchart Gardens at Tod Inlet.

The Stacy family rented the site as a marina shortly after the cement company moved. In the 1940s the Halls took it over and built the majority of the buildings that now stand there. They later bought the land from the cement company.

Pender Islands

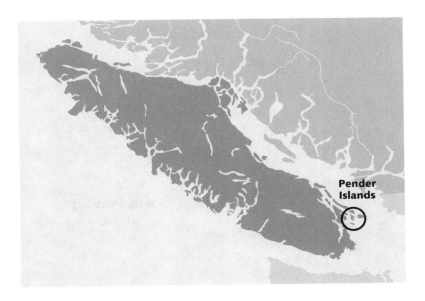

Pender
Islands

With a dry climate and laid-back feel, "the Penders"—as the locals call their islands—are a great place to get on the water. There are several places to explore on the two neighbouring islands, and they can also be used as a launching spot to get to other islands in the area including Prevost Island.

Difficulty levels:
> ➤ Port Browning to Beaumont Marine Provincial Park: Novice
> ➤ Other areas: Intermediate to advanced

Approximate travel times:
> ➤ Port Browning to Beaumont Marine Provincial Park: Half day (or longer)
> ➤ Other areas: Half day to multiple day
> ➤ North Pender Island can be circumnavigated in approximately 8 hours if you are travelling at a good steady pace, and South Pender in 4 hours.

Approximate distances:
> ➤ Hamilton Beach (Port Browning) to Beaumont Marine Provincial Park: 7.2 km (4.6 mi) round trip
> ➤ Circumnavigating North Pender: 29 km (18 mi)
> ➤ Circumnavigating South Pender: 16 km (10 mi)

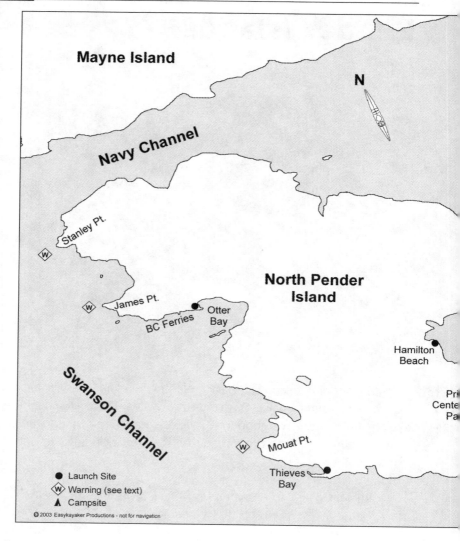

CHS chart: 3462—Juan de Fuca Strait to Strait of Georgia

Tidal reference port: Fulford Harbour

Marine weather and sea conditions reference:
➤ Strait of Georgia
➤ East Point (Saturna Island)

Prevailing winds: Southeasterlies, though the southeast coast of South Pender is exposed to southerlies. It is often windy around the Penders on summer afternoons.

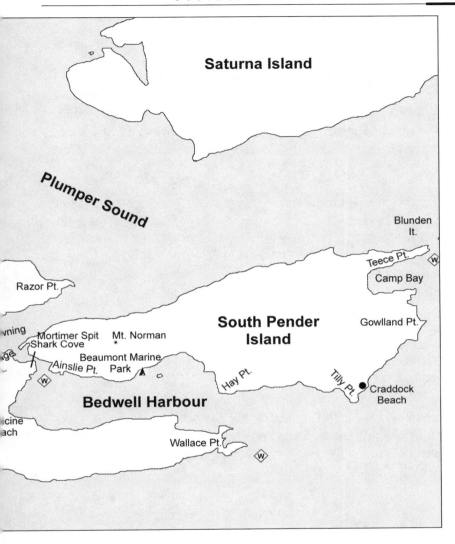

Warnings:

➤ Given the number of headlands and areas with currents, tidal rips and standing waves, it is essential you know how to read tide and current tables if you are paddling outside Port Browning and Bedwell Harbour without a guide.

➤ There are strong currents on the exposed southern end of North Pender Island in Swanson Channel.

➤ Watch for ferries and ferry-generated waves in Swanson and Navy channels.

➤ Currents in Navy Channel can be strong.

➤ Currents are noticeable at headland areas including Tilly Point and

Teece Point.

➤ Currents are considerable at Blunden Islet during peak ebb and flood tides.

➤ Wallace Point can experience fast current and frequent crosswaves.

➤ Currents, ferry wash and southerlies can converge at Mouat Point.

➤ Fairly strong currents can be found at James Point and Stanley Point.

➤ Currents under Pender Bridge in Pender Canal can run up to 3 knots.

➤ Medicine Beach is a sensitive saltwater marsh protected by the Islands Trust.

Getting there: There are regular ferry crossings to the Pender Islands from Swartz Bay (Victoria), Tsawwassen (Vancouver) and Saltspring, Mayne and Galiano islands. For schedule information call 1-888-223-3779 (in BC), 250-386-3431 (outside BC) or go to *www.bcferries.com*. Reservations can be made on-line or by calling 1-888-724-5223 (in BC) or 604-444-2890 (outside BC).

Recommended launch sites:

➤ **Hamilton Road Beach**: This site is on North Pender in Port Browning. From the ferry terminal follow Otter Bay Road to the right until you reach Bedwell Harbour Road, turn right, then turn left on Hamilton Road.

➤ **Thieves Bay**: On North Pender, this site has public parking and a picnic area. Drive past Hamilton Road on Bedwell Harbour Road (which becomes Canal Road), turn right on Aldridge Road, then right again on Schooner Way.

Hawkins Islet, about a half-hour paddle from Pender toward Saltspring

➤ **Craddock Beach**: Follow Canal Road south on South Pender Island to Spalding Road. Turn right on Spalding and then turn left on Gowlland Point Road. Turn right on Craddock Road.

Other launch sites:
➤ **Otter Bay Marina** near the ferry terminal on North Pender ($5 launch fee)
➤ **Medicine Beach** on North Pender (limited parking)
➤ **Mortimer Spit** on South Pender (no overnight parking)

Accommodations: Various B&Bs and resorts. Information is available in brochures on the ferries.

Camping:
➤ Beaumont Marine Provincial Park on South Pender: Accessible by boat or by a 20-minute hike from Mount Norman Regional Park parking lot. Reservations are not available.
➤ Prior Centennial Provincial Park on North Pender Island: The park is 6 km (4 mi) southeast of the Otter Bay ferry terminal off Canal Road. To reserve a site call 1-800-689-9025 or book on-line at *www.discovercamping.ca*.

Travel notes (Paul)

Gary and I took a roundabout route to the Penders, catching a ferry at Crofton to Saltspring Island, then a second ferry from Saltspring to North Pender Island. After exploring the islands and visiting friends, we unloaded our kayaks on the sand beach at the end of Hamilton Road. Moments later we were paddling in a mild headwind along the shores of Port Browning to Aldridge Point. We turned into the narrow channel between Aldridge and Mortimer Spit and then entered Pender Canal. We were expecting to be pulled quickly under the one-lane bridge, but hardly even felt the current as we passed between the pilings.

We examined the banks of the canal, aware that the ancient midden here was the site of one of BC's largest archeological digs. The canal was fairly protected from winds, but as we paddled around Ainslie Point we encountered a headwind that stayed with us all the way to Beaumont Marine Provincial Park.

The Penders generally have a Mediterranean microclimate and receive little rain compared to Vancouver. On this day, however, as a cold rain struck us just before we reached Beaumont in Bedwell Harbour, all thoughts of the Mediterranean were washed from my mind. Ahead I could see a few solitary trees on a rocky knoll, joined to the park by a midden beach. To escape the stiff wind, Gary and I pulled up on the lee side of this little peninsula.

We left our boats and scouted the provincial campsite. This 58-hectare (143-acre) park has scenic trails, swimming and camping, and you can get provisions at the nearby Bedwell Harbour village. A shoreline trail heads toward Ainslie Point and into Mount Norman Regional Park. Even under a dark grey cover of clouds, the park was beautiful. Garry oak, arbutus, fir, and bigleaf maples surrounded the campgrounds.

Pender Canal and Bridge. Looks can be deceiving. The current beneath the bridge wasn't as strong as we expected.

We had planned to explore the coastline past the village of Bedwell Harbour on South Pender and the saltwater sanctuary of Medicine Beach on North Pender, but the strong winds made travelling farther south hazardous, and we were chilled by the rain and wind.

As we launched, waves rolled into our cockpits before we managed to secure our sprayskirts around the coaming. We had a quick return trip, aided by wind and waves. Boat traffic was heavy as we neared the bridge, but the tide was high enough for us to pass between some pilings near shore, leaving the main

Razor Point on North Pender Island

channel open for a large RCMP cruiser. If there was any current as we passed under the bridge, it was well disguised by the wake from the cruiser and three other boats.

Prevost Island

Sue Konen, a guide with Kayak Pender Island, has several ideas for trips around Pender Island including a paddle to Prevost Island from James Point. For more information on Prevost see page 74, under Saltspring Island.

Difficulty level: Intermediate to advanced

Approximate travel time: 45-minute crossing (one way)

Approximate distances:
> Otter Bay to Point Liddell on Prevost Island: 4.5 km (2.8 mi) one way
> Point Liddell to James Bay (Prevost Island): 6.5 km (4.0 mi) one way

Recommended launch site:
> **Otter Bay Marina** is the closest launch site. You can walk-wheel a kayak to this launch site from the ferry (0.5 km/0.3 mi) or you can drive right to the launch. There is a $5 fee to launch from here.

Camping:
➤ James Bay: In the Prevost Island Protected Area (see page 65—Saltspring Island).

Local History

Pender Island was named after Daniel Pender, a master of the vessel *Plumper* in 1857. Typical of early industry on many Gulf Islands, the Penders once had a herring saltery, a brick factory, a fertilizer plant and logging. The Penders now have a population of 2,000—making it the second most populated Gulf Island after Saltspring.

You may have noticed that "the Penders" are often referred to as "Pender Island." This is because an isthmus originally joined North and South Pender Islands. In 1902 the isthmus was dredged to create a canal large enough for the steamship *Iroquois* to easily pass through on its way from Hope Bay on North Pender to Sidney. The canal made the route shorter and safer by avoiding the currents at the southern, exposed end of the Penders. A one-lane bridge built in 1955 now connects the two islands.

During the summers of 1984 and 1985, the largest archeological dig in the Gulf Islands took place under the bridge on North Pender. Searching through the midden, archeologists from Simon Fraser University uncovered hundreds of artifacts including a slate burial box. Some of the items date back 5,000 years.

Northern Saltspring and Galiano Islands

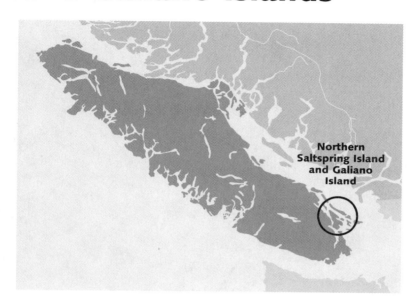

Northern Saltspring Island and Galiano Island

Visitors to Saltspring Island often sense a special energy, common to many of the Gulf Islands. It springs from the local residents, who enjoy an easygoing lifestyle in a holiday paradise, and is intensified by the peaceful landscape of farms and forests. The island is home to a thriving arts community and great eateries, and offers many attractions, including farm tours, fishing, hiking, swimming, farmers' markets, craft fairs, music and much more.

The largest of the southern Gulf Islands, Saltspring is also the most populated, with 11,000 residents. There are three towns or villages: Ganges, Vesuvius and Fulford. Ganges is the largest and is alive with activity, especially on Saturdays from April until October when it hosts the weekly craft market in Centennial Park.

Saltspring has many good launch sites, beautiful beaches and easy access to good kayak camping. From the northeastern portion of the island it's easy to reach other popular kayaking destinations including Montague Harbour Marine Provincial Park (on Galiano Island), Prevost Island Protected Area and Wallace Island Marine Provincial Park.

CHS Chart: 3442 North Pender Island to Thetis Island

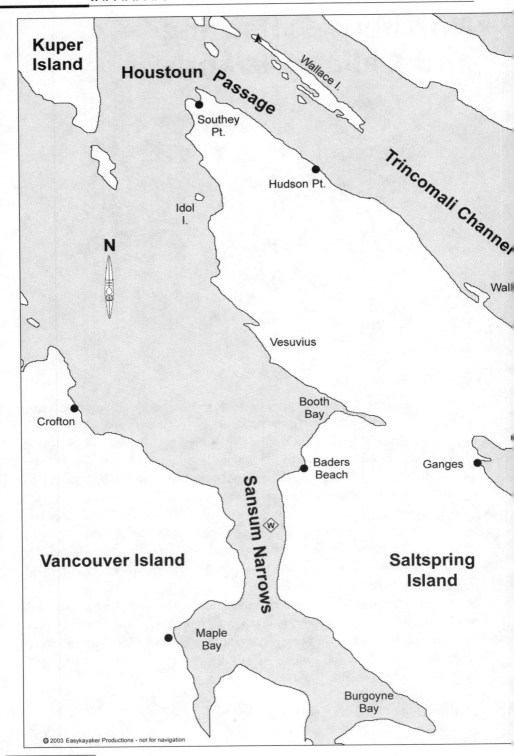

Kuper
Island

Houstoun Passage

Wallace I.

Southey
Pt.

Trincomali Channel

Hudson Pt.

Idol
I.

N

Wal

Vesuvius

Booth
Bay

Crofton

Baders
Beach

Ganges

Sansum Narrows

W

Vancouver Island

Saltspring
Island

Maple
Bay

Burgoyne
Bay

© 2003 Easykayaker Productions - not for navigation

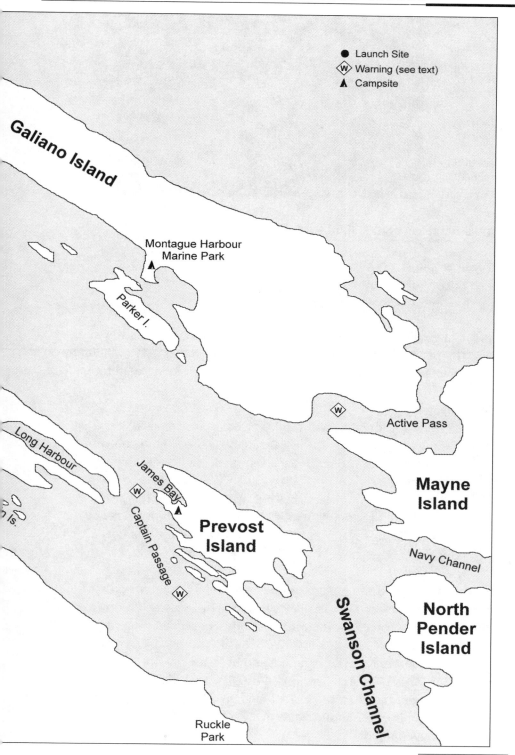

Launch Site
W Warning (see text)
▲ Campsite

Galiano Island

Montague Harbour
Marine Park

Parker I.

Active Pass

Long Harbour

James Bay

Captain Passage

Prevost
Island

Mayne
Island

Navy Channel

North
Pender
Island

Swanson Channel

Ruckle
Park

63

Burgoyne Bay. Paddling from the head of Burgoyne Bay to Baders Beach takes about 90 minutes.

Tidal reference port: Fulford Harbour

Weather and sea conditions reference:
- East Point (Saturna Island)
- Strait of Georgia

Prevailing winds: Southeast, often windy in afternoon during the summer. The eastern portion of Houstoun Passage sometimes gets a bit bumpy on summer afternoons as the current and wind are funnelled through here.

Warnings:
- Watch out for large boat traffic, including BC Ferries.
- Many local islets are fragile habitat and should be treated with care.
- Many reefs are seal pullouts—keep far enough away that you do not disturb them.
- Many of Saltspring's launches are boat ramps built using volunteer labour and funds from boating clubs and organizations. Whenever possible, keep your kayaks off to the side to allow power boaters use of the ramps.

Getting there: Saltspring Island can be reached by ferry from Crofton (Vancouver Island), Swartz Bay (Victoria), Tsawwassen (Vancouver) and many of the other Southern Gulf Islands. For schedule information call 1-888-223-3779 (in BC) or 250-386-3431 (outside BC), or go to *www.bcferries.com*. Reservations can be made on-line or by calling 1-888-724-5223 (in BC) or 604-444-2890 (outside BC). Local water taxis can also pick up and deliver you and your kayak. Saltspring is only a short paddle away from many launch sites on eastern Vancouver Island.

Accommodations: Luxury resorts and numerous B&Bs. Call the Saltspring Island Visitor Information Centre at 250-537-5252 or 1-866-216-2936, or go to *www.saltspringisland.bc.ca.*

Camping:

➤ Ruckle Provincial Park, Saltspring Island: From the Fulford-Ganges Road, turn onto Beaver Point Road and follow it to the end.

➤ At the time of writing, camping was being planned for Burgoyne Bay Provincial Park, Saltspring Island.

➤ There is also camping at Chivers Point on Wallace Island, at James Bay on Prevost Island and at Montague Harbour on Galiano Island.

Note: Difficulty levels, approximate travel times, distances, location-specific warnings and launch sites are listed under specific paddling areas.

Baders Beach, Booth Bay, Burgoyne Bay and Idol Island

Located on the more protected west side of the island, Baders Beach is a great place to launch. If it's blowing at Ganges, it may be calm here.

A treat at high tide is a paddle in nearby Booth Bay, a long, skinny inlet with a large mud flat at its entrance. There's only one problem. If your timing is off, you may end up with a portage when you try to paddle back out.

Just south of Baders Beach is the beginning of Sansum Narrows. If you catch an ebb tide you can use the current to take you to Burgoyne Bay Marine Provincial Park. Time your trip to catch a flood tide back or you will get a vigorous workout. Look for small sea caves on both shores along the way.

If it's one of those days when the tides don't fit your schedule, consider

Be sure to time the tides. A mud flat appears at the entrance to Booth Bay when the water level falls.

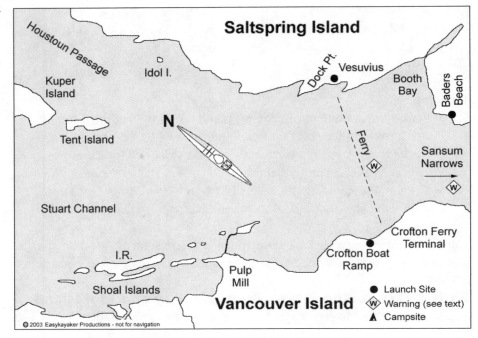

paddling north toward Southey Point and Idol Island. When you paddle north out of Baders Beach, look for an eagle's nest in a tall tree right at the shoreline as you round the first point. There are lots of pullout spots between Baders Beach and Southey Point, which are handy for paddlers should weather conditions change. The nice thing about local weather is that, after an hour or two, the sea has often returned to calmer conditions. We found Dock Point was a great lunch spot.

Difficulty levels:
> ➤ South of Baders Beach: Intermediate (due to Sansum Narrows)
> ➤ North of Baders Beach: Novice

Approximate travel times:
> ➤ Baders Beach to Burgoyne Bay: About 60 to 90 minutes each way if the current is helping
> ➤ Baders Beach heading north: Half day (or longer)

Approximate distances: From Baders Beach (one way)
> ➤ To the head of Booth Bay: 2 km (1.2 mi)
> ➤ To the head of Burgoyne Bay: 8 km (5 mi)
> ➤ To Southey Point: 12 km (7.5 mi)
> ➤ To Idol Island: 8 km (5 mi)

Warnings:

➤ Watch for ferry traffic going to and from Vesuvius (between Dock Point and Booth Bay).

➤ Current in Sansum Narrows.

➤ Idol Island is a culturally significant First Nations site. You should not land on it.

Getting there/launching: The Baders Beach launch is near the end of Collins Road. Take Rainbow Road from downtown Ganges, then left on Collins. Alternatively, you can take Lower Ganges Road west from Ganges, turn left onto Canal Road, and you'll merge with Rainbow Road. Parking is plentiful and beach access is easy.

Southey Point, Tent and Kuper Islands and the Secretary Chain

From Southey Point the coastline is interesting in both directions, especially to the south, where you paddle by the small but intriguing Idol Island (see under Baders Beach). In general, currents are minor in the entire area; on flood tides they flow north and on ebb tides they flow south. Just off the tips of both Southey Point and Penetakut Spit (on the northeast corner of Kuper Island) there are minor tidal rapids. They look exciting on a flat calm day, but really won't give you much of a thrill. When it's a little choppy out you don't see or feel the current unless you stop paddling and drift with it.

If you paddle southwest, you will come to Tent and Kuper islands. These are both First Nations land and most of the coastline is unsettled and quite beautiful.

Motorboats and sailboats generally stay away from the north end of Wallace Island at Chivers Point.

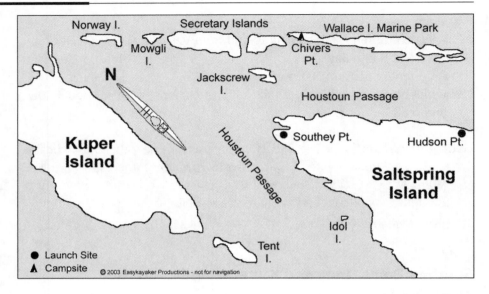

Our favourite option is paddling to the Secretary Chain (Wallace, Jackscrew, North and South Secretary, Mowgli and Norway islands). The crossing from Southey Point to Jackscrew takes about 10 minutes and only once have we had to deal with choppy seas in this area. Once you reach Jackscrew, you can avoid open water and paddle in the shelter of the many islands. There is a great little cove with a beautiful sandy beach, ideal for swimming, on the west side of Jackscrew Island. This cove is well protected, even on a windy day.

Most of Wallace Island is a provincial marine park. It has good campsites and hiking trails. Kayakers mainly keep to the north end of Wallace Island at Chivers Point, while the motorboats and sailboats go to Conover Cove on the south end. It takes about an hour to walk the length of the island on an old road.

Difficulty level: Novice to intermediate

Approximate travel times:
- ➤ Tent and Kuper islands—Half day
- ➤ Secretary Chain—Full day to multiple day

Approximate distances: From Southey Point
- ➤ To Jackscrew Island: 1 km (0.6 mi) one way
- ➤ Around Kuper Island and Tent Island: 21 km (13 mi) round trip

Warnings:

➤ Kuper and Tent islands are owned by the Penelakut First Nation.

➤ Houstoun Passage (between Wallace and Saltspring islands) tends to become windy in the afternoon during the summer, but the waves aren't usually too big.

➤ Except for Wallace Island, all the islands in the Secretary Chain are private property and clearly marked as such.

Getting there/launching: The Southey Point launch site is easy to find. Just take any of the three roads that go to the northern end of Saltspring Island (Sunset, North End, or North Beach roads). When you get to the northern tip of the island you'll come to Southey Point Road. Arbutus branches off Southey, and at the end of Arbutus there is a great launching beach. You can drive right down to the gently sloping beach. The only downside is that the turnaround is poor and parking is almost non-existent right at the beach.

Hudson Point

Hudson Point is at the east end of Houstoun Passage, directly across from the east end of Wallace Island Marine Provincial Park. There are good pullouts along the shore in both directions from Hudson Point, making this a fairly safe area to paddle. The water is usually calmer near the shore.

For those who like to go with the current, this is a good launch site for visiting Montague Harbour Marine Provincial Park on Galiano Island when the tide is ebbing. Crossing from Saltspring to Galiano this far north also lets the paddler avoid the traffic and fast water of Captain Passage. (For information on Montague Harbour see page 76.)

Though not much of a point, Hudson Point is a good launch area with beach access.

Difficulty level: Novice to intermediate

Approximate travel times:
> ➤ Hudson Point area: Half day
> ➤ To Montague Harbour (Galiano Island): Full day to multiple day

Approximate distances:
> ➤ From Hudson Point to Montague Harbour (Galiano Island): 13 km (8.1 mi) one way. Go to the southeast tip of Wallace Island, over to Retreat Cove on Galiano Island, and southeast to Montague Harbour.
> ➤ Hudson Point to James Bay (Prevost Island): 13.5 km (8.4 mi) one way
> ➤ Hudson Point to Walker Hook: 8 km (5 mi) round trip

Warning: Houstoun Passage sometimes gets a bit bumpy as the current and wind both get mildly funnelled here.

Getting there/launching: Hudson Point is not much of a point, but it's a good beach access. It's located off North Beach Road and has a highly visible sign. The access is a steep boat ramp. The beach area is small at high tide and extensive at low tide. The parking area on North Beach Road at the top of the boat ramp will accommodate quite a few cars, and you can find more wide spots for parking up and down the road.

Long Harbour

Long Harbour is a wonderful place to paddle. It's 5 km (3.1 mi) long at high tide and 3 km (2 mi) at low tide. This is probably the best launch site if you're going to Prevost Island Protected Area (see page 74), and is also a great launch site for a trip to Montague Harbour Marine Provincial Park on Galiano Island if there is a flooding tide (see page 76). Another nice paddle is to round Scott Point and explore the Chain Islands of Ganges Harbour (see page 73). There is a great beach and lunch spot on Third Sister Island.

Difficulty levels:
> ➤ Exploring Long Harbour: Novice
> ➤ Long Harbour to James Bay (Prevost Island): Novice to intermediate
> ➤ Long Harbour to Montague Harbour (Galiano Island): Novice to intermediate

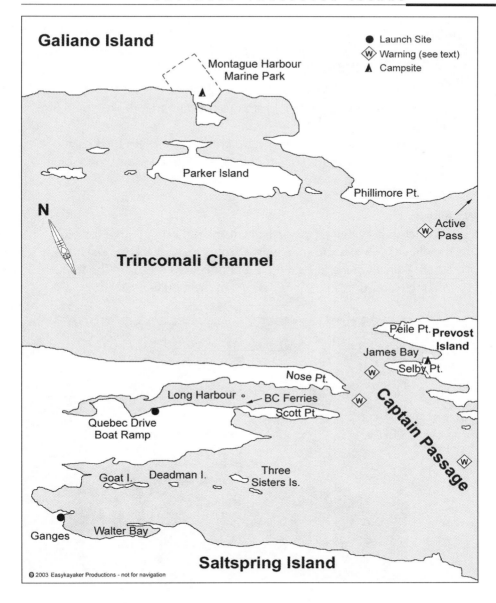

Approximate travel times:

> ➤ Exploring the length of Long Harbour: Half day
> ➤ Long Harbour to James Bay (Prevost Island): Half day to multiple day
> ➤ Long Harbour to Montague Harbour (Galiano Island): Multiple day
> ➤ Long Harbour to Chain Islands: Full day

Approximate distances:

➤ Exploring Long Harbour: 6 km (3.75 mi) at low tide and 10 km (6.3 mi) at high tide (round trip)

➤ Long Harbour to James Bay (Prevost Island): 5.5 km (3.4 mi) one way

➤ Long Harbour to Montague Harbour (Galiano Island): 10 km (6.3 mi) one way

➤ Long Harbour to Chain Islands: 16 km (10 mi) round trip if circum-navigating the Chain Islands group; 12 km (7.5 mi) round trip if only visiting Third Sister Island

Warnings:

➤ Watch out for ferries, particularly at the mouth of Long Harbour—they have little room to manoeuvre. You should check the schedule before launching. Ferries sound their horns before leaving the terminal in Long Harbour, and they can be heard from quite a distance.

The foot of Quebec Drive has a gentle slope, allowing you to drive to the water's edge to launch.

➤ Currents in Captain Passage (3 knots)

➤ Watch for turbulence around Nose Point and Selby Point when the current is running.

Getting there/launching: There is a great little boat ramp at the end of Quebec Drive, which is off Long Harbour Road. The launch site has a gentle slope. You can drive to the water's edge and there is parking nearby.

Locals call this beach on Third Sister Island, Chocolate Beach.

Ganges Harbour

Except for the boat traffic, which is mostly concentrated in its centre, the harbour is a paddler's paradise of small islands, interesting coves and unique homes. Goat, Deadman, First Sister, Second Sister and Third Sister islands make up the Chain Islands in Ganges Harbour (map pg 71). It's fun to paddle around them, but they are all private property. However, there is a beach on Third Sister Island you can pull up on for a break.

Difficulty level: Novice

Approximate travel time: Half day

Approximate distance: Exploring Ganges Harbour and the islands: 8 to 10 km (5 to 6.3 mi)

Warnings:
> ➤ Watch for boat traffic.
>
> ➤ The spit and Walter Bay on the south side of the harbour are a bird sanctuary and paddlers are asked to stay a good distance offshore when paddling by.
>
> ➤ The five Chain Islands are privately owned. Please respect private property.

Getting there/launching: There's a dinghy dock and a government dock in Ganges Harbour, as well as a ramp between Centennial Park and Grace Point for launching kayaks. The only problem is that this area can be extremely busy during weekends. If you're going on an overnight trip, you will need to find a place to park that isn't in the heart of Ganges.

Prevost Island Protected Area

The James Bay portion of Prevost Island is a protected area, part of the Pacific Marine Heritage Legacy, and is managed by BC Parks (map pg 63, 71).

Hiking trails lead from the head of James Bay to the north shore of the island. The camping area is a cell phone dead zone, so if you must talk to someone on your cell you will have to climb to a high spot or paddle out past Selby Point.

James Bay at low tide. Hiking trails beginning at the head of the bay lead to the north shore of the island.

Prevost has lovely pebble beaches with a shallow slope. On a sunny day they absorb heat and then warm the water as the tide floods, making this an ideal place to swim.

James Bay provides good anchorage, so even though you may be the only camper, there will likely be other people in the area. We were there on a three-day weekend and there were only two other tents and about 10 boats anchored in the bay. We couldn't see the other tents from our campsite and only saw a few people. That same weekend Montague Park was full and had at least 100 boats anchored nearby.

Difficulty level: Novice to intermediate due to current and boat traffic

Approximate travel time: Half day or longer

Approximate distances:
- ➤ From Long Harbour: Less than 6 km (3.75 mi)
- ➤ From Ganges: About 7.5 km (4.6 mi)
- ➤ From Hudson Point: 14 km (8.7 mi) to James Bay
- ➤ Note that the only open-water crossing is less than 1 km (0.6 mi)

Warnings:
- ➤ Watch for boat traffic.
- ➤ Currents in Captain Passage can reach 3 knots for periods of one to four hours on days when the moon is new or near full.
- ➤ There can be strong tidal flows where Captain Passage meets Trincomali Channel, especially on a flood tide. You should time your paddle for slack current.
- ➤ There can be turbulence at Nose and Selby points.
- ➤ Peile Point is a bird sanctuary and is off-limits to the public.

Getting there/launching: The closest launch is in Long Harbour (see under Long Harbour for details).

Camping: Camping is allowed in a large meadow at an orchard site on the island. The meadow extends to the beach, so you don't have to pack your gear very far. There are no developed campsites, but there is space for tents between the old fruit trees and there is an outhouse at the south side of the meadow. At the time of publication, camping was free. There is no drinking water available at the park, so make sure you bring your own.

Montague Harbour Marine Provincial Park (Galiano Island)

At 28 km (17.4 mi) long and 6 km (3.75 mi) across at its widest point, Galiano is the second largest of the Southern Gulf Islands and is said to be the driest (map pg 63, 71). It's an interesting place to visit and has been described as an island of artists. Its restaurants run from basic to five star and there is a full range of accommodations available.

Established as BC's first marine park in 1959, Montague Harbour Marine Provincial Park is 89 hectares of white sandy beaches, open meadows, large trees, craggy headlands and protected harbours. Visitors can observe middens in many areas along the shoreline. These First Nations shellfish refuse heaps date back 3,000 years. They are protected under BC law. Please do not disturb these archaeological sites.

Dionisio Alcala-Galiano, a Spanish naval commander, arrived in the area in 1792 and is credited with being the first European to visit the Southern Gulf Islands. The name Montague Harbour, which first appeared on surveying charts in the 1850s, commemorates a British naval officer. Forty years later, Captain Gray settled on what's now known as Gray Peninsula and cultivated an orchard. His produce was shipped to Victoria. Some signs of the orchard still remain within the park.

Montague Harbour Marine Provincial Park makes a great base for exploring Galiano's southern shoreline and the five nearby islands. You can also paddle over to Prevost Island for some hiking and exploring.

Difficulty levels:
> ➤ Around Montague Harbour: Novice
> ➤ To/from Prevost Island or Saltspring Island: Intermediate

Approximate travel time:
Multiple days for a round trip from Saltspring Island

Approximate distances:
> ➤ Montague Harbour to Prevost Island: 14 km (8.7 mi) round trip
> ➤ Montague Harbour to Long Harbour (Saltspring): 10 km (6.3 mi) one way

Warnings:
> ➤ **Do not paddle in Active Pass.** There are very strong currents and a high amount of large boat traffic. If you paddle too close to the entrance of the pass, you could end up being sucked into it. A kayaker can paddle up to 4 knots/hr, but the pass can run at 8 knots/hr. This is

the most heavily used marine passage in the Southern Gulf Islands.

➤ Watch for boat traffic in Montague Harbour.

Getting there/launching: Ferry service is available from Vancouver, Victoria and Saltspring Island, so it's easy to get to Galiano, even though it's not always a quick trip. For schedule information call 1-888-223-3779 (in BC) or 250-386-3431 (outside BC), or go to *www.bcferries.com*. You can make reservations on-line or by calling 1-888-724-5223 (in BC) or 604-444-2890 (outside BC). You can also get to Galiano by kayak from Saltspring.

Camping: As there is road access to Montague Harbour Marine Provincial Park, it can be a busy place. Fortunately you can go on-line to *www.discovercamping.ca* or phone 1-800-689-9025 to reserve a camp-site. There is a fair amount of space between the sites and many have tent platforms. This park has running water, trash cans and firepits, but no showers. There are cafés and restaurants nearby. Camping currently costs $15 per party per night. There are about 25 drive-in and 15 walk-in campsites. Kayakers will have to pack everything uphill from the beach, with a bit of a walk to even the closest campsite.

Travel notes (Gary)

We did not plan our first paddle from Saltspring Island to Prevost Island Protected Area and Montague Harbour Marine Provincial Park well, but it was a lot of fun. Even though the weather looked iffy, we decided to go prepared to camp, know-ing that it might end up just being a day paddle. We didn't spend much time packing, and food consisted of high-octane trail mix with lots of chocolate and dried fruit mixed in, some granola bars, fruit juice and pop.

Neither of us are strangers to Saltspring Island but we certainly don't know it as well as the kayak outfitters who live and operate there. After we left the ferry we looked at several launch sites along North End Road and in Long Harbour, then travelled to Ganges to talk to Jack Rosen of Island Escapades and Bill Elford of Sea Otter Kayaking, who gave us a lot of sound advice. Paul and I had a large lunch, knowing this might be our last real meal for a while.

Time to paddle. We launched at the foot of Quebec Drive around 2:30 p.m. and paddled up Long Harbour. The ferry was due to depart at 4:00 p.m. and slack current would be about 3:55 p.m. Ideally we wanted to be just behind the ferry when we crossed over from Long Harbour to Prevost Island. This would keep us out of the ferry's way, and the current would be just starting to flood, giving us a gentle push.

We ended up at the crossing early, but the current wasn't very strong even though it was against us. We had been warned about the turbulence off Nose and Selby points. I watched as a large sailboat motored by Nose Point and bobbed noticeably. As we neared the point we saw why. The light wind was blowing against the current and there was an impressive set of standing waves.

Boat traffic was wild! We headed across toward Selby Point, dodging boats travelling in all directions. The crossing only took about 10 minutes. There were small standing waves at Selby Point, too, but we paddled through them to take a closer look at the shore before rounding Selby Point into James Bay.

James Bay is protected from the prevailing winds that blow in from Juan de Fuca and Haro straits, but it is exposed to westerlies from Trincomali Channel. Today had been typical, with the winds blowing from the southwest between 1 and 5 p.m. Once in James Bay the water was like glass.

We landed at the orchard and checked out the camping area. Next we paddled over to the head of James Bay and went for a short walk. We were tempted to set up camp here, but the purpose of our trip was to explore, and we had paddled less than 6 km (3.75 mi). It was only 5 p.m., so we decided to carry on to Montague Harbour.

We quickly rounded Peile Point, and it took about 30 minutes to complete the crossing to the entrance to Montague Harbour. Just before we reached the other side, we were hit by the wake from a large sailboat travelling almost parallel to our course. We should have turned and crossed it, but instead we rode it. It started interacting with the currents from Active Pass and seemed to get bigger, and then it started breaking. It was moving slowly, probably due to the currents, so we paddled out and stayed just ahead of it, but that was tiring. We didn't want to turn and get broadsided by breaking waves, so we slowed and let it pass us.

The current and wind flowing into Montague Harbour gave us a free ride, and about 30 minutes later we were at the provincial marine park. Our original idea was to find a campsite, set up and paddle over to a café for supper—but the campground was full. So we explored the campsites, had a snack of goat pepperoni that I got in trade for a copy of our book, *Easykayaker*, paddled around the park and visited some of the beautiful white sand beaches.

Coasting into Montague Harbour. This provincial marine park is home to some spectacular white sand beaches.

At 6:30 p.m. we set out against the light wind and mild current to the navigational light at Phillimore Point. There we stopped on a patch of pure white, ground-up oyster shell beach for some trail mix and psyched ourselves up for the crossing back to Prevost Island. The crossing turned out to be serene. There was no wind or noticeable current, and no boat traffic other than a picturesque view of a ferry coming out of Active Pass and heading away from us toward Victoria.

Our trip had started at 8 a.m., and we had been either paddling or hiking since 2:30 p.m. It was now about 8 p.m. and we were three-quarters of the way across to Prevost, not far from pitching camp. But we seemed to be going in slow motion. We put on a final burst of speed. It didn't last long, but it made a difference. The light at Peile Point loomed closer, and soon we were past it and into James Bay.

We had listened to the latest weather update on my VHF radio as we paddled over. Showers were predicted for the night. We set up the tents, had a snack as dusk fell, watched the beautiful evening colours and saw a deer wander into the orchard meadow. After paddling 19 km (11.8 mi) and doing some hiking, we both slept well.

Sunday morning I was awake early, as usual, and got up around 6:45 a.m. to blue skies and sunshine. I went for a wonderful hike, but lost my trail on the way back and ended up doing some interesting detours.

By the time I was back at camp, the sky was darkening and it looked like the deluge would start at any moment. We had a quick breakfast and packed up. The tides were unusual. Normally there are two highs and two lows each day. On this day there was one very long high tide and one normal low tide. The high tide had peaked during the night, and the long period of slack current and tide would last until about 10:30 a.m. We checked the BC Ferries schedule and saw that we wouldn't be competing with the ferry. The crossing was smooth; there was almost no boat traffic, no turbulence at Nose and Selby points and it even looked like the sky was clearing.

The tide was high enough to provide some interesting paddling in Long Harbour just inside Nose Point. There are a couple of buildings on an islet here. Near the buildings there is a little rocky area that had a striking display of blue camus, pink sea blush and bright yellow stonecrop plants in bloom.

Just after we passed the islet a headwind hit us. It seemed unfair to have to fight this hard after the light headwind we'd had the day before going the other direction. We crossed over to the southern shore. The sky was darkening again, and we hugged the shore, paddling under boat ramps to avoid the breeze. Paul watched a mink run down one of the ramps only a metre above my head. It stopped for a moment on a nearby float and stared at Paul. About three-quarters of the way down Long Harbour the wind quit and the water surface turned to glass. Rain started to sprinkle just as we reached our landing spot and the journey's end.

Even though this was a rushed trip, we both had a great time. As we made our way to the ferry terminal at Vesuvius, we were already planning a return trip for more paddling. One of these days I would love to spend four to six days paddling all the way around Saltspring Island. There are lots of campsites and B&Bs at well-spaced intervals to make this a very fun trip.

Central Vancouver Island

Bamfield Area

Bamfield Area

The Bamfield area, on the southern side of Barkley Sound, has something to offer kayakers of all levels. For those who enjoy leisurely paddling in calm conditions, Poett Nook, Bamfield Inlet and Grappler Inlet are jewels. Pachena Bay can be a great place to play in the surf. Spend a day exploring along Mills Peninsula in Trevor Channel or cross the channel to the Deer Group Islands for an extended camping trip. No matter where you go you are bound to see phenomenal West Coast scenery and wildlife. If you're lucky you may even spot grey whales in Trevor Channel.

CHS chart: 3671—Barkley Sound

Tidal reference port: Tofino

Weather and sea conditions reference:
- ➤ Cape Beale
- ➤ Pachena Point
- ➤ West Coast Vancouver Island South

Prevailing winds: Afternoon winds from the west. These winds can cause waves from the southwest in Trevor Channel. Winds in the area can rise suddenly, so it's essential to have up-to-the-minute marine forecasts for any exposed area.

Warnings:

➤ Crossing Imperial Eagle Channel by kayak to the Broken Group Islands is not recommended, as this area can quickly become very rough.

➤ Do not try landing south of Brady's Beach on Mills Peninsula. This area has dangerous surf.

➤ The water around Cape Beale can be extremely rough, and weather conditions here can change rapidly. There are few places to land as the coastline is mostly exposed rock cliffs. There are strong currents, overfalls, tide rips and a hidden reef. Only very experienced kayakers should try to paddle in this area and we do not recommend it.

➤ The west side of Diana Island (Deer Group) can be hazardous.

➤ Bears populate the area. Do not store food in tents or kayaks when camping—hang food from trees.

➤ There is First Nations territory in most paddling areas. You should not land on it without permission from the local band office. For information call 250-728-3414.

➤ When travelling to Bamfield, be prepared for rain. Bamfield receives an average of 270 cm (106 in) of rainfall per year. July and August are the driest months.

Brady's Beach

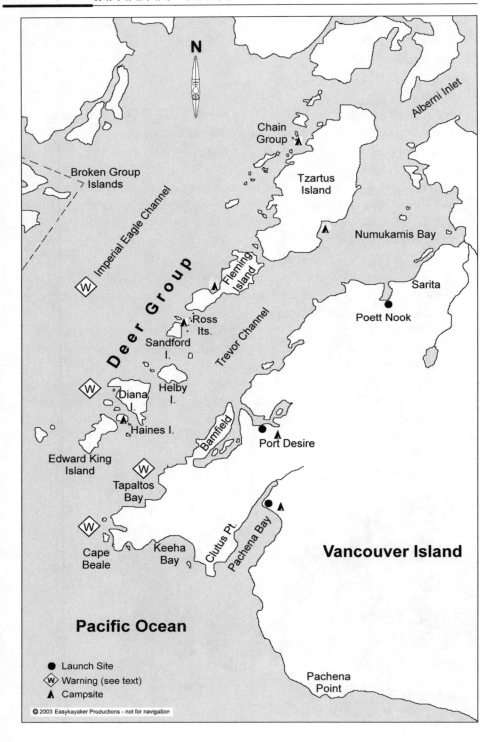

N

Alberni Inlet

Chain Group

Tzartus Island

Broken Group Islands

Imperial Eagle Channel

Numukamis Bay

Sarita

W

Deer Group

Fleming Island

Poett Nook

Ross Its.

Sandford I.

Trevor Channel

W

Helby I.

Diana I.

Bamfield

W

Haines I.

Port Desire

Edward King Island

W

Tapaltos Bay

Vancouver Island

W

Cape Beale

Keeha Bay

Clutus Pt.

Pachena Bay

Pacific Ocean

● Launch Site
Ⓦ Warning (see text)
▲ Campsite

© 2003 Easykayaker Productions - not for navigation

Pachena Point

Getting there:

➤ The easiest and most scenic way to reach Bamfield is by travelling aboard the MV *Lady Rose* or the MV *Frances Barkley*. At the time of writing, Lady Rose Marine Services provided transportation on these two historic ships from Port Alberni to Bamfield five days a week during the summer and three days a week during the off-season. Information is available at *http://www.ladyrosemarine.com/* or 250-723-8313. In the summer months we recommend that you reserve space for yourself and your kayak in advance. There is a fee for transporting kayaks.

➤ Pachena Bay Express provides a charter van service from Port Alberni to Pachena Bay. Information is available at 250-728-1290. Pachena Bay Express also provides transportation between Pachena Bay and Bamfield, a 4-km (2.5-mi) trip. It does not transport kayaks.

➤ Driving to Bamfield can be quite an experience. For those travelling from Nanaimo and areas north, take the Bamfield Road from Port Alberni. For those travelling from Duncan and areas south, take the Nitinat River Road from the west end of Cowichan Lake. Both roads are well signed for Bamfield, as are the turnoffs along the way. Both routes require about 85 km (53 mi) of travel on active logging roads that can be in rough shape. Pull over and stop well off the road for all logging trucks. These oversized trucks carry long, wide loads of logs and are particularly dangerous on curved sections of road. Normally the trucks are not used on Saturdays and Sundays, so these are safer days to travel. Drive with headlights on at all times. Fuel up at either Port Alberni, Duncan or Lake Cowichan before heading off on the industrial roads, and make sure your spare tire is inflated and ready for use. Sarita Lake Recreational Site is a great place for a rest stop.

Accommodations: Lodges, cottages and B&Bs. In the summer contact the Bamfield Tourist Information Centre (250-728-3006) or the Bamfield Chamber of Commerce (*www.bamfieldchamber.com*) for more information, or call Tourism BC, 1-800-435-5622, to make a reservation.

Note: Difficulty levels, approximate travel times, distances, location-specific warnings, launch sites and camping information are listed under specific paddling areas.

Pachena Bay and Keeha Beach

The Pachena Bay Campground, owned and operated by the Huu-ay-aht First Nation, is a good launching place for day paddles, and there are several hiking trails in the vicinity. Pachena Bay has a lovely white sand beach edged by rain forest. Nearby Keeha Beach, in Keeha Bay, has been described as one of the most beautiful beaches along the West Coast (map pg 84).

Though beautiful, be careful—Keeha Beach is subject to rapid changes in winds and wave height.

Difficulty levels:
➤ Pachena Bay: Novice to intermediate
➤ Pachena Bay to Keeha Beach: Intermediate to advanced

Approximate travel times:
➤ Exploring Pachena Bay: Half day
➤ Pachena Bay to Keeha Beach: Full day

Approximate distance: The midpoint of Keeha Beach is approximately 6 km (3.75 mi) from Pachena Bay.

Warnings:
➤ Weather and sea conditions can change very rapidly in this area.
➤ Possibility of strong surf. Paddlers must be comfortable doing surf launches and landings.
➤ Both Pachena Bay and Keeha Beach have a southwesterly exposure and are subject to rapid changes in wind and wave height.

Getting there: Pachena Bay is 4 km (2.5 mi) southeast of Bamfield on the Bamfield Road. To get to Keeha Beach by kayak, follow the coastline around Clutus Point. You can also access Keeha Beach by rough trail through Pacific Rim National Park.

Launching: There is a great place to launch kayaks between campsites T6 and T7. You can back your vehicle to the logs just above the high-tide line, unload your kayaks and then park near the beach access.

Camping: Pachena Bay Campground, 250-728-1287

Travel notes (Paul)

Our most recent trip to Bamfield coincided with excellent weather. The island's rugged west coast, with its sandy beaches and lush rain forest, is beautiful in any weather, but on hot sunny days it's paradise. The dirt road to Bamfield, however, is hellish. Bamfield receives 2.7 m (9 ft) of rain annually, so the chances are high that the road will be potholed from a rainstorm. The road's condition also depends on how long it has been since it was graded. Unfortunately we hit it under worst case conditions— potholed and ungraded—and had to do most of the trip in first gear. The locals said they'd never seen it so bad.

The sun was only a few degrees above the trees on the western shore when we laid our boats at the edge of the incoming tide in Pachena Bay. Gary and I slipped into our kayaks and paddled toward the surf, which was breaking at a height of 40 cm (16 in). I paddled vigorously through the surf and watched it break along the top edge of my sprayskirt, soaking the sleeves of my T-shirt. Gary got even wetter.

We glided along the western shoreline, admiring the small caves on the north shore of Pachena Bay, enjoying the evening paddle. We were surprised to find a sailboat anchored in a small cove. Because the weather and wave conditions here can change in as little as 20 minutes, most sailors will not anchor in this general area. A sailor could row ashore and then find the incoming waves have changed to West Coast rollers backed by strong winds, making it dangerous to return to the boat.

As we neared Clutus Point the winds began to pick up and we found ourselves in a bit of a swell. With the sun now falling behind the trees we caught a few waves and paddled back to the beach. Playing in the surf is easier said than done. Gary entered the breakers first and his boat turned sideways as the biggest wave crested and lost its energy to the underlying sands. I rode the next wave in and watched as Gary rolled over in slow motion. Fortunately he suffered no more than sand up his jacket and a thorough soaking.

We pulled our boats up onto a sand dune and walked over to the Pachena River, which enters the bay on its western side. A fairly deep channel has cut through the sand at the mouth. The only obstacle for a kayak entering the river would be breaking surf. On a higher tide we probably would have been tempted to paddle up the river.

Mark Hall, former general manager of Seaward Kayaks, demonstrates his technique in the surf.

Note from Gary

Playing in the surf is a gas, but rolling over in shallow water can be hard on the body. I knew to ride in on a breaking wave, but I was having so much fun racing the surf I got carried away. As I was only 6 m (20 ft) from the beach, the backflow caught me and pulled me back and sideways into a 60- to 75-cm (2- to 2.5-ft) wave, which instantly lifted me up and turned me upside down as it broke. That didn't bother me. What made me mad was that I didn't brace or even try to roll back up. One of these days, I'll head back with my wetsuit or drysuit and get some more practice playing in the surf.

West Coast Trail (including Pachena Point Lighthouse) and Cape Beale Trail

The former West Coast Lifesaving Trail was reopened as a 77-km (50-mi) hiking trail in 1969, renamed the **West Coast Trail** and, a year later, made part of Pacific Rim National Park. It has since become one of the most popular hiking routes in Canada. It was beginning to deteriorate due to the sheer numbers of hikers until Parks Canada developed a booking system for those hardy souls planning to hike the full length of the trail. You don't need reservations for day hikes, but you're supposed to let the park office know of your intentions. The trail office is at the end of the Pachena Bay campsite road. You can walk in from the campsite or drive in from the main Bamfield road.

Gary on the West Coast Trail, one of the most popular trails in Canada. Those who wish to hike its full length must make reservations.

Several daytime hikes are available in this area:

The return hike to **Pachena Point Lighthouse**, located 10 km (6.3 mi) along the trail, takes approximately six hours. The path here is quite wide and level. For hikers travelling the entire West Coast Trail it's either a picturesque start or, if they started in Port Renfrew, an easy end to the trip. (If you've ever carried a 32 kg/70 lb backpack over narrow, muddy trails or up a series of ladders, you know what we mean). The round trip to the lighthouse is an exquisite day walk. There are several viewpoints along this spectacular coastline. A good portion of the hike is slightly inland rather than directly along the beach. Along the way you might spot remains of the old telegraph line that followed this course. The Pachena Point station was built in response to the *Valencia* disaster and other shipwrecks. It was made of wood because its location high above the water and far from any sandy beaches made building a concrete lighthouse impractical. It is the only eight-sided wooden lighthouse on the West Coast.

The turnoff to the **Cape Beale Lighthouse, Keeha Bay** and **Tapaltos Beach trails** is located approximately 2.5 km (1.5 mi) from the Pachena Bay exit as you travel toward Bamfield. Turn left at the powerhouse. The trailhead to the three destinations is less than 2 km (1.2 mi) farther down the road. The trail to Keeha Bay is 3.5 km (2.2 mi) one way. The 6-km (3.7-mi) trail to the lighthouse ends short of its destination, which can only be reached at low tide. Gary and I have not hiked these trails but have been told they are fairly rough and very muddy.

Valencia

Over the years, the stretch of coast known as the "Graveyard of the Pacific" has swallowed dozens of ships and claimed hundreds of lives. Of all

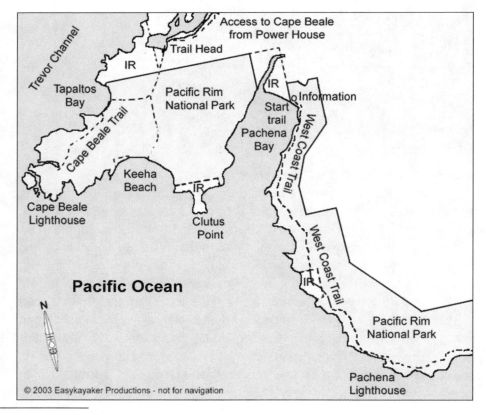

© 2003 Easykayaker Productions - not for navigation

the shipwrecks to take place here, the most famous one is the *Valencia* disaster. On January 22, 1906, the steamer, carrying 104 passengers and 64 crew, missed the beacon and foghorns at Cape Flattery and the entrance to the Juan de Fuca Strait and ran aground near Pachena Point. This marked the beginning of a 40-hour ordeal that has been described as the most shameful incident in Canadian maritime history. It seems confusion and panic aboard ship, combined with the lack of courage of other vessels' captains, who would not launch boats to go to the foundering steamer, led to the deaths of most people aboard the *Valencia*. The ship, with a gaping hole in its hull, soon lost its engines and lights to rising water. Huge waves crashed over the vessel. The poorly trained crew improperly timed the launching of lifeboats, and in minutes the sea crushed the boats like wooden matchsticks against the hull of the ship. In the end only 36 people survived.

Tapaltos Bay

Tapaltos Bay, located about 3 km (1.9 mi) northeast of Cape Beale, has a westerly exposure to the Pacific Ocean. Liz Isaac, owner of Bamfield Kayak Centre, calls Tapaltos a "dumping surf beach" because of its steep slope. She says it's treacherous on both low and high tides. As a paddler approaches the shore it is not obvious how far the drop is from the surf to the sand.

Gary and I heard about two Vancouver policemen who approached the shoreline unaware of the dangers. Suddenly the surf dropped them onto the inclined beach and rolled over them. They both survived the incident, but took away dislocated shoulders and a near-deadly lesson in West Coast beaches.

Liz also ran into trouble in the surf here. Evidence of her experience hangs on the wall of her kayak business. After striking the beach as the Vancouver policemen's boats had done, her kayak rolled with enough force to snap the Greenland paddle she owned. The scary thing is she wasn't paddling with it— it was a spare paddle secured under a bungee cord on her kayak!

Bamfield and Grappler Inlets

The sheltered waters of Bamfield and Grappler inlets have something for everyone: small coves and nooks to explore, lush islands, the remains of boats and buildings from earlier times, wildlife and a terrific view across Trevor Channel to the Deer Group Islands. The two inlets meet Trevor Channel at the same point, making them easy to explore on one trip.

Looking south from the Bamfield government docks.

Difficulty level: Novice

Approximate travel time: Half day to full day

Approximate distances:
➤ Exploring Grappler Inlet from the Port Desire launch site: 5 to 7 km (3 to 4.5 mi) round trip, depending on tide
➤ Exploring Bamfield Inlet from the Port Desire launch site: 8 to 10 km (5 to 6 mi) round trip, depending on tide
➤ Exploring both inlets: 16 km (10 mi) round trip for the length of both inlets including all the nooks and crannies

Warnings:
➤ Watch for boat traffic.
➤ If you paddle into Trevor Channel, be aware that weather and sea conditions can change quickly and may require stronger kayaking skills than you need for travelling the inlets. Do not try to land south of Brady's Beach along Mills Peninsula. The surf here is not visible until too late and the results can be deadly (see Tapaltos Bay warning, page 91). Paddling is more sheltered in the other direction towards Roquefeuil Bay and Poett Nook.
➤ The beach at the head of Bamfield Inlet is on a designated Indian Reserve. Do not land here without permission from the local band office. For information call 250-728-3414.
➤ Please respect private property.
➤ You can't reach the head of either Bamfield or Grappler Inlet or paddle on the northwest side of Burlo Island during low tide.

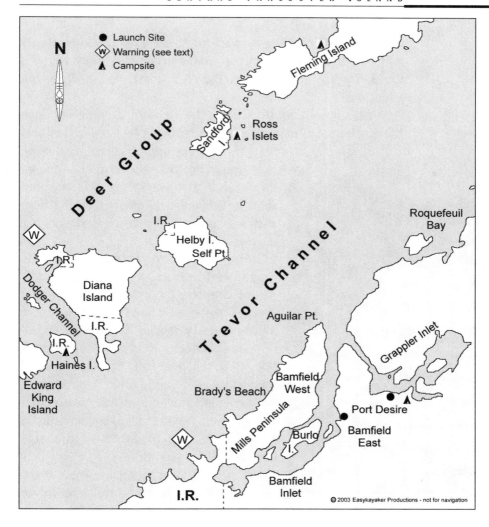

Recommended launch site: The boat ramp at Port Desire. (There is a small charge for launching, which you pay at the Centennial Park/Tourist Information Centre office.)

Other launch site: Bamfield East's government dock

Camping:
  ➤ Centennial Park/Campground: Located near the Port Desire boat ramp. Check in at the Info Centre. Call 250-728-3006 for information.
  ➤ Seabeam Fishing Resort and Campground: Turn right just before the Port Desire boat ramp. Call 250-728-3286 for information.

Travel notes (Gary)

I started my morning by checking to see if my quick-dry shorts and T-shirt were dry from my tumble in the surf. They weren't. Quick-dry is a relative term on the West Coast, also known as the Wet Coast.

Port Desire launch site

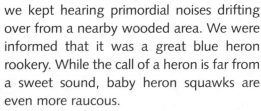

We discovered our truck had a flat tire from the gruelling drive the day before, and while the tire was being repaired in Bamfield we kept hearing primordial noises drifting over from a nearby wooded area. We were informed that it was a great blue heron rookery. While the call of a heron is far from a sweet sound, baby heron squawks are even more raucous.

With our tire fixed we headed down the road to Port Desire. Our plan was to paddle out of Grappler Inlet, take a look around Trevor Channel, visit Bamfield Inlet and save exploration of Grappler Inlet for the end of our paddle, which would coincide with high tide. It was a trade-off. Both Liz Isaac at Bamfield Kayak Centre and Sheryl Mass at Broken Island Adventures had told us that Grappler was the best place to see bears at low tide, but much more of the area would be accessible at high tide.

We paddled over to Aguilar Point at the tip of Mills Peninsula and out into Trevor Channel. We could see the Deer Group only a short 2-km (1.2-mi) crossing away, and the Broken Group Islands were a short but dangerous 11-km (6.8-mi) trip from us.

As we headed up Bamfield Inlet we saw a mixture of new and old buildings lining the shore, with boats of varying types and ages tied to the docks. Bamfield West, on the west side of the inlet, is not accessible by road, and a picturesque winding board-walk follows the shoreline.

The tide was too low for us to travel up the west side of Burlo Island, but it was just as well that we were forced to the east side as we were treated to the sight of a bear and cub on the beach as we paddled along.

After we passed Burlo and Rance islands, the inlet became

much wilder and almost unpopulated. We passed a number of abandoned and overgrown houses from days gone by. Old boats in various stages of decay slumped along the shores. Some were no more than keels and a few ribs, while others were almost intact. We knew the remains of fallen longhouses were also nearby but unseen and decaying in the dense growth.

We landed for lunch at a muddy beach near the head of the inlet. This land is on an Indian Reserve (IR), so you must get permission from the Huu-ay-aht Band to explore it. Otherwise you should stay below the high tide line. This beach is at the narrowest point of Mills Peninsula, and we could hear the surf on the other side of the jut of land. The welcoming poles that once graced the village here are now in the lobby of the Royal British Columbia Museum in Victoria. Similar poles have been erected outside the House of Huu-ay-aht, the band's community hall near Pachena Bay.

House of Huu-ay-aht. You must get permission from the Huu-ay-aht band before exploring land marked IR in this area.

On our way back we tried once more to go on the west side of Burlo Island. The tide was higher, but still not high enough—we would have needed to do a short portage to complete the trip. Partway down the west side we saw another mother bear and her cub. This cub was smaller than the one we saw earlier. It was standing on its hind legs, picking berries and looking teddy-bear cute. In comparison, Mom looked very strong as she turned rocks and small boulders over with one paw and ate the little crabs that hid below these rocks. We saw her attempt to turn a large rock that finally required the use of both front paws. I slowly paddled closer to take a photograph, but the hair on the back of Mom's neck went up—a signal that I had invaded her comfort zone. The water wasn't very deep and I know how fast a bear can bound through shallow water, so I eased away.

My photos were disappointing, but the experience of watching the bear and her cub was great. The light breeze was causing us to slowly drift towards the southern end of Burlo Island, the same direction as the bears were travelling, so we sat and enjoyed the show for quite a while. Eventually we paddled around the southern tip of the island and spoke to a man working on a boat at the only house in the area. I asked if the bears gave him any trouble. He said he'd never seen one there. When we told him there was a mom and cub about 100 m down the shore and coming his way, his expression changed noticeably.

After stopping in Bamfield West to visit the Net Loft Gallery and buy a Bamfield Kayak Festival T-shirt, we took a short walk along the boardwalk and then returned to our kayaks and paddled to Grappler Inlet.

Paddling towards the Bamfield boardwalk, where the weary paddler can relax and explore shops.

The mouth of Grappler Inlet is narrow, but it opens up at Port Desire. A charming islet, appropriately named Flower Isle, is opposite Port Desire, appearing as a dot on our chart. A house on the islet hangs partly over the water; the wharf, walkways and flowerbeds are built from stone, and there are flowers everywhere. I spoke with the owners as they puttered about the gardens—a full-time job in the summer judging by the size of their display. An article in *Cottage Magazine* stated that in the 1940s a Spanish couple squatted here and built a small cabin. The next owner floated an old cannery or logging bunkhouse alongside and joined up the two buildings. The current owners, the Gisbornes, have done extensive renovations and repairs. The cabin now has a proper septic system, electricity and running water, which comes via a black plastic pipe that runs underwater about 300 m up a nearby creek. The local bears like to gnaw on the pipe, causing the occasional leak.

The high tide allowed us to poke into all the nooks and crannies of this mostly uninhabited inlet. We found the narrow area about halfway up the inlet especially beautiful, though the entire inlet was picturesque. We toured the head of Grappler clockwise, explored the mouths of the creeks and circumnavigated the large island. There were hundreds of California gulls, which we were later told was unusual for the area.

All day long we had met other kayakers, some guided, but most out on their own. We had also visited with locals along the shores. Paul described it as very social kayaking, but we were starting to feel the effects of paddling 16 km (10 mi) under a very warm sun. It was time to return to the truck.

Paul at entrance to Poett Nook, an ideal launching spot.

Back at Pachena Bay, my quick-dry shorts were finally dry after almost 24 hours. We grabbed some refreshments, then headed out onto the beach to catch the evening sun and sunset. Sitting not far from the small breakers, we could gaze down the wide sandy beach and look out to sea. It was a perfect way to end the day and rest before our next day's trip to Poett Nook and the Sarita River delta.

Poett Nook and Sarita Bay Area

Described as the most sheltered place in Barkley Sound, Poett Nook is an ideal launching spot for kayakers and fishermen, as well as a favourite launch for accessing the northern Deer Group and Chain Group Islands (see Deer Group, Tzartus Island and Chain Group, page 100). From the opening of Poett Nook there is a great view of Trevor Channel and Barkley Sound. There are lots of seabirds around the Sarita River delta and great crabbing in Sarita Bay, which is tucked into the east side of Numukamis Bay. Those wanting to extend their trip can paddle north from the Sarita River delta and investigate Hosie and Congreve islands.

Difficulty levels:
> ➤ Poett Nook: Novice
> ➤ Poett Nook to Sarita Bay: Intermediate

Approximate travel time: Half day

Approximate distances:

➤ Poett Nook to the Sarita River delta: 9 km (5.6 mi) round trip

➤ Sarita River delta to Congreve Island: 2 km (1.2 mi) to the southern tip of Congreve, 7.5 km (4.6 mi) round trip from the Sarita River delta if you circumnavigate Congreve

Warnings:

➤ Weather in Trevor Channel can change in as little as 20 minutes, creating rough sea conditions. You should check the weather forecast before heading out.

➤ On a low tide you will need to go around the outside of Santa Maria Island.

Getting there/launching: Poett Nook is located approximately 70 km (45 mi) from Port Alberni and 2.4 km (1.5 mi) off the Bamfield Mainline Road. There is a nominal fee to launch your kayak at this easy launch site and campsite. Pay the fee to the camp manager at the small store. There is another fee for leaving your vehicle overnight.

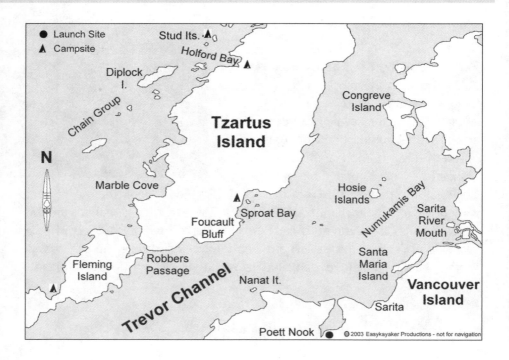

Travel notes (Paul)

We were immediately enthralled by Poett Nook as we settled our kayaks into its protected waters. The nook has a narrow opening to Trevor Channel and we paddled intently in the first minutes to see what lay beyond. The view of Trevor Channel and Barkley Sound was panoramic. Nearby Tzartus Island towered over the other islands, impressing us with its size.

From Poett Nook we headed for the Sarita River. We paddled past a small bay that contained a log landing and dryland sort yard, where bundles of logs were sliding down a skidway of peeled timber. We passed the bay in a few minutes and slowly left the engine noise behind.

A short jaunt later we reached a narrow channel filled with eel-grass between Santa Maria Island and the Vancouver Island coastline. We kayaked carefully through the channel, enjoying this natural crab habitat.

The Sarita River empties into Trevor Channel just northeast of Santa Maria Island. The river has filled the delta with sand. Beneath the surface of the water there is a drop from about 2 to 24 m (7 to 72 ft) in depth at the river mouth. A number of bird species frequent the river delta. We observed California gulls, ducks, bald eagles, hawks and a golden eagle. We could easily imagine bears foraging here.

We paddled about 150 m (492 ft) up the southern fork of the river until we hit some light rapids. I paddled a little farther upstream, watched a small troop of ducks disappear around a corner and under a log, and noticed what looked like a golden eagle perched on a stump. Seconds later it shot about 5 m (16 ft) above the water. It seemed to be having difficulty hanging in the breeze. Then I saw its intent—a mother duck and her flock of ducklings were madly swimming toward the protection of an earth overhang. The golden eagle flew up and started its plunge down toward the ducks when suddenly a bald eagle swept across the flats, distracting the golden eagle from its attack. The golden eagle agilely recovered at water level and made a quick exit in the opposite direction while the bald eagle continued on its way. By this time the river had turned my kayak, and I struggled to align it downstream.

We returned to Poett Nook with a light westerly brushing our cheeks. About 2.5 km (1.5 mi) west of Poett Nook is Nanat Islet and a point of land. Many paddlers cross Trevor Channel from here to Tzartus Island.

After following the coastline to Nanat Islet, we returned to explore Poett Nook and discovered a small stream entering it along the southwestern shore. The stream could probably be navigated for a short distance on a fairly high tide.

This beautiful sunny day was the end of our Bamfield area trip. We tied the kayaks onto the truck and headed back to Youbou and Cowichan Lake along a road that had been graded since our arrival and was, thank goodness, much improved.

Deer Group, Tzartus Island and Chain Group

The Deer Group Islands, Tzartus Island and Chain Group Islands are located to the north and northeast of Bamfield in Barkley Sound between Trevor and Imperial Eagle channels (map pg 84, 98). Compared to the nearby Broken Group Islands, this paddling area attracts only a small number of kayakers. Its popularity is growing, however, due to its spectacular beauty.

Southern Deer Group Islands

We have not yet been lucky enough to travel to the Deer Group, but we've heard about the islands' rock formations, sea caves, arches, sandy beaches, beautiful forests and wide variety of bird life. It is possible to circumnavigate Diana Island and return in one day. If you travel counterclockwise from Self Point (on Helby Island) around Diana you should avoid the afternoon headwinds. If it is gusty, Seppings Island and Edward King Island at the entrance to Dodger Channel provide shelter from the wind. Dodger Cove, now known as Dodger Channel, was once the site of a thriving village on Diana Island.

View of the Deer Group from Brady's Beach

Difficulty level: Intermediate to advanced

Approximate travel time: Full day to multiple day

Approximate distances: Distances for crossings under 500 m (0.3 mi) are not given. Many of the islands are less than 300 m apart.
➤ Aguilar Point on Mills Peninsula to Self Point on Helby Island: 2 km (1.2 mi) one way
➤ Bamfield or Port Desire to Helby Island and around Diana Island: about 15 km (9.3 mi) round trip
➤ Circumnavigation of Diana Island from Self Point on Helby Island: 8 km (5 mi)
➤ Self Point (Helby) to Sandford Island: 1.75 km (1 mi) one way

Warnings:
➤ Crossings of Trevor Channel must be carefully planned. Ocean swell and wind-whipped waves can strike paddlers broadside. A change in conditions from calm waters to whitecaps can occur in a 20- to 40-minute period. According to John Mass of Broken Island Adventures, you know the weather is going to change for the worse when you see a black line approaching from Effingham Island in the Broken Group Islands bringing wind and waves. Liz Isaac of Bamfield Kayak Centre says the conditions are fairly dependable on long, hot summer days. The winds start to blow at noon each day and rarely blow harder than 15 to 20 knots.
➤ The western side of Diana Island is exposed to the Pacific. Waves striking against the rocky shore rebound and generate choppy sea conditions.
➤ Voss Point (southern tip of Diana Island) and Kirby Point (northwest tip of Diana Island) are exposed to westerly winds.
➤ A strong westerly wind can pin you on the shore in any exposed area.
➤ Kirby Point on Diana Island is First Nations land. You are not allowed to camp here. However, you can seek permission from the camping attendant on Haines Island to visit during the day. There is a beautiful meadow and forest beyond the beach.
➤ The entire southern section of Diana Island is First Nations land.

Getting there/launching: Paddlers generally reach the Deer Group by kayaking from Bamfield or Port Desire to Helby Island. The crossing from

Aguilar Point on Mills Peninsula to Self Point on Helby Island should take about 30 minutes. Once you have crossed to the Deer Group you can travel southwest toward Diana Island or north along Helby's coastline toward Sandford Island. As westerlies typically blow in the afternoons, it's best to make this crossing in the morning. Local outfitters can also drop you off at almost any location in the islands.

Camping:

➤ Sandford Island: There are three campsites on the northeast shoreline of Sandford, which is northeast of Helby Island.

➤ Ross Islets: These islets, between Sandford and Fleming islands, are popular with kayakers looking for a place to camp.

➤ Fleming Island: A large bay on the north side of Fleming offers a beautiful beach with camping spots.

➤ Haines Island: This island, between Diana and Edward King islands, is owned by the Huu-ay-aht First Nation, but you can camp here for a fee. Make sure each paddler in your group is carrying at least $10 cash. Someone will come and collect the fee from you.

Strong kayakers required. Beware, sea and weather conditions change quickly in Trevor Channel.

Tzartus Island and the Chain Group

Tzartus, at the northeast end of the Deer Group, is the largest island in Barkley Sound. It is located adjacent to where Trevor Channel meets Alberni Inlet. Numerous sea-arches around Marble Cove and sandy beaches in Robbers Passage make it a favourite destination. We have not yet been here, but locals describe it as a wonderful place to get away from it all.

Difficulty level: Intermediate to advanced

Approximate travel time: Full day or multiple day

Approximate distances:
- ➤ Poett Nook to Nanat Islet: 2.5 km (1.5 mi) one way
- ➤ Nanat Islet to Foucault Bluff on Tzartus Island: 1.5 km (0.9 mi) one way

Warnings:
➤ Trevor Channel is subject to rough waters if westerlies blow. If westerlies begin to pick up it's best to head toward either Sproat Bay, where an oyster lease is located, or to Robbers Passage with its protected location and sandy beaches.

➤ Much of the easterly side of Tzartus Island consists of bluffs.

➤ You are requested not to camp on Tzartus Island beaches near oyster leases. There is clearly a problem in some of the campsites on this island, especially by late August, caused by kayakers' poor sanitation. Please use a honey bucket and pack your waste out. If you don't have a honey bucket, dig a deep cat hole in the woods, or dig a hole and defecate below the tide line on a beach far from any oyster leases.

Getting there/launching: Tzartus Island can be accessed from Poett Nook (see page 98) or from the southern Deer Group Islands.

Camping:
➤ Sproat Bay: You can camp in Sproat Bay if you don't interfere with the oyster lease.

➤ Holford Bay: There are campsites at this bay on Tzartus Island.

➤ Stud Islets: These islets in the Chain Group, just northwest of Holford Bay, are a popular camping area. There is reasonable protection on the lee side of the islets and islands from a westerly.

Enjoy your paddle in this area and please leave it clean for the next kayaker!

Local History

The first inhabitants of the Bamfield area were the Huu-ay-aht people. The village of Kiix?in, near the current site of Bamfield, was the Huu-ay-aht capital until the 1880s. Then the villagers moved away, and the village has remained untouched ever since. The federal government recently declared it a national historic site. Massive hand-hewn cedar posts and beams from several bighouses are still visible in the rain forest. The Huu-ay-aht Band (previously the Ohiat Band) is developing plans to allow tourists to visit the area by 2006, but at the time of writing it was off-limits to visitors.

The Huu-ay-aht had established trading links with the Europeans by the late 1700s. In 1859, Eddy Banfield set up a trading post and became the government agent until he died three years later. At first it was thought that he drowned in a boating accident, but later stories surfaced of murder. His alleged murderer was tried in Victoria and acquitted due to lack of evidence. Banfield's name remained associated with the area, though gradually it became changed to Bamfield.

After the Canadian Pacific Railway chose Bamfield as the terminus of the Trans-Pacific Telegraph Cable, electricity, tennis courts, a cinema and a dancehall appeared in this remote community. The Canadian Pacific Railway began constructing the Bamfield Cable Station, designed by Victoria architect Francis Rattenbury, in 1901. The cable ship *Colonia* began laying the 10,353-km-long (6,430-mi) telegraph cable at Bamfield on September 19, 1902. Part of the longest submarine telegraph cable system in the world, it went from Bamfield to Fanning Island in the South Pacific. From there another cable ran to New Zealand and Australia. The first messages were sent on November 1, 1902. The Bamfield cable was connected to telegraph wires running east to Vancouver, Montreal, Halifax and another cable under the Atlantic to London.

The Bamfield area is part of a dangerous stretch of coastline between Port Renfrew and Ucluelet known as the "Graveyard of the Pacific." In the 40 years between 1866 and 1906, 56 ships were destroyed here and 711 people died. The West Coast Lifesaving Trail (now the popular West Coast Trail) was built in response to these disasters. It gave marooned sailors a chance to walk to civilization, and a lifesaving station—equipped with a sail-and-oar-powered lifeboat—was established at Pachena Bay in 1906. In 1907 the first powered lifeboat in Canada was commissioned and the station moved to Bamfield.

On June 20, 1959, the last message was sent from the Bamfield Cable Station. The cable was rerouted to Port Alberni and the station closed. In 1972 the site and remaining buildings became the Bamfield Marine Station, which is owned and operated by Western Canadian Universities Marine Biological Society. The Bamfield Marine Station provides research facilities and technical assistance for scientists, graduate and undergraduate courses in marine and coastal sciences, and programs for schools and other interested groups. Bamfield now boasts a population of 300.

Ucluelet Inlet

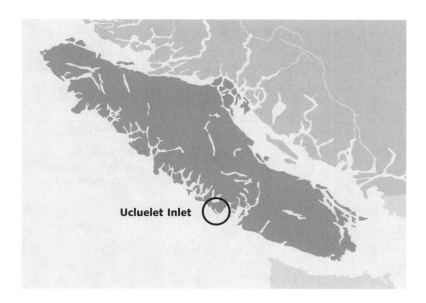

Ucluelet Inlet

Ucluelet, a quaint fishing port and town with a protected harbour on one side and the wild Pacific Ocean on the other, is an ideal location for kayaking, whale watching, storm watching and bear spotting. The town, located on the Ucluth Peninsula, boasts a population of about 1,700 people.

Ucluelet Inlet has an ambience similar to Bamfield's. It is a historic seaport that hasn't been overly commercialized for the tourist trade yet. A few small parts may have entered the 21st century, but much of the town still feels like

The Ucluelet coast

it's from yesteryear. The 8-km-long (5 mi) inlet shows few signs of settlement, though occasional relics dot the shore. As you paddle between Ucluelet and Hyphocus Island you will see houses on stilts, built by gold prospectors in the 1890s. A few fish-processing plants attract sea lions and eagles. You will likely encounter boat traffic in the area between the boat basin and the mouth of the inlet. The other half of the inlet is shallow and a good place to view bears, especially in the evening. Ideally you want a high tide to explore the shallow waters and coves at the head of the inlet. At low tide, on the other hand, there are white sandy beaches at the mouth of the inlet.

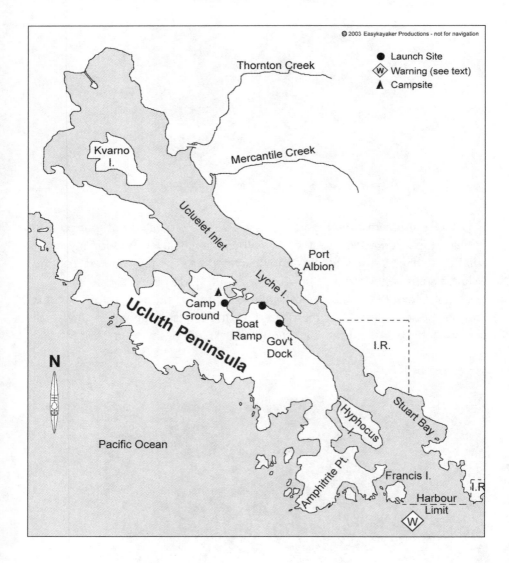

Difficulty levels:
> Inside the inlet: Novice
> Outside the inlet: Advanced (unless with a guide)

Approximate travel time: Half day to full day

Approximate distances:
> From Island West boat ramp to Port Albion: 0.7 km (0.4 mi) one way
> From Port Albion to Mercantile Creek: 1.5 km (0.9 mi) one way
> Exploring the inlet: 25 km (15.5 mi) if you're hugging the shoreline

CHS charts:
> 3671—Barkley Sound
> 3646—Plans Barkley Sound (Ucluelet Inlet)

Tidal reference port: Tofino

Weather and sea conditions reference:
> Amphitrite Point
> Lennard Island
> West Coast Vancouver Island South

Prevailing winds: Winds from the northwest during the summer from 11 a.m. to 5 p.m.

Warnings:
> Do not venture out past the Harbour Limit (Francis Island) as strong nor'westerlies can come up suddenly, making it hard to get back inside.
> Watch for large boat traffic in the southern portion of the inlet.
> Fog can roll in quickly and limit visibility.
> The area marked IR near the Harbour Limit (see map) is culturally significant to the local First Nations and should not be landed on. Sea caves there are ancient burial spots.
> The narrow channel between the government wharf and Lyche Island is a busy place with large boat traffic.
> The flats between Mercantile Creek and Thornton Creek are a sensitive shellfish habitat.
> Ucluelet is home to a healthy population of black bears—be bear smart.

Getting there: Ucluelet is 100 km (62 mi) west of Port Alberni and 295 km (183 mi) north of Victoria. The most scenic way to reach Ucluelet is by traveling aboard the MV *Lady Rose* or the MV *Frances Barkley*. Lady Rose Marine Services currently uses these two historic ships to offer trips from Port Alberni to Ucluelet. Information is available at *http://www.ladyrosemarine.com/* or 250-723-8313. We recommend that you reserve space for yourself and your kayak in advance. There is a fee for transporting kayaks.

Recommended launch sites:

➤ **Stairs at Government Wharf**: The government wharf and the Ucluelet Information Centre are both located at the foot of Main Street. Nearby a wide set of concrete steps leads down to a good but rocky launch site. You

can unload in front of the Info Centre and then usually find parking just a stone's throw away.

➤ **Island West boat ramp**: This launch site, part of the Island West Fishing Resort, is hidden just around the corner when you hit the foot of Bay Street. Once your boats and gear are off-loaded, park against the embankment in the gravel area on the other side of the building that houses Island West's marine store and the Eagle's Nest Marine Pub.

➤ **Ucluelet Campground** (for guests only): Owned by Island West, the campground has a good beach for launching. Turn left onto Seaplane Base Road just as you enter Ucluelet. You will see the entrance to the campground almost immediately on the right.

➤ **Coastal Knights** (for guests only): A little way past Port Albion, on the opposite side of the inlet from Ucluelet, is Coastal Knights B&B, which offers nice rooms, a great view and a nice launch site for guests. The owners also have a small kayak fleet and offer guided tours.

View from Coastal Knights, a kayaker-friendly B&B.

Other launch site: Thornton Creek at fish hatchery (useable at high tide)

Accommodations: Luxury resorts, motels and numerous B&Bs. Call the Visitor Information Centre at 250-726-4641.

Camping: Ucluelet Campground is a nice campground with large trees and a bit of elbow room between campsites. For reservations call 250-726-4355.

Travel notes (Gary)

Paul, his wife Imelda and I arrived in Ucluelet on a sunny afternoon. After checking into our motel we headed out to hike the Wild Pacific Trail and visit the lighthouse at Amphitrite Point, which is at about the midpoint on this very scenic trail.

Amphitrite Point Lighthouse is a historic but still important station, marking the entrance to Barkley Sound.

Wild Pacific Trail

The Wild Pacific Trail starts at He-tin-kis Park, located just past Roots Lodge on Peninsula Road near Coast Guard Road. Three trails actually start here and it can be a bit confusing. The trail on the right, closest to Roots Lodge, goes down to a pretty little protected beach called Terrace Beach. The middle trail is the start of the boardwalk portion of the Wild Pacific Trail. The trail on the left goes through He-tin-kis Park and connects with the Wild Pacific Trail.

Hiking the 2.5-km (1.5-mi) Wild Pacific Trail is well worth your time. The forest and ocean views are fabulous, and the lighthouse is squat but picturesque. When you start at the boardwalk end, you will find a viewing platform with a picnic table not far down the trail. From there a set of stairs leads to a small beach and cove protected by reefs and small islands. This is a good place

View from Wild Pacific Trail

to investigate tide pools. The climb back up to the trail is guaranteed to get the cardiovascular system into high gear. The section of the trail past the lighthouse offers views of Bamfield and the Broken Group Islands. Most of the trail is well situated for wave and storm watching. There are plans to extend the trail another 6 km (3.75 mi) north along the west coast.

Pictured above is the Amphitrite Point Lighthouse near Ucluelet. Its predecessor, a similar-looking wooden building, was washed away by a tidal wave on January 2, 1914. The current light, built close to the original location in 1915, and the lighthouse at Cape Beale are important stations on a treacherous coastline as they mark the entrance to Barkley Sound.

In 1919 James Frazer maintained the Amphitrite Point Lighthouse from Ucluelet's lifeboat station. He received only a $10 monthly stipend to keep the lamp wick burning. During all kinds of weather he hiked one mile to light the lamp each day at sunset. At midnight he returned to wind the machinery and trim the wick. He made a third trip at sunrise to snuff out the light.

After our hike we spent some time in the residential and business areas to get a feel for Ucluelet.

Then we drove over to the Port Albion side for a visit to the fish hatchery at Thornton Creek. When I had last been there the salmon were running and the black bear were fattening up on them in preparation for a long winter's nap. My photos of black bears in the evening shade hadn't turned out too well, so now, as we walked the boardwalk to the waterfall, I had my good camera with a telephoto lens—but the bears were somewhere else.

We carried on to Port Albion and Coastal Knights B&B to visit the proprietors, Randy and Cathy. Some of their clients were just paddling in after a guided day trip of the harbour.

Back in Ucluelet we had a meal to remember at the Peninsula Motor Inn and Restaurant. It's owned by Donnie Dong, the

grandfather of one of Paul's Grade 5 students, Kelsey. Donnie very graciously cooked us several specialty Chinese dishes.

Ucluelet from Port Albion

After supper we launched near the stairs by the government wharf and went for a short paddle. The afternoon winds had been late that day and were still blowing strong from the head of the inlet toward the mouth of the inlet (a northeast wind). We started off into the wind and then rode it back. Even though the wind was quite fresh, the waves didn't get much of a chance to build.

At 9 p.m. it was still light and warm, so we headed over to meet Tracy Morben of Majestic Ocean Kayaking to learn about Ucluelet paddling from her. Paul and I seldom visit pubs, but later that night we visited Island West's Eagle's Nest Marine Pub and watched dusk descend on the now still waters of Ucluelet Inlet.

As usual I woke up early the next morning, itching to be out on the water on such a warm day. Just before breakfast the fog rolled in, but it only lasted a few minutes. Typical West Coast weather. In a blink, fog can roll in, enveloping sea and land together and often reducing visibility to a few metres or less.

Today Imelda and I would be paddling together, leaving Paul on shore to hike, mind his inflamed wrist and enjoy a cappuccino. We launched from Island West's boat ramp and headed across the inlet toward the mouth of Mercantile Creek. The crossing is only about half a kilometre, but we made a couple of detours: first when we heard the barking of a sea lion and then to see an eagle on a piling. Both were near the fish plant at Port Albion. There's also an eagle's nest along the shore a short way northwest of the fish plant.

As we paddled I thought back to the previous November when I was fortunate to spend a day with the local aboriginal community. Old photographs of elders stared out from the walls of the community hall, and one seemed to keep calling me—I must have glanced at his photo a hundred times that day. During breaks I gazed at the beautiful white beaches of Stuart Bay and the George Fraser Islands through a window. Today, out on the water, I kept thinking of that elder and what life must have been like here in his time.

We travelled up Mercantile Creek as far as the depth would permit. Our quest was to photograph bear. Tracy had mentioned there was a waterfall a short distance up the creek, but we decided not to hike in to see it. Instead we went back to the inlet and made our way along the coast to Thornton Creek. I was scanning the area for bears using a great little monocular my wife gave me for Christmas. I find it much handier than binoculars when kayaking.

No bear, and time was running out, so we crossed over to the western shore and investigated the sun-bleached hulks of wooden boats from yesteryear that dot the shoreline. Even

Now a luxury hotel and restaurant, the MV Canadian Princess, a.k.a. the Willie J, carried out top secret assignments for the Royal Canadian Navy during the war.

though we could see the fog bank threatening to spill in from three different directions, we were in hot sunshine and loving it.

On our way back we made a detour into the boat basin and over to the MV *Canadian Princess*. This 72-metre (236-ft) floating hotel was the flagship of the Canadian Hydrographic Service from 1932 till 1975. Built as a steam ship, the *William J. Stewart*, in Collingwood, Ontario, in 1932, it came through the Panama Canal and up the West Coast. *Willie J*'s homeport was Victoria, and with a crew of 55 sailors and seven officers it worked the entire BC coast from mid-April to mid-October. During the war it carried out top-secret assignments for the Royal Canadian Navy. *Willie J* hit Ripple Rock on Vancouver Island's east coast on June 11, 1944, and was beached in the mud of Plumper Bay. It took almost a month to refloat the ship, but *Willie J* went on surveying the coast for another 31 years. On September 20, 1975, it retired to Patricia Bay in Victoria. A few years later the Oak Bay Marine Group purchased and restored the vessel, and this piece of West Coast history now makes up the heart of Ucluelet's Canadian Princess Resort, offering accommodation and a restaurant. We can thank ships like this one for the marine charts that so many mariners rely on.

On our way back around the breakwater we encountered a couple of sea lions, which one local referred to as "sea dogs." The fish plants all seem to have sea lions nearby, and there are now pilchards for them to feed on. Pilchards, or Pacific sardines, were abundant here until they mysteriously disappeared in the 1930s. They have recently and just as mysteriously returned; studies are being done to see if there are enough fish to support a commercial pilchard fishery. But back to the sea dogs. These sea lions are very different from those we have run into elsewhere. They're used to people and although they may be aggressive, they aren't as openly threatening as some we've met. As we paddled along from the breakwater, one joined us and swam most of the way to the boat ramp in line between my boat and Imelda's.

I'm sure this won't be the last time we paddle Ucluelet Inlet. Like so many other locations highlighted in this book, our time there was all too short, but enough to whet our appetite for more.

Local History

"Ucluth," in the language spoken by the local Nuu-chah-nulth people, means "safe harbour." The safe harbour in pre-contact times was home to a large population of Nuu-chah-nulth. This aboriginal community still lives here in the two locations marked I.R. (Indian Reserve) on the charts. Later, the name "Ucluth Inlet" was shortened to "Ucluelet."

The first non-Natives to arrive were fur sealers in the 1860s. Two of them, Captain Peter Francis and Captain William Spring, established a trading post at Spring Cove. During the 1880s some permanent settlers arrived, like William and James Sutton, who built a shingle and sawmill at what is now Port Albion. The Sutton Lumber Company did well and the Suttons eventually opened a general store.

Ucluelet was first serviced and supplied by the SS *Maud*, a Canadian Pacific Railway (CPR) boat, and then in 1913 the SS *Princess Maquinna* took over. These ships steamed up from Victoria three times a month. A First Nations elder from the old coastal village of Nitinat, along what is now the West Coast Trail, said that when the weather permitted, his people used to paddle out into the open ocean to drop off mail and passengers when the ship sailed by on its way from Victoria to Ucluelet.

In 1890 a rumour that a road was going to be built and the lure of excellent fishing encouraged more settlers to locate in the Ucluelet area. Gold was also discovered in Wreck Bay during the 1890s, which brought prospectors to Ucluelet. Unfortunately the gold was too fine and in too little quantity to be profitable.

By 1898 Ucluelet had a doctor and a mission school. A settler of note about this time was George Fraser, a Scottish horticulturalist, who spent more than 50 years developing hybrid rhododendrons and azaleas. His gardens were known to horticulturists around the world.

Ucluelet was connected to the rest of the world by telegraph in 1903, and around 1906 a lifeboat station and the Amphitrite Point Lighthouse were built. By the 1920s fishing was a major local industry and a reduction plant was built to process pilchards. When the pilchards disappeared in the late 1930s, the reduction plant began processing herring.

It wasn't until August 1959 that a road connecting Ucluelet to Port Alberni was finally finished, though it was a gravel road that the public could only use on weekends and evenings. When Pacific Rim National Park was created in 1970, the connection was upgraded from a logging road to a narrow and sometimes twisting paved highway.

Clayoquot Sound

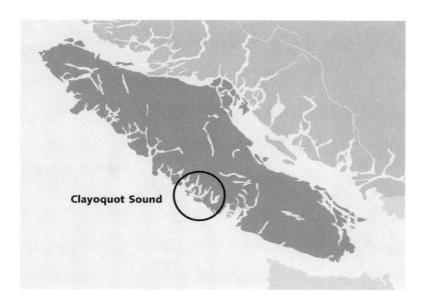

Clayoquot Sound

Rugged beauty, sandy beaches and many waterways make up the busiest sound on Vancouver Island's west coast. The area includes part of Pacific Rim National Park and a number of provincial parks including Dawley Passage, Epper Passage, Vargas Island, Gibson Marine, Flores Island, Maquinna, Sulphur Passage, Sydney Inlet and Hesquiat Peninsula.

With so many protected places to explore, it's not surprising that Clayoquot Sound is one of Vancouver Island's most popular kayaking destinations. There are dozens of possible trips here, ranging from a day paddle to the sandy beaches of Vargas Island to an extended trip to the soothing thermal pools at Hot Springs Cove.

Tofino, a town of 1,400 people, is the gateway to Clayoquot Sound. Tofino is as hip as it is remote. Although small, the town boasts luxurious resorts, cozy B&Bs, cafés where you can sit and sip cappuccinos, and stores that carry everything from surfboards to fine jewellery. For years the mainstay of the local economy was logging and fishing, and while these industries continue to be a source of employment for locals, the creation of nearby Pacific Rim National Park in 1970, combined with the paving of the only road into town, transformed Tofino into one of the top tourism destinations in British Columbia. Much of its appeal is its eco-tourism: hiking, kayaking and whale watching. Nearby beaches are also famous among surfers.

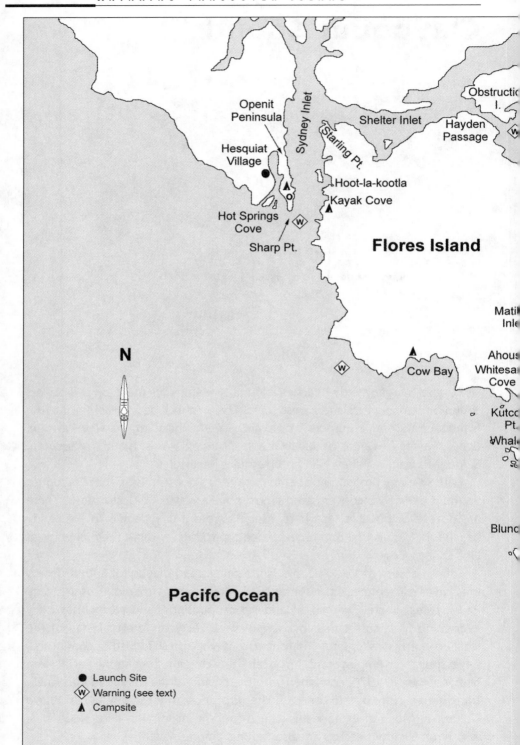

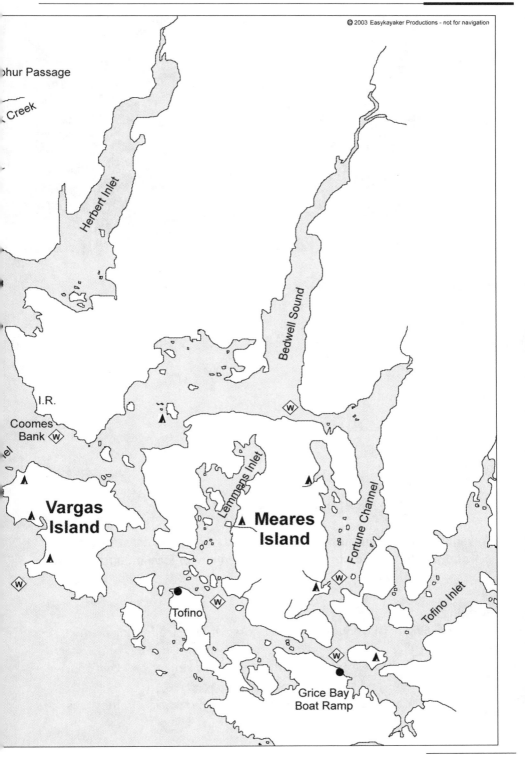

Tofino Inlet

CHS charts:
> ➤ 3673—Clayoquot Sound to Tofino Inlet
> ➤ 3685—Tofino, for extra detail
> ➤ 3674—Clayoquot Sound to Millar Channel, for Flores Island and Hot
> Springs Cove

Tidal reference port: Tofino

Weather and sea conditions reference:
> ➤ Amphitrite Point
> ➤ Tofino
> ➤ Lennard Island
> ➤ West Coast Vancouver Island South

Prevailing winds: Winds usually rise in the afternoon and are westerlies or northwesterlies, although due to the proximity of local mountains they can be quite variable.

Warnings:
> ➤ Paddling in Clayoquot Sound is *not* recommended for beginning kayakers unless they are guided. Lemmens Inlet, Grice Bay and Tofino Inlet may be the exceptions to this warning as long as paddlers understand currents and avoid narrows and passages.
> ➤ Weather and sea conditions change quickly, especially in the areas exposed to the Pacific Ocean.

➤ There are tidal currents, tidal rips and whirlpools in some areas.

➤ Currents affect much of the area's paddling. Many places also have back eddies and those with local knowledge can use them to grab a free ride when going against the current in a channel. Passages with strong currents are listed under specific paddling sections.

➤ If you end up travelling with the current in fast-flowing narrows, keep well away from turbulence and whirlpools caused by back eddies. Try to stick to where most of the water is flowing in the same direction. Although there is often more boat traffic and faster water in the centre of a channel, there is also often a more uniform water flow. Sometimes the water close to shore looks calmer, but it can be boiling just under the surface with whirlpools created by the current interacting with rocks, reefs, shallows, points, or the shore. Many narrows do have safe easy water right along the shore, but you need local knowledge to find safe routes through each set of narrows and often these safe routes change with flow direction and speed.

➤ Do not paddle across kelp beds! Should your kayak capsize, you could be pulled down, become tangled in bull-kelp and drown.

➤ Watch for high levels of boat traffic in Browning Passage, Maurus Channel and Calmus Passage.

➤ Fog can roll in quickly and limit visibility. It's often foggy even in August.

➤ Be aware there are black bears, cougars and wolves in some areas. In July 2000, two wolves attacked a camper on Vargas Island. Although those wolves were destroyed, campers should exercise caution and use wildlife safety practices. See the BC Parks web site for information on safety around wildlife, *http://wlapwww.gov.bc.ca/bcparks/index.htm*.

➤ Respect First Nations land (marked IR on charts). Do not disturb these lands or archeological sites.

➤ You may need insect repellant at camping areas away from the Pacific.

Emergency contacts: The village of Ahousat monitors VHF channel 68, the Hesquiaht First Nation at Hot Springs Cove monitors channel 66, Coast Guard and other boaters monitor channel 16, local fish farms monitor channels 8, 10 or 80. Search and Rescue Emergency can be reached at 1-800-567-5111 or by dialing *311 on your cell phone. Tofino Coast Guard Radio is at 250-726-7716, 250-726-7777 or 250-726-7312.

Tofino village launch site. Launch close to or during slack tide periods to avoid strong currents around the dock.

Getting there: It's a 200-km (125-mi) trip from Nanaimo to Tofino. Drive northwest on Highway 19, then turn west on Highway 4 and continue on past Port Alberni, along a twisty section of highway, until you reach a T-junction. Turn right and follow the road to Tofino.

Recommended launch sites:

➤ **Grice Bay boat ramp**: The boat ramp is on Grice Bay Road, which has a well-marked turnoff on Highway 4 north of the Green Point Campground and Tofino's airport, and south of Radar Hill. It's best to launch at slack tide or during minor tidal changes from this ramp in Pacific Rim National Park. You'll need to get a parking permit, which costs $8 per day or $42 for the year. You can buy a permit at Green Point Campground or at automated machines in various parking lots (note that some machines only sell day passes). If you're going out for more than six days, buying a season pass costs less, but this has to be done through park headquarters. You may want to buy a one-day permit and leave a note on your vehicle's dashboard explaining that you've gone kayaking for a few days, but you should check with Parks staff about their current policy for kayaker parking. Staff people have told us that if a vehicle exceeds the time paid for, they will ticket it and fine the driver, but will not tow the vehicle. They do not want to have someone rush to get back through dangerous sea conditions to avoid having their car towed.

➤ **Tofino government dock**: This dock is located at the end of 1st Street, and there is parking in a gravel lot at the corner of Main and 3rd streets. Launch near slack tide; there are strong currents near the dock during peak tide flow, and Browning Passage can be rough if the tide is running against the wind.

Tofino accommodations: There are many B&Bs, hotels, motels and resorts. The Visitor Information Centre (run by the Tofino–Long Beach Chamber of Commerce) is open from March to September, Monday through Friday, 11 a.m. to 5 p.m. Phone 250-725-3414, e-mail *tofino@island.net*, or visit *www.island.net/~tofino*. If local accommodation is unavailable you may wish to try the Ucluelet Visitor Information Centre, 250-726-4641.

Camping: There are many wilderness and marine park camping areas within Clayoquot Sound. These are listed with the information for each specific paddling area. Keep the following safety precautions in mind when staying at these sites.
➤ Cache food in trees, away from tents and kayaks.
➤ There are many streams and creeks to provide fresh water, but you may need to treat the water before you drink it. You can buy water-treatment devices at many kayak and outdoor stores for $200 or so. (Note that boiling doesn't always do the trick.)
➤ Fires are discouraged but are currently permitted below high tide line.
➤ Pack out all garbage.
➤ Many areas do not have outhouses, so you'll need to make provisions for disposal of human waste.

Tofino area camping:
➤ Bella Pacifica Campground and Resort: At 400 MacKenzie Beach Road, on the west side of Highway 4, 3 km (1.9 mi) south of Tofino. Reservations available. Phone 250-725-3400, e-mail *campground@bellapacifica.com* or visit the web site at *www.bellapacifica.com*.
➤ MacKenzie Beach Resort Campground: This is at 1101 Pacific Rim Highway, on the left side of Highway 4 as you drive north to Tofino. Reservations available. Phone 250-725-3439, e-mail *macbeach@tofino-bc.com*, or visit *www.tofino-bc.com/macbeach*.
➤ Crystal Cove Beach Resort: At 1165 Cedarwood Place, this resort is located on MacKenzie Beach, on the left side of Pacific Rim Highway as you drive north to Tofino. Reservations available. Phone 250-725-4213, e-mail *crystalc@alberni.net*, or visit *www.crystalcovebeachresort.com*.

➤ Green Point Campground: This is in Pacific Rim National Park, 10 km (6.3 mi) north of the park information centre on the left-hand side of Highway 4. Reservations are available for drive-in campers only and are recommended for groups. Phone 1-800-689-9025 or 604-689-9025, e-mail *pacrim_info@pch.gc.ca*, or visit *http://parkscan.harbour.com/pacrim/camp2.htm*.

➤ Long Beach Golf Course: There are campsites on this golf course, at 1850 Pacific Rim Highway. As you drive north on Highway 4, turn right onto Grice Bay Road. Reservations are taken after 1 p.m. by phone only at 250-725-3314. For more information e-mail *golf@island.net* or visit the web site, *www.longbeachgolfcourse.com*.

Note: Difficulty levels, approximate travel times and distances, location-specific warnings, tide and current information, as well as accommodation and camping information for areas other than Tofino are listed under specific paddling areas.

Grice Bay, Tofino Inlet and Heelboom Bay

If you are looking for an easy and fairly safe day paddle, launching at Grice Bay and paddling up Tofino Inlet is one option. Ideally you would want to ride the flood tide as it rises up the inlet and return on the ebbing tide. A good route would be to go from Grice Bay to Indian Island, cross over to Island Cove, tuck behind Warne Island, explore the waterways near McCall Island and Ridout Islets, then cross over to Kennedy Cove, at the mouth of Kennedy River. This cove is worth exploring. Plan to return on the ebb tide following the southern shore. Most of this area has been extensively logged, but it has greened up and looks much better than it did 20 years ago. The mouth of Kennedy River is a good fishing spot.

Another paddle from Grice Bay, which can be done in a day or stretched to an overnight trip, is to travel to Heelboom Bay and back. Heelboom Bay was a focal point of the 1983–84 protests against MacMillan Bloedel, a forestry company that planned to clear-cut large sections of Meares Island. The trip is fairly short, but requires more advanced paddling skills due to the currents in Dawley Passage. Read the travel notes for Meares Island to learn more about paddling around Heelboom Bay.

Difficulty levels:
➤ Tofino Inlet and Grice Bay (not including narrows): Novice
➤ Grice Bay to Heelboom Bay: Intermediate

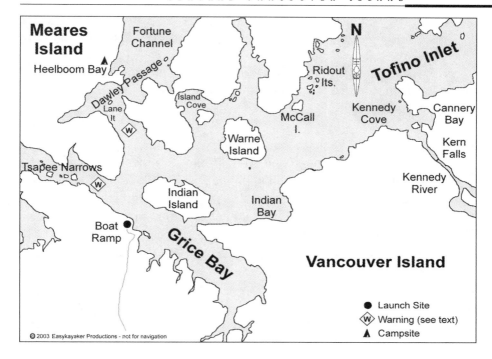

Approximate travel time: Full day to multiple day

Approximate distances:
> Grice Bay to Indian Island: 0.6 km (0.4 mi)
> Grice Bay to Kennedy Cove (along proposed route): 19 km (11.8 mi) round trip, but it should feel like less if you go with the mild current
> Grice Bay to Heelboom Bay: 5.5 km (3.4 mi) one way

Tidal reference port: Tofino. When calculating tidal flow for Kennedy Cove (off Tofino Inlet), you must add 30 minutes for high tide at Tofino and add 40 minutes for low tide. In other words, if the tide table says high tide at Tofino is at 13:30, then the high tide for Grice Bay and Tofino Inlet would be about 14:00. If you are using *Canadian Tide and Current Tables*, Vol. 6, you should also add an hour for daylight saving time if applicable (i.e., 14:00 becomes 15:00). Slack low tide lasts over an hour and slack high is also quite long here, though slack times in the narrows and passages are short.

Warnings:
> Tidal flows are fairly gentle in Grice Bay and Tofino Inlet, but do not get too close to Dawley Passage or Tsapee Narrows during an ebbing tide.

➤ Dawley Passage runs up to 3 knots and has a strong tidal rip by Lane Islet.

➤ Tsapee Narrows, northwest of Grice Bay, can run at 4 knots. There are a few islands in and just west of the narrows that can cause some turbulence.

Camping:

➤ Matt and Ben's Campground: This is a privately owned campground on Indian Island. For information phone 250-726-8578.

➤ Heelboom Bay: There are several campsites here and a cabin you can stay in. You'll need a portable treatment system to drink the local water, and there's no outhouse.

➤ Windy Bay: We've heard from two sources that there is a nice camping area at the head of the bay.

Meares Island

North and west of Tofino looms Meares Island with peaceful coves, old-growth forest and towering hills. Killer whales and porpoises swim off its shores, eagles nest in its trees and salmon spawn in some of its streams. The area's history is visible in the 5,000-year-old midden at Opitsat village, the bare strip of beach in Adventure Cove where a boat was launched in the 1790s and, most recently, the campsite in Heelboom Bay where environmentalists camped during the 1983–84 Meares Island protests.

It's possible to take in some of Meares' highlights during a day paddle from either Tofino or Grice Bay, or you can spend a few days circumnavigating the island. Lemmens Inlet is a good place to explore if you have limited time. Near its mouth is the Big Tree Trail, a popular hiking route through old-growth forest. On the way here, you'll see Morpheus Island. The local First Nations used it as a cemetery island and it later served the same purpose for residents of Tofino from the late 1800s until around 1950.

Difficulty levels:

➤ Tofino to Big Tree Trail and Lemmens Inlet: Novice to intermediate (if following recommended route during slack tides)

➤ All other areas: Intermediate to advanced

Approximate travel time: Full day to multiple day

Approximate distances: Distances of less than 500 m are not noted.

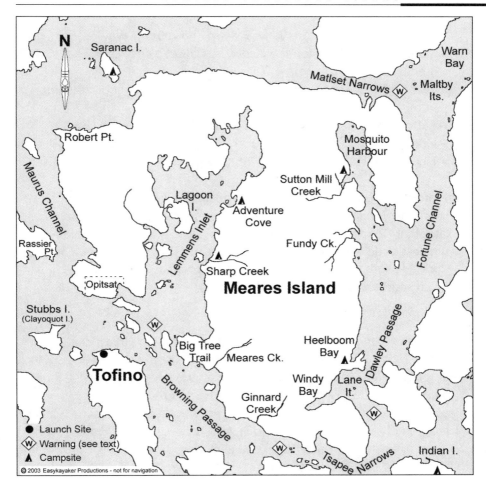

> Tofino to the Big Tree Trail (along recommended route): 3 km (1.9 mi) one way
> Tofino to Sharp Creek (Lemmens Inlet): 5 km (3.1 mi) one way
> Grice Bay launch site to Big Tree Trail: 8.6 km (5.4 mi) one way
> Big Tree Trail to Sharp Creek: 3 to 5 km (1.9 to 3.1 mi) one way depending on tide level
> Sharp Creek to Adventure Cove (Lemmens Inlet): 2.2 km (1.3 mi) one way
> Adventure Cove to the head of Lemmens Inlet: 3 km (1.9 mi) one way
> Tofino to Opitsat: 2.3 km (1.4 mi) one way
> Opitsat to Robert Point: 6.7 km (4.2 mi) one way

➤ Robert Point to Saranac Island: 2.4 km (1.5 mi) one way
➤ Saranac Island to easternmost cove in Matlset Narrows: 9.2 km (5.8 mi) one way
➤ Matlset Narrows to Sutton Mill Creek (Mosquito Harbour): 8.6 km (5.4 mi) one way
➤ Sutton Mill Creek to Heelboom Bay: 6.5 km (4.1 mi) one way
➤ Heelboom Bay to Grice Bay launch site: 5.5 km (3.4 mi) one way
➤ Heelboom Bay to Tofino: 13.5 km (8.4 mi) one way

Tidal reference port: Tofino. Fortune Channel tides are about 20 minutes later than Tofino times and Grice Bay times are about 30 to 40 minutes later than Tofino. It is important to know these tide table deviations for timing a paddle through Tsapee Narrows and Dawley Passage. Low slack tide lasts for over an hour in these two areas, but slack current is much shorter in the narrows and passages.

Currents:
➤ Meares Island lies in the middle of a large tidal flow that fills and drains Tofino Inlet. Think of Tofino Inlet, Grice Bay and Kennedy Cove as a bottle with two necks. One neck is a little larger, but it's also three times longer. Each neck has a couple of narrow places. Throw in some points, rocks, islets and coves and you get some very interesting water movement in and out of this bottle. All this water movement can work for or against you. It may leave you exploring and/or sitting on the beach for a couple of hours as you wait for the tide to turn. If you want

There are many narrow channels and fast-flowing currents between Meares and Tofino.

Meares Island

to test your theories about currents, circumnavigating Meares can be an illuminating trip. Because there are so many narrow channels with fast-flowing current around Meares, the ideal time to attempt this trip is during the first or third quarter of the moon during neap tides (smaller tide changes). The following information should help you plan your trip.

➤ Tsapee Narrows: Floods 4 knots southeast toward Grice Bay; ebbs flowing northwest.

➤ Browning Passage: Floods southeast toward Grice Bay, ebbs flowing northwest.

➤ Duffin Passage (north of Tofino): Floods up to 3 knots from Felice Island east through centre of passage; ebbs 3 knots west along Tofino shoreline to Felice Island.

➤ Riley-Morpheus Islands Channel (between Tofino and the Big Tree Trail area): Floods 5 knots south and ebbs 5 knots north into Lemmens Inlet. There are whirlpools at times.

➤ Lemmens Inlet: Floods north into inlet, ebbs south. The entrance is affected by Heynen Channel.

➤ Heynen Channel (north of Tofino and west of Lemmens Inlet): Floods 2 knots east near Stockham Island.

➤ Maurus Channel (between Meares and Vargas islands): Floods 2 knots north near Rassier Point (Vargas Island) and 1 knot for rest of channel area. Ebbs south.

➤ Matlset Narrows (north end of Meares Island): Floods 4 knots east toward Warn Bay and Fortune Channel; ebbs 4 knots west with a tidal rip near Maltby Islets. There are two coves on the north end of Meares

Island in Matlset Narrows. Kayakers waiting for a tide change often use the eastern one. Water flowing in and out of the coves creates a little turbulence in the narrows, but it should be easy to enter the coves if you need to.

➤ Dawley Passage (east side of Meares): Floods 3 knots south toward Grice Bay and ebbs 3 knots north, with a tidal rip near Lane Islet.

Prevailing winds:

➤ There is a good likelihood of westerlies or southwesterlies blowing in from Calmus Passage and/or Father Charles Channel.

➤ The north and northwest sides of Meares are open to winds off the Pacific.

➤ Fortune Channel can receive winds off Kennedy Lake, but it is more sheltered than the Pacific side of the island.

➤ There is wind in Dawley Passage from Windy Bay.

Warnings:

➤ Beginner paddlers should *not* try to circumnavigate Meares Island without a guide.

➤ Watch for strong currents, tidal rips and whirlpools. Be especially attentive in Tsapee Narrows, Matlset Narrows and Dawley Passage (especially near Lane Islet).

➤ There can be whirlpools between Morpheus and Riley islands.

➤ Do not cross from Tofino to Lemmens Inlet during peak tide changes.

➤ The passage between Beck and Stone islands is a main boating lane, but is the best route from Tofino to Lemmens Inlet.

➤ Watch for boat traffic in Maurus Channel.

➤ The entrance to Lemmens Inlet is affected by Heynen Channel. Weaker paddlers may find it difficult to paddle in or out of Lemmens Inlet against the current.

➤ Tidal flats in Lemmens Inlet area are a resting place for seabirds—do not disturb resting birds.

➤ Chum salmon spawn in Meares Creek, Sharp Creek and an unnamed creek on the west side of Lemmens Inlet from mid-October to late November. Do not disturb the fish or streambeds.

➤ Windy Bay lives up to its name.

➤ The mud flats near Ducking Island (in Browning Passage) and the Arakun Islands (in Lemmens Inlet) are huge. If you are caught in the wrong place here on a falling tide, your portage may be a long one.

Paddling in and out of Lemmens Inlet can be a work-out against the current.

(Note: These are referred to locally as the Ducking and Arakum mud flats. Neither are named on CHS charts.)

Getting there/launching:

➤ From Tofino to the Big Tree Trail area/Lemmens Inlet: The recommended route is to head northeast over to Arnet Island, north between Beck and Stone islands and then east over to Meares. En route you might want to take a side trip to Deadman Islets (west of Beck Island) where there is an eagle's nest. When you look at a map it might appear that an easier route is to paddle down to Usatzes Point, over to Riley Island and then to Morpheus Island and Meares, but this is *not* recommended unless you want to risk getting sucked into a whirlpool and 5 knot currents.

➤ From Tofino to Opitsat: Take the same route as above, going between Stone and Beck islands or via Deadman Islets.

➤ From Grice Bay to Big Tree Trail, Opitsat, or Lemmens Inlet: Travel

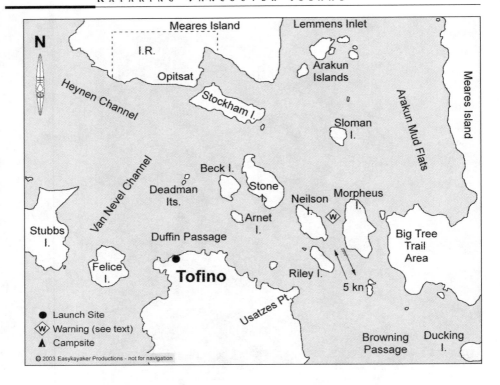

during the early part of an ebb tide through Tsapee Narrows and follow Browning Passage to the narrow passage between Morpheus Island and the Big Tree Trail area of Meares Island. If you are travelling past the Big Tree Trail, head for the west side of Sloman Island and then carry on to Opitsat or Lemmens Inlet.

Camping: Meares' shoreline offers an occasional rest area and, in a pinch, an emergency campsite for one or two tents, especially if tides aren't too high at night. The following is only a partial list of potential campsites.

➤ Sharp Creek (Lemmens Inlet): There are three potential camping sites near the mouth of Sharp Creek, two to the north and one to the south. Each site will hold a few tents. This area has a nice beach and a stream. Trails behind it lead into old-growth forest.

➤ Robert Point: When we visited we found the campsite overgrown, but some of the beach area might be useable.

➤ Saranac Island: We camped at the top of a beach in a small cove, but we barely had room for our three tents above the high tide line. There likely would not be space to camp on a really high tide.

➤ Matlset Narrows: There are two coves on the north end of Meares

Island in Matlset Narrows. The one farthest east can be used as a campsite in a pinch.

➤ Mosquito Harbour: There are two good campsites, one near the mouth of Sutton Mill Creek and one at the head of the harbour. The one at Sutton Mill Creek has a rough camping shelter and outhouse and space for more tents in the woods.

➤ Heelboom Bay: The camping area here can support quite a few tents. There is a cabin you can stay in as well. You'll need a portable treatment system to drink the local water, and there's no outhouse.

➤ Windy Bay: We've been told by two sources that there is a nice campsite at the head of the bay.

Travel notes (Gary)

We tackled a trip around Meares Island during the spring tides of a new moon, when the tide changes reached almost 3.7 m (12 ft). The four of us—Paul, our friends Dave and Celia, and I—debated which direction to travel around Meares. We decided on clockwise because we were concerned about wind from the west or southwest during the most exposed portion of our trip, as we crossed the top of Meares Island. We wanted to travel with the current and wind as much as possible, and except when we hit the occasional back eddy, we paddled with the current about 80 percent of the time. We passed through three of the four narrows within an hour of slack, and the fourth at full run.

Gary at Ginnard Creek

Grice Bay to Sharp Creek

We launched at the Grice Bay boat ramp about an hour and a half after high tide and headed through Tsapee Narrows into Browning Passage. Fortunately there was only a minor tide change of about 1 m (3.6 ft). Tsapee can run at 4 knots, but at the moment it was only at 1 or 2 knots. There are a few islands in and just west of the narrows, which can cause some turbulence.

Mindful that water is usually smoother in the centre of a passage, we stayed in the middle, keeping an eye out for boat traffic. Our intention was to ride the ebb as far as the Big Tree Trail and hike until low tide. Then we would ride the flood tide into Lemmens Inlet. However, when we saw a pretty little waterfall at the mouth of Ginnard Creek, we couldn't resist paddling across the sand flats to the fall for a short break. After travelling with the current in Browning Passage, navigating the back eddy in the shallows (less than 30 cm/1 ft deep) made it seem like we were paddling in slow motion. As we stopped we spotted waterspouts in Browning Passage. They were high enough to be from a whale, but looked similar to those from sea lions or porpoises.

The Hanging Garden Tree, so named because of the numerous plants that grow on its bark, is one of many gigantic old-growth trees along this trail.

After our break, as we paddled away from Ginnard Creek we started running out of water and quickly headed out to find a channel before we got stranded on the Ducking Island mud flats. When we neared the Big Tree Trail area we slipped into the little channel between Morpheus Island and Meares. The paddle in this narrow channel was very calm and we easily found the start of the trail by the sheer volume of traffic going to and from it. Water taxis deliver people about every 30 minutes, and kayak tours seem to stop as often.

Hiking Among Giants

The Big Tree Trail leads hikers through an old-growth forest. The trees here are estimated to be between 1,000 and 1,500 years old, making them among the oldest—and biggest— life forms on earth. There are cedars along this trail that are over 18 m (60 ft) in circumference. For many people the highlight of the hike is the Hanging Garden Tree, so named because so many other plants grow on it. The first part of the trail is boardwalk and then it becomes a muddy path. The boardwalk connects to the beach in two locations where water taxis drop off their customers. To the right is a small pebbly beach for kayakers. The trailhead is almost invisible, but once on the beach you can see its rocky start at the base of a large cedar tree.

At low slack we were back in our kayaks and starting up Lemmens Inlet, on the lookout for a campsite we had heard was located near the mouth of Sharp Creek. Due to the low tide we had to paddle three-quarters of the way to Opitsat, then make a dogleg to Mona Island and turn 90 degrees to cross the inlet to Sharp Creek. This transformed a 3-km (1.9-mi) trip as the crow flies into 5 km (3.1 mi) of paddling. Once again the (tidal) force was with us as the current gave us a gentle push for those 5 km. We approached the camp area at a fairly low tide, so we chose to come in on the north side of Sharp Island. At a very low tide, there is a long portage.

Launch at Sharp Creek

After quickly exploring the three potential campsites, we chose the centre site because it had enough room to spread out, a nice little beach and easy water access for bringing in the kayaks. There was also the sound of a babbling brook to lull us to sleep.

After setting up camp we dined on, of all things, Subway sandwiches we had picked up in Port Alberni. It felt odd to be sitting on the beach with little sign of humankind, eating fast food. After a dessert of almond squares we ran some lines over tree branches and hung up the rest of our food in case we were visited by bears.

We didn't see any bear sign when we hiked the trails behind the campsite. Nor did we discover any signs of an outhouse. Fortunately we had my little camp shovel, so could make do.

As dusk settled in we retired to our tents to read and then

sleep. There would be no point in rising early, as the tide wouldn't be high enough to launch until about 10 a.m.

Sharp Creek (Lemmens Inlet) to Saranac Island

After a peaceful night and breakfast, we packed up our boats and headed back out on the water. Our plan was to ride the flood up to Adventure Cove—the former location of Fort Defiance—visit the historical site, explore a bit more of Lemmens Inlet and then fight the current out of the inlet and paddle to Robert Point or Saranac Island.

It didn't take long to cover the 2.2 km (1.3 mi) to Adventure Cove, where we met some kayakers who had spent the night at the great little campsite in the cove. (Because this area is an archeological site, we recommend it for visiting but suggest people don't camp here. It is illegal to disturb a historic site.) There were two sailboats moored in the cove, one of which, the *Ariel*, was from Portland, Oregon. There was also a float home in the northeast corner of the cove. As we paddled into the little cove we tried to imagine what it would have been like for Captain Robert Gray to sail his ship in here more than 200 years earlier.

Fort Defiance

In 1791 Captain Robert Gray, an American fur trader, sailed his 220-ton ship *Columbia* from the eastern United States, around the tip of South America to Vancouver Island. He arrived at Meares Island, which he had visited two years earlier, and once there directed the construction of Fort Defiance in Adventure Cove. The fort was two storeys, 11 by 5.5 m (36 by 18 ft) and constructed from logs. There were no bastions or palisades, but the fort was well situated for defence and had two cannons and loopholes for muskets. Gray's men also constructed a blacksmith shop, carpenter's shed and two saw pits.

The cove's original name was Clickscleuctsee and it was described as "form'd by an Isle and the SE shore Clioquot sound, so small that when the ship was moor'd you might throw a stone upon the beach in any direction." On September 19, 1791, Lieutenant John Boit, the 16-year-old fifth officer, wrote in his diary: "Captain Gray went with two longboats up the sound for to seek a convenient cove. In the evening the Capt. returned having found a place to his mind 1 league from where the ship lay." The next day *Columbia*, under tow and under sail, was moved into what the Americans were already calling

Paddling into Adventure Cove, site of the old American Fort Defiance.

Adventure Cove, for the winter. According to Boit, vast numbers of the local Natives joined to watch this and "appeared pleas'd with the idea of our tarrying with them for the cold season."

Christmas 1791 was celebrated with decorations and a feast of 20 fat geese, a huge huckleberry pie and quantities of rum. Chief Wickaninnish and his men took part in the ceremonies. Native custom did not allow women to attend, but the chief had his slaves carry some of the goodies to the women waiting at the canoes.

Chief Wickaninnish threw a celebration in turn on January 1, 1792, but only Boit and a small crew attended. Lieutenant Boit writes, "As soon as the king saw me I was called toward him, and seated upon his right. This house was about 80 feet long, and 40 feet broad, and about 18 feet high with a flat roof. The king was elevated about two feet higher than the company with a canopy over his head, stuck full of animals teeth. The company consisted of above 100 men, all considerably advanced in years..."

Boit was "strongly invited to partake" in the refreshments, "but the smell was enough—therefore pleaded indisposition... The king informed me there was going to be a dance in the evening, and wished me to stay. However, I declined, and returned on board."

Native/non-Native relations went downhill after this. Several times warning shots were fired, and in early March some visiting chiefs were observed talking to a boy who had joined the *Columbia* in the Sandwich Islands. Captain Gray questioned the boy and learned that he had been asked to wet the ship's powder and steal shot for the natives. The *Columbia* was up on the ways, being cleaned, and the men were ordered to finish the job as soon as possible. Several canoes arrived that night and the occupants started shouting what sounded like war cries, but the ship's company, all armed, stood guard during the night, and the next day *Columbia* was refloated.

Meanwhile, the men had been using local timber to build a 45-ton trading sloop, and on March 22, 1792, the *Adventure* was launched. You can still see the smooth section of beach where the rocks were removed to give the ship an easy passage to the water. The sloop was prepared for a four-month journey to the Queen Charlotte Islands, but as Captain Gray sailed out past the First Nations village of Opitsat, he extracted revenge that would taint Native/non-Native relations for many years.

Boit writes, "I am sorry to be under the necessity of remarking that this day I was sent with three boats all well mann'd and armed to destroy the village of Opitsatah. It was a command I was in no way tenacious of, and am grieved to think that Captain Gray should let his passion go so far. This village was about half a mile in diameter, and contained upwards of 200 houses, generally well built for Indian... ev'ry door that you enter'd was in resemblance to an human and beast head, the passage through the mouth, besides which there was much more rude carved work about the dwellings some of which was by no means inelegant. This fine village, the work of ages, was in short time totally destroy'd."

After a six-month trading season, Gray sold the *Adventure* to the Spanish captain Quadra at Nootka for 72 sea otter pelts (about $4,000). Gray then sailed south and "discovered" the Columbia River, which he named after his ship, and continued on to China and then Boston. This made *Columbia* the first American ship to circumnavigate the globe.

The location of Fort Defiance (i.e., Adventure Cove or Clickscleuctsee) was a mystery for about 175 years until Ken Gibson, a Tofino resident, and a group of helpers found the remains of the fort using information from the ship's log and Boit's diary. On December 9, 1967, the cove and 55 hectares surrounding (135 acres) were designated an archeological site, and the next year a team from the University of Victoria conducted a dig.

(Information for this sidebar came from *Ghost Towns and Mining Camps of Vancouver Island*, by T.W. Paterson and Garnet Basque; *Paddling Through Time*, by Joanna Streetly; *Pacific Yachting's Cruising Guide to British Columbia*, Vol. IV, by Don Watmough; and *Exploring Vancouver Island's West Coast*, by Don Douglas.)

We didn't stay in Adventure Cove as long as we would have liked because we wanted to get out of Lemmens Inlet and catch the flood tide through Maurus Channel. As we passed by Lagoon Island we thought about going into the cove to look at the ancient stone fish trap, but kept on paddling. Another time we'll get back and spend a couple of days in Lemmens Inlet, exploring all its shoreline, and if the weather's good and jellyfish few we'll swim in the warm waters of Lemmens' little northwest cove.

Paddling out of Lemmens Inlet was an uphill battle against a flooding tide. The GPS showed that we were crawling along at only 5 km/hr (3 mph). Our fight against the flood ended as we reached Stockham Island, and we cut inside toward Opitsat. Until the last moment this looked like a landlocked cove, but we put our trust in the chart, which showed a passage. As we paddled by Opitsat we admired the two totem poles near the water at the centre of the village.

Totem poles near water at Opitsat, a First Nations village.

Stubbs Island (a.k.a. Clayoquot Island) was on our left a little over a kilometre away as we left Opitsat. We could see and feel the current as we headed up Maurus Channel between Vargas and Meares islands. We had hoped to make it to Robert Point before the tide changed, but that didn't happen. Instead we took a break for lunch, pulling onto the beach opposite the channel light about 2.5 km (1.5 mi) short of the point.

Fortunately the ebb current isn't very strong north of the navigation light, and we soon made Robert Point once we were back in our boats. We had planned to camp either here or on Saranac Island for the night. The campsites at Robert Point were quite over-grown, and we knew we had a long paddle ahead of us the next day, so we decided to head for Saranac and look for a better camping spot there.

Once around Robert Point we had the afternoon wind at our

backs and a mild current against us. This created some wave action and minor whitecapping where the current was most pronounced. As we crossed the channel the waves hit us from behind at about 45 degrees. With the help of the wind we quickly reached Saranac Island, our last-chance camping spot. Our Coast Recreation Map didn't show any camping spots for another 9 km (5.6 mi), and we had paddled over 19 km (12 mi) already that day, some of it against currents. We were tired and ready to set up camp.

There were three promising-looking beaches. The best was a small cove, sheltered from the afternoon breeze. A small fire ring of rocks on the beach indicated that others had camped here, but there was only one possible tent site in the woods. We paddled over to the next beach to the south. It was worse. We had seen a beach to the north as we approached the island, so off we went,

but it wasn't any better. Spirits were dropping quickly. We were tired and didn't want to backtrack to Robert Point or Vargas Island. We would have a long enough paddle the next day even if we stayed here.

We returned to the first beach in the small cove and looked at it with less critical eyes. Out came the tide tables. We studied flotsam levels of seaweed on the beach and predicted where the tide would rise to. Then we looked at vegetation to find salt vs. non-salt habitat indicator plants. Heads were scratched and the sound "ummmm" was heard more than once. The tide was now about 2.7 m (9 ft) and would rise to 3.6 m (11.8 ft) at 00:35.

Saranac Camp close call. When we awoke the water line was lapping at our tent doors.

Finally we picked three sites at the top of the beach, gathered rocks to build a wall at the low side and started shovelling with a very small camp shovel to build up level platforms for our three tents. By the time the tents were set up, we were all saying it would be okay. Secretly, I think we all had doubts. Nonetheless, it was a great beach, a wonderful view and a great spot to camp. There wasn't an outhouse, but there were a few private alcoves below high tide where there was easy digging. Firewood was dry and plentiful.

When it was time to turn in, Dave, Celia and Paul's kayaks

were high on the beach and well tied. Mine was on a log, elevated above the sand. We drifted off to sleep, listening to the gentle lapping of the water. I woke a little before midnight but couldn't hear the water, and when I shone my feeble flashlight out the tent I didn't see water. At high tide, about a half hour later, I rolled over and felt the bottom of my tent. It was dry and there was still no sound of water. How close was it?

We had hoped that bears wouldn't frequent this small island. On the other side of Saranac is a fish farm and this certainly can be a bear attraction. Saranac is not far from Meares Island, so a bear could easily swim here. I did a bit of a jungle walk looking for signs and found none. We went to sleep that night prepared, but were pretty sure a bear wouldn't bother us. At 4 a.m. I was awakened by a noise. My flashlight and sandals were ready so I was able to get outside quickly. I had left a pot and lid by my tent to use as noisemakers. I shone my light around, realized the sound had come from nowhere near the kayaks, food or tents and decided that all was well. The next morning, Dave told me he had heard two woofs and a splash and concluded that we had been visited by a sea lion.

When we woke, we had a laugh. The wet tide line was touching the door of Paul's tent. It was about a foot from Dave and Celia's and about two feet down the sand from mine. If one large boat had gone by during high tide, its wake would have soaked all of us. It's amazing how flat calm and silent the ocean was during the night, with not even a ripple to make noise. The same can't be said for the early birds—five crows that decided we should wake up.

Saranac Island to Mosquito Harbour

We had ideal conditions for our paddle from Saranac Island to Matlset Narrows. The water was like glass. As we paddled we came across a large floating red sea urchin. I tried to avoid touching its sharp spines as I gently lifted it onto my kayak. It wasn't until I caught up with the rest of the group that we realized it was still alive. After we had a good look at it, I placed it back in the water where it could drift in the mild current.

We were planning to reach the narrows about an hour before high tide, but the current and good water conditions increased our travelling speed and we reached them at peak current, much

Playing dead. When we realized this red sea urchin was alive, I carefully returned it to the water.

sooner than we had planned. I had the GPS on deck and was watching our speed, which averaged about 7.5 km/hr (4.6 mph). As Matlset Narrows is wide and straight, we decided to risk going through at full run. It's funny, but it didn't feel like we were going fast unless we looked at the shore. The GPS went from 7.5 to 10 to 14 km/hr (6 to 8 mph). We decided to see how fast we could go and got up to 15.5 km/hr (9.6 mph) for a few minutes. The shore was whizzing by.

There are two coves on the Meares Island side of the narrows. Kayakers waiting for a tide change often use the one farther east. In a pinch it can be used as a campsite. The coves cause a little turbulence in the narrows, but it looked like it would be easy to enter either of them should you choose to. We stayed well away from shore and the kelp beds that lie east of the coves. As mentioned above, the combination of kelp and current scare me, as it can be deadly.

As we left the narrows the fast water that had been very calm collided with a large body of slow-moving water. The result was a series of funny little swirls as hundreds of small currents went gently off in all directions. The effect on the kayak was minor considering that the narrows were running at least 4 knots.

The next hour found us in back eddies part of the time, crawling along at about 5.5 km/hr (3.4 mph). The threat of rain was overshadowed by the excitement of watching two or three harbour porpoises go by in the opposite direction. We were happy to round the point into Mosquito Harbour and even happier at the return of the warm sun.

As we approached Sutton Mill Creek, a series of pilings marked the location of the Sutton Mill site. The Sutton Lumber Company of Seattle established a mill at Sutton Creek in Mosquito Harbour in 1906. It became one of the largest sawmills in British Columbia and had an 11-m (36-ft) bandsaw, but now the mill site is overgrown with thorny brush. Paul and I tried to penetrate it wearing shorts and T-shirts and soon gave up. Later that day the *Ariel* pulled into Mosquito Harbour and the owners set out to explore in their Easyrider double kayak. They were dressed more appropriately and made their way through the thick brush to find many rusting hunks of machinery.

There are two camp areas in Mosquito Harbour, one at the old midden on the north bank of Sutton Mill Creek and the other at the head of the harbour. We chose the one at Sutton Mill Creek, as it was the closest. This site could hold a lot of tents with a little work, but rain forests have a way of taking over. Paul opted for the grassy knoll, while Dave, Celia and I pitched our two tents just inside the woods where the trail forks to go to the cabin or to the outhouse. The cabin is a rough camping shelter that looks to be about 15 years old and never really finished. The outhouse, I'm happy to report, was working fine. The walls are only 1.4 m (4.5 ft) tall, though, making it the shortest roofed outhouse I've ever visited.

I set up my tent so it did not block the trail, passing on a site next to ripe thimbleberries. A squirrel had laid claim to the berries and spent most of the daylight hours jumping from branch to branch. The thimbleberry branches could barely support its weight.

Sutton Mill Creek camp. Be warned: Mosquito Harbour comes by its name honestly.

Sutton Mill Creek is worth exploring at high tide, but be warned: Mosquito Harbour comes by its name honestly. While life isn't too bad on the water or at the water's edge, you may be eaten alive in the woods. As a result, we spent most of our time at the beach or in our tents.

We had company at the beach. A group of large garter snakes

had a favourite sunning spot but were rather shy and would leave if anyone got within about 2 m (6.5 ft). As soon as we moved away, they came back. Our mouse friend wasn't nearly so shy and would come through the grass to check each of us out. At breakfast the next morning mouse and snakes were both back.

We told bear stories as night closed in. When I walked up the beach toward the head of the harbour for a final leg stretch, though, I picked up a marginal trail back through the large old-growth trees and as I neared our grassy knoll I saw three piles of old bear scat. (Well, the scat was old, but the bear could have been any age.) The rest of the group joined me to dissect the scat and we were relieved that no garbage showed up. Celia noted that this bear trail avoided the human trails plus the outhouse and cabin—a good sign.

We all shortly retired with items nearby in case of bear. We had paddled 17 km (10.5 mi) that day and were ready for sleep.

Mosquito Harbour to Grice Bay

The next morning found us without water at the beach—the tide was way out. Paul and I joined Dave, who had walked out to an islet. The noise of thousands of clams greeted us as we walked through the tidal flats. We sat on the islet and waited for the tide to start rising. Slack low tide seemed to last for over an hour. Before slack tide ended, we joined Celia for breakfast, broke camp and started off toward Heelboom Bay and home.

Although the wind from Kennedy Lake can whip over the low-lands and along Fortune Channel, this body of water is fairly protected. The highlights of our paddle through this channel were the sight of a large group of porpoises and a stop at the ancient stone fish trap near Fundy Creek. We were anxious to visit Heelboom Bay, as this was the site of the Meares Island logging protests and the camp of the protesters. We joined the couple from the *Ariel* on the beach to explore the campsite. In a nearby cabin there is a notebook that contains interesting accounts written by earlier visitors. One was a tale of four tree planters who set off to jungle-walk the entire island. Unfortunately, they hiked to an islet patrolled by bears and ended up spending the night there. The next day they had to build a raft to get off the island.

There's a carved wooden sign proclaiming *Meares Island Tribal Park* across Heelboom Bay from the camping area. On April 21,

1984, the Clayoquot Band signed a declaration to create the park. In it the band states it is prepared to share Meares Island with non-Natives for hiking, camping, fishing, whale watching and gathering restricted amounts of seafoods and shellfish.

The tide was coming in quickly and we were moving the boats every few minutes, expecting the tide to crest or at least slow at any moment. High tide in Tofino would be at 2:25 p.m. and we wanted a bit of push through Dawley Passage, but not too much.

At 2 p.m. the *Ariel* lifted anchor and we lifted paddles. We were quicker out of the bay, but *Ariel* passed us going into the narrows, which turned out to be a good thing. We followed the boat through the narrowest point rather than going around the right side of Lane Islet and into the mouth of Windy Bay. I've read that Windy Bay deserves its name, and it certainly was windy when we went by.

Created in 1984 by local First Nations, this park is shared with non-Natives for hiking, camping, fishing, whale watching and gathering restricted amounts of seafoods and shellfish.

Ariel was trying to go on the left side of Lane Islet, but as we watched it got pulled sideways to the right by a strong tidal rip and was getting perilously close to the islet. At this point we could hear the roar of the tidal rip and see its influence on the surface.

As the old saying goes, "When handed lemons, make lemonade," and that's what we did. Our group was still a little way from the rip, so we swung left until we hit the rip and then turned right and travelled with it. It gave a comfortable free ride past the islet and we then turned and paddled toward Grice Bay. The rest of the trip was in light chop as the afternoon breeze was doing its thing.

It is always sad when a great trip ends, so we postponed the finish by driving up Radar Hill and viewing our paddling route from 123 m (403 ft) above sea level.

Vargas Island

Vargas Island is probably the most popular paddling destination in Clayoquot Sound. It has expansive sandy beaches and about half of its coastline is provincial park, including most of the southern and western sides of the island. For those who enjoy hiking there is an old telegraph trail that crosses the island through stunted trees and muskeg from near the Vargas Island Inn to Ahous Bay.

You can take a great day trip from Tofino to the southern tip of Vargas Island where there is a nice beach to explore. On the way, you can stop for a break at one of the beaches on the southwest part of Stubbs Island (a.k.a. Clayoquot Island). Captain Pinney established a trading post here in 1875, and Stubbs became the first non-Native settlement of Clayoquot Sound. It was considered the unofficial capital city of Vancouver Island's west coast until around 1900, when many people relocated to Tofino.

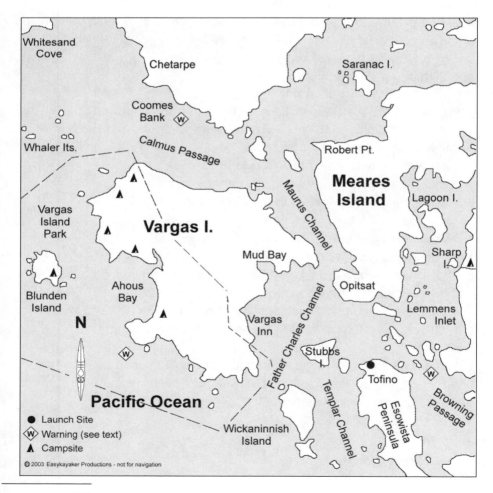

Vargas Island

The most common Vargas Island kayak trip is a multi-day paddle leaving Tofino, crossing over to Opitsat on Meares Island, and then heading north up Maurus Channel and west along the top of Vargas Island in Calmus Passage to Vargas Island Provincial Park. Some people choose to finish their trip by circumnavigating Vargas, but the trip down the west side is for experienced paddlers only.

Difficulty levels:
> ➤ Tofino to the southern tip of Vargas Island: Intermediate
> ➤ Tofino to northwest corner of Vargas Island: Intermediate
> ➤ West side of Vargas Island from Ahous Bay south: Advanced

Approximate travel time: Full day to multiple day

Approximate distances:
> ➤ Tofino to the southern tip of Vargas Island: 11 km (6.8 mi) round trip
> ➤ Tofino to first campsite in Vargas Island Provincial Park (northwest corner of island): 12 km (7.5 mi) one way

Currents:
> ➤ Van Nevel Channel (between Felice and Stubbs islands): Floods 3 knots northeast toward Meares Island, ebbs 3 knots southwest.
> ➤ Maurus Channel (between Meares and Vargas islands): Floods 2 knots north near Rassier Point and 1 knot for rest of channel area, ebbs south
> ➤ Calmus Passage (north of Vargas): Floods 2 knots east and northeast between Vargas, Morfee and Dunlap islands

Prevailing winds: Westerlies or northwest winds often prevail in the after-noon. Paddlers can get pinned down in Calmus Passage, but things usually calm down in the evening or early morning, allowing paddlers to escape to more sheltered locations.

Warnings:
➤ The area just south of Ahous Bay can get quite rough.
➤ You need favourable weather and sea conditions to paddle past Wickaninnish Island to the southern tip of Vargas Island.
➤ Paddlers visiting Vargas Island must be comfortable doing surf landings and launches.
➤ Conditions can change quickly.
➤ Watch for boat traffic.

Getting there:
➤ Tofino to the southern part of the island: On an ebb tide from Tofino, travel along the east side of Felice Island to its southern tip, then head for the southern shore of Stubbs Island. From Stubbs Island, the crossing to Vargas Island is only about 1.5 km (0.9 mi). A flood tide may require a 2.5 km (1.5 mi) (one way) longer route that goes from Tofino heading through the Deadman Islets and then crossing over to Vargas Island before heading south along Vargas's shoreline.
➤ Tofino to the northwest corner of the island: From Tofino on a flood tide or minor ebb tide, paddle north to Opitsat and go up Maurus Channel. If the tide is ebbing fairly strongly, instead of heading for Opitsat some kayakers choose to round the southern tips of Felice and Stubbs islands and cross over to Vargas Island before heading north along its eastern shoreline. On a flooding tide you get a better ride on the Meares side of Maurus Channel; if it's ebbing follow the Vargas Island shore. Ideally you should ride the flood tide going north in this channel and return to Tofino on the ebb tide. If you stick close to the shore in Calmus Passage you can avoid some of the wind that blows through here. Several islets provide a break from the surf for landing.

Accommodations: On the east side is the Vargas Island Inn, a quaint, rustic-but-comfortable getaway. Phone 250-725-3309. Reservations are avail-able for guided groups only.

Camping:

➤ Vargas Island: There are many possible camping spots on the north end of Vargas, but many of these are on private property, so be careful where you land. The nicest beaches are in Vargas Island Provincial Park, which starts near the northwest corner of the island. This area has green throne-type outhouses. BC Parks installed these low-maintenance out-houses a few years ago after a wolf attack on the island—the wolf started chewing the head of a kayaker who was sleeping outside. Wolves dig up and feed on human waste, and this, as well as being fed directly by humans, may have prompted the attack.

➤ Blunden Island: There is a small camping area on Blunden, which is part of Vargas Island Provincial Park. This is a location for experienced paddlers who don't mind getting trapped here if the winds start to howl.

Travel notes (Gary)

My family took a semi-luxury trip to Vargas Island many years ago. It was in our early kayaking days, and our daughter Katherine was nine years old at the time. Ten people had signed up for a three-day Vargas Island trip with one of the many outfit-ters who provide guided trips in Clayoquot Sound. Six of us were family in one form or another, and there were four strangers who quickly became friends. Katherine and I were in the "banana-yak," a short yellow double that we owned.

Our first day out we landed in minor surf on a large sandy beach on the southwest corner of Vargas Island. The guides and one experienced paddler landed first. A wave caught the paddler as his kayak grounded in the sand, and he rolled onto his side in the water. The guides were in place to help the rest of us. During the lunch break, Katherine had a great time playing at the tide line, but she also got a scolding when my wife, Teesh, discovered the sleeves of her only long-sleeved shirt were wet.

After lunch we were back in the double kayak, sitting at the tide line and waiting for the next big wave. When it arrived the guides gave our boat a shove and off we went climbing over the first breaker. Like most of the other doubles, we were still descending from the first breaker when we hit the second breaker. Instead of rising up over the second breaker, we dove through it. It was only slightly higher than the top of Katherine's head. A few seconds later we were clear of the small breakers and I watched the water drip from my daughter's hair, shoulders and arms. Katherine spit out some salt water and said, "And Mom was mad I got my sleeves wet!"

The last to launch was one of the guides. He put his boat in shallow water, got in and quickly did up his sprayskirt as a wave came in and floated him. As the next breaker rolled over his deck, the sprayskirt popped loose and he had a lap and boat full of water. Fortunately, the warm summer breeze helped us all dry quickly. We certainly gained an appreciation for the dangers of surf landings and launches.

We paddled a short distance up Father Charles Channel and landed at the Vargas Island Inn. Enter this rustic lodge and take a step back in time—although a 21st-century touch is the solar power. The owners live next door, so we had the complete run of the lodge including the kitchen. Supper was a crab feed on the beach supplied by the inn's owners. Later that first night we had a sauna on the beach. Needless to say we slept well.

Flo, the inn's Labrador puppy, many years ago during our very first trip to Vargas Island.

Katherine and Teesh opted out of the second day's paddle so that Katherine could do schoolwork and play with Flo, the inn's Labrador puppy. It was only April and Katherine was playing hooky from her class at school, which, ironically, was taught by Paul. The rest of us paddled up the east side of Vargas and along its north end. On our way back we had lunch at a sandy beach near Mud Bay. Our return leg in the afternoon was against a strong headwind, but the distance wasn't far and the sea conditions

Ahous Beach

were mild. It was still early when we returned, so we all hiked the old telegraph trail across the island to Ahous Bay.

Ahous Beach is unbelievably beautiful. It is very picturesque, 3 km (2 mi) long, wide and made up of white sand. The trail getting there is something else, especially in April. It is only about 3 km long, but runs mostly through muskeg, and many of the hunks of wood that make up the corduroy trail are slightly submerged. As the wood is evenly spaced you can usually guess where to step. BC Parks decided the one bridge was unsafe and removed it, making that short section of the trail a bit more challenging.

Earlier, Katherine got her one pair of shoes wet and was again in trouble with her mother. Now we were on a very muddy obstacle course and we all made some missteps that caused us to sink up to a foot in mud. Most of us fell several times. Katherine had the shoes sucked off her feet more than once, and we would search in the mud to find them. The trip was great fun and I was determined to get back to Ahous Beach for a longer stay.

The next morning we paddled out past Wickaninnish Island to experience the ocean swell, then kayaked over to a sandy/gravel beach on the west side of Stubbs Island for lunch. From there we crossed over to Felice Island and paddled from this island to the Esowista Peninsula at slack tide to land at Tofino.

Sixteen months later, eight of us took a whale-watching boat as a water taxi to Ahous Beach and spent five wonderful rainy days—the only people there. The weather changed the first day, so when we were picked up the water taxi arrived from the north. This meant that we got to finish our trip by circumnavigating Vargas Island by Zodiac.

Southern Flores Island

Those who enjoy paddling, hiking, swimming, beachcombing and camping in less crowded conditions will appreciate Flores Island's long beaches and lush forests. On the south end of the island are the unforgettable sandy beaches of Whitesand Cove and Cow Bay. Whitesand Cove is in Gibson Marine Park, and Cow Bay is part of the 7,113-hectare (17,576-acre) Flores Island Provincial Park, a large wilderness area that includes three undisturbed watersheds and stands of Sitka spruce (map pg 116, 144).

From Whitesand Cove it is a pleasant half-hour walk through the rain forest to the village of Marktosis, one of the largest all-Native communities on the BC coast. There's a large modern grocery store here where you can stock up on provisions. Across Matilda Inlet is the non-Native town of Ahousat with a small store and marina. Note that most locals refer to both the Native and non-Native town as Ahousat. This is also the name of the First Nation band in the area. O-tsus-aht was the name of the original winter village here, while Maaqtusiis means "moving from one side to another," which describes how the village spans the neck of land it's on.

Difficulty level: Intermediate to advanced

Approximate travel time: Multiple day

Approximate distances (one way):
➤ Tofino to northwest corner of Vargas Island: 12 km (7.5 mi)
➤ Crossing Brabant Channel from the northwest corner of Vargas Island to Whaler Islets: 2.5 km (1.5 mi)
➤ Whaler Islet to Kutcous Point on Flores: 2.5 km (1.5 mi)
➤ Ahousat to Whitesand Cove: 10 km (6.3 mi)
➤ Whitesand Cove to Cow Bay: 8 km (5 mi)

Warnings:
➤ The trip from Tofino to Flores Island is *not* for beginning paddlers. However, you can also get here by water taxi (see "Getting there").

➤ If you're going to paddle from Ahousat to Whitesand you should be able to do surf landings and be prepared to get pinned down for several days if a southwest wind comes up.

➤ Even experienced paddlers should *not* try to paddle farther west than Cow Bay along the coast of Flores Island. This shoreline is rocky and subject to rough sea conditions. There are few landing spots and more than one paddler has gotten into trouble here.

➤ The shallow water of Coomes Bank (the Vancouver Island side of Calmus Passage) can be rough until you reach the Indian Reserve at Chetarpe. We recommend you *not* paddle here.

➤ Watch for rough water near Kutcous Point.

➤ If you are fortunate enough to spot a whale, stay at least 100 m (330 ft) away. If your observation lasts over 30 minutes, move to at least 300 m (1,000 ft) away.

Getting there:

➤ Water transportation to Ahousat is provided by scheduled water taxis that leave every hour or so from the government dock at the foot of 1st Street in Tofino. The taxis are affordable, but the price will rise quite a bit if you want to be dropped off at the beach. All can transport a limited number of kayaks. For information call the Ahousat Band Office, 250-670-9531.

➤ Many people take the water taxi to Ahousat and then paddle around to Whitesand Cove. From there you can paddle to Cow Bay.

➤ For those paddling from Tofino to Flores Island, the recommended route is to go to the northwest corner of Vargas Island (see page 145),

Sunset at Cow Bay. You may need to explore a little before landing to avoid the surf.

cross Brabant Channel to Whaler Islets, then paddle toward Kutcous Point on Flores Island. Turn west to get to Cow Bay (you may need to paddle a while to find a landing spot where you can avoid the surf) or east if you want to go to Whitesand Cove. Some paddlers may be tempted to follow the north shore of Calmus Passage instead of making the two crossings, but the water can be rougher here. You should have a GPS with the coordinates for Whaler Islets (126W04.2' 49N13.4') and for Kutcous Point on Flores Island (126W04.9' 49N14.8'). The water in Brabant Channel is usually calmer in the morning. Flooding tides also give smoother water as the prevailing breeze is from the west. There are sandy beaches on all sides of Whaler Islets, so it is almost always possible to land here in the lee of the wind.

Accommodations:

➤ Vera's Guest House: This is in Marktosis, just up the hill from the hydro dock. Call 250-670-9511 for reservations or e-mail *verasguesthouse@canada.com*.

➤ Hummingbird International Hostel: You can contact this hostel in Ahousat at 250-670-9679, by e-mail *info@hummingbird-hostel.com* or on the web *www.hummingbird-hostel.com*.

Camping:

➤ Cow Bay: Undefined beach campsites, no amenities

➤ Whitesand Cove: Undefined beach campsites, no amenities

➤ Whaler Islets: In a pinch you can camp here

Flores Island Trails

The Wild Side Heritage Trail is a great alternative for those who want to experience this area without the expense of taking a kayak. This trail leaves Marktosis and runs less than 2 km (1.2 mi) to Whitesand Cove. Much of the hike is on a boardwalk. From Whitesand Cove you can continue on to Cow Bay and then follow the trail a total of 16 km (10 mi) to the spectacular views from the top of Mt. Flores (elevation 902 m/2,960 ft). If you plan to hike this trail, make sure you let the water taxi crew know so they will let you off at the correct dock.

There is a hiking/camping fee to use this First Nations heritage trail, which was completed in 1995. The two creeks often go dry by midsummer, so plan

Wild Side Heritage Trail, a great way to experience the area without a kayak.

on packing in all your drinking and cooking water. For those who want to learn more about the trail, we recommend Stanley Sam Sr.'s *Ahousat Wild Side Heritage Trail Guidebook*. For more information about water taxis, guided walks, trail fees, etc., contact the Ahousat Band Office at 250-670-9531.

Hot Springs Cove

The ultimate Clayoquot paddling adventure is a one-way trip to Hot Springs Cove (map pg 116), From Whitesand Cove or Ahousat (Flores Island), the excursion usually takes two days with an overnight stop in Sulphur Passage Provincial Park. On the way to Hot Springs Cove you'll travel through two of Vancouver Island's deepest fjords, Millar Channel and Shelter Inlet, pass spectacular creeks and islets, and see where Sydney Inlet meets the open Pacific on the west side of Flores Island. From here it's a short paddle (or walk) to Hot Springs Cove, home of the Hesquiaht Band and the location of some well-known thermal pools. The Hesquiaht people used to live farther west until the tsunami following the 1964 Alaskan earthquake washed their homes out to sea. No lives were lost, but an elder said you could see some of the homes half-floating for days.

These soothing thermal pools are a popular natural attraction.

Except for the Hesquiaht's small reserve and two other chunks of land, most of Hot Springs Cove is part of the 2,667-hectare (6,590-acre) Maquinna Provincial Park. The Hesquiaht run the campground at Hot Springs Cove, which is across the inlet and a bit south of their reserve. There is a 30-minute walk to the hot springs from the park dock and camp area via a boardwalk trail. For those arriving by water, you pass the springs just a short way inside Sharp Point, which you round when entering Hot Springs Cove.

Approximately 380 litres (100 gallons) of water come out of the ground each minute, heated to 50 degrees Celsius (122 degrees Fahrenheit), and cascade down a 6-m (20-ft) waterfall into a series of natural soaking pools. Each pool is a little cooler than the one above, and at high tide the lower pools mix with salt water. The water smells of sulphur but is clean and refreshing. The pools can be crowded during the day thanks to all the charters that bring folks here, but in the morning and evening or late at night you will often find the place deserted.

That these springs are part of Maquinna Provincial Park is partially due to the generosity of Ivan and Mabel Clark, who donated the land to the province in 1954. They established a general store in the cove around the 1930s, but the Hot Springs store, post office and school are long gone. First Nations people used the springs for hundreds and maybe even thousands of years to treat a variety of ailments.

On your way up Millar Channel it's worth exploring Shark Creek, which has a beautiful waterfall. In the early 1990s basking sharks were sighted here almost daily; now they are nearly extinct. Basking sharks are the world's second largest fish. They can grow to 10 m (33 ft) long. That's a lot longer than your kayak. Fortunately they aren't aggressive and don't have large teeth. If you see one of these critters, please report it to the Pacific Biological Station in Nanaimo.

Difficulty level: Intermediate to advanced

Approximate travel time: Multiple day

Approximate distances (one way):
- ➤ Tofino to Whitesand Cove: 18.2 km (11.3 mi)
- ➤ Whitesand Cove to Sulphur Passage: 14 km (8.7 mi)
- ➤ Sulphur Passage campsite to Hot Springs: just under 20 km (12.4 mi)

Currents:
- ➤ Hayden Passage: Flood and ebb of 4 knots (some sources say 2.5 knots); directions and timing can vary
- ➤ Sulphur Passage: We have no first-hand information regarding this passage, but the *BC Marine Parks Guide* states currents can run up to 4 knots

Warnings:
- ➤ Conditions can be quite rough when you exit Sydney Inlet into the open Pacific to round Sharp Point into Hot Springs Cove.
- ➤ The channels in northern Clayoquot Sound, behind Flores Island, are steep-sided fjords While protected from ocean swells, these fjords funnel wind and are often rough and strewn with whitecaps.
- ➤ Landing sites are few, and campsites are even fewer. Large groups should not travel in this area, as campsites that are there cannot accommodate many tents. Even small groups must plan their trip carefully in case they arrive to find a campsite already taken and must push on to the next possible site.

➤ We have no first-hand information regarding Sulphur Passage. The cruising guides recommend using local knowledge and mention the passage has many rocks affecting navigation and current flows. *Paddling Through Time* speaks about the beauty of this passage and says it is fairly protected from wind.

➤ Do not use soap in the hot springs.

Getting there/launching:

➤ Hot Springs Cove is serviced by the *Matlahaw* water taxi (phone 250-670-1106 or 1-886-670-1106) and Homiss Enterprises (250-670-1110 or 888-781-9977). Both can transport a limited number of kayaks. The *Matlahaw* makes one scheduled trip daily leaving from Hot Springs Cove around 1:30 p.m. and from Tofino at 3:00 p.m.

➤ Most people paddle from Tofino and take the *Matlahaw* back. This way, if the weather doesn't co-operate, paddlers can turn back to Tofino or Ahousat. The standard route is Tofino to Vargas Island to Whitesand Cove (see under Vargas Island and Flores Island). From Whitesand Cove, paddle up Millar Channel past Matilda Inlet where the twin villages of Marktosis and Ahousat are located. Farther along, Shark Creek is on the east side of the channel. From here it's a short paddle to Obstruction Island and Sulphur Passage Provincial Park. You can go through either Hayden Passage or Sulphur Passage to Shelter Inlet, then into Sydney Inlet and around the Openit Peninsula into Hot Springs Cove. Should sea conditions prevent you from entering Hot Springs Cove, you can climb the Openit Peninsula and radio the *Matlahaw* or Band office on VHF channel 66 to arrange a pickup.

➤ For a book-length description of a paddle from Tofino to Meares Island

Shark Creek, the location of this magnificent waterfall, was once a popular hangout for the now nearly extinct basking shark.

and on to Hot Springs Cove, read Joanna Streetly's *Paddling Through Time: A Kayaking Journey Through Clayoquot Sound*.

Accommodations:

➤ Hot Springs Lodge: This small motel is perched partially on pilings across from the peninsula, a two-minute walk from the Hesquiaht village. Phone 250-670-1106 or 1-800-670-1106 or e-mail *bgsabbas@hotmail.com* for reservations.

➤ The InnChanter B&B: This "boatel" is at the park's dock in winter and anchored about 100 m (300 ft) from shore in spring and summer. Breakfast and dinner included in the rates. Phone 250-670-1149 for reservations or visit the web site: *www.innchanter.com*.

Camping:

➤ There is a good camping spot for kayakers on the southeast side of Sulphur Passage.

➤ Many kayakers choose to camp on the beaches near the hot springs along Sydney Inlet, on the Openit Peninsula, instead of rounding Sharp Point and paddling the last kilometre or two to the provincial campground. There are minor trails that connect these beaches to the hot springs' main boardwalk trail. As there are so many minor trails, make sure you mark yours for the return trip.

➤ There is good camping in a little cove referred to as Kayak Cove by the book *Exploring Vancouver Island's West Coast*. It is almost landlocked and its entrance is not easy to see. It's located on the east shore of Sydney Inlet on Flores Island a short way south of the areas locally known as Baseball Cove and Hoot-la-Kootla. Other local names for this beach, according to *Paddling Through Time*, are Crazy Eagle Beach, Ann's Beach, Sandy Beach and Half Moon Bay.

➤ The campground run by the Hesquiaht Band is situated north of the dock in Hot Springs Cove. There is water available from a hand pump on shore just north of the pier. There are outhouses at the camp area and near the springs. For more information contact the Hesquiaht Band office at 250-670-1100.

Northern Valdes Island (Wakes Cove)

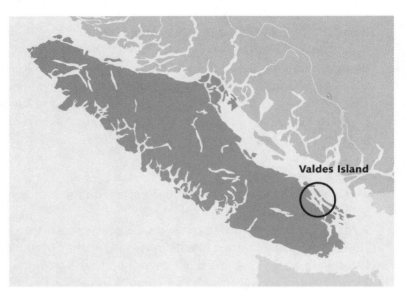

Valdes is in the middle of a chain of islands that includes Gabriola, Galiano, Mayne and Saturna. Between this chain and Vancouver Island are some of the best paddling waters in the world. While small passes between the islands have fast-moving currents, the waters west of the chain are relatively protected from wind and large waves, and paddlers can spend many enjoyable days exploring the myriad small islands. There are interesting rock formations almost everywhere, and the most interesting are along the cliffs of Valdes Island.

Valdes has one of the lowest ratios of population to land area in the Gulf Islands. Most of the southern half of the island is forest company land. There is a small First Nations village at Shingle Point, but it sees little use. Until recently, the northern half of the island was either private property, Crown land or First Nations land (indicated by the notation IR on charts). While the amount of kayaking in this area has increased at a dramatic rate, camping space has not.

In June 2002 the provincial government purchased a large parcel of land at Wakes Cove and announced the creation of Wakes Cove Provincial Park, which will offer some much-needed camping space for kayakers and other small boaters. This park features an old-growth forest interspersed with arbutus trees, Garry oaks and endangered plant species.

Difficulty levels:
- ➤ Wakes Cove and Flat Top Islands: Novice to intermediate
- ➤ Gabriola Passage: Intermediate to advanced
- ➤ Cedar-by-the-Sea boat ramp to Link Island and through Gabriola Passage: Advanced

Approximate travel times:
- ➤ Drumbeg Provincial Park to Flat Top Islands: Half day to full day
- ➤ Drumbeg Provincial Park to Wakes Cove: Half day to multiple day

Approximate distances:
- ➤ Drumbeg Provincial Park to Wakes Cove: 1.2 km (0.8 mi)
- ➤ Drumbeg Provincial Park to Dogfish Bay (proposed camping area): 1.5 km (0.9 mi)
- ➤ Wakes Cove to Dogfish Bay: 1.5 km (0.9 mi)
- ➤ Drumbeg Provincial Park to closest Flat Top Island (Breakwater Island): 0.7 km (0.4 mi)
- ➤ Exploring Flat Top Islands (circumnavigating the entire group including Kendrick—round trip from Drumbeg): 10 km (6.3 mi)
- ➤ Cedar-by-the-Sea boat ramp to Link Island and through Gabriola Passage to Dogfish Bay: 9 km (5.6 mi) one way

Drumbeg Park launch site

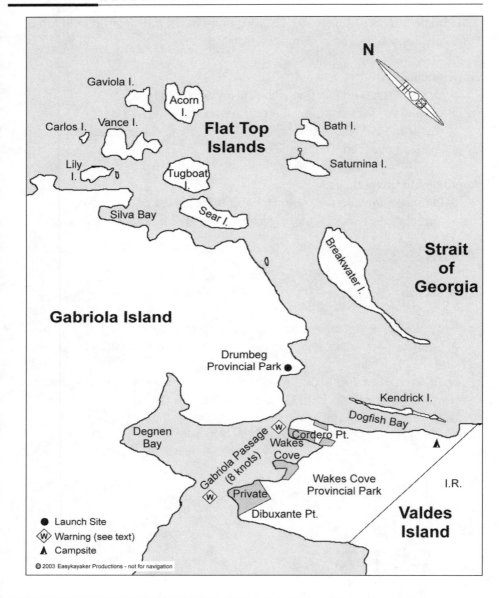

CHS charts:
- ➤ 3443—Thetis Island to Nanaimo
- ➤ 3475—Stuart Channel (Dodd Narrows)
- ➤ 3463—Strait of Georgia (Southern Portion)

Tidal reference port: Point Atkinson

Current reference station: Gabriola Passage

Weather and sea conditions reference:
➤ Strait of Georgia
➤ Entrance Island

Prevailing winds: Northwest or southeast; winds can be variable.

Warnings:
➤ Tidal currents up to 9 knots, tidal rips and whirlpools in Gabriola Passage (between Gabriola and Valdes islands). Currents flood east and ebb west.
➤ Tidal currents up to 10 knots, tidal rips and whirlpools in Porlier Pass (between Valdes and Galiano islands). Currents flood northeast and ebb southwest.
➤ Tidal currents up to 5 knots in False Narrows (between Gabriola and Mudge islands). Currents flood northwest and ebb southeast.
➤ Slack current in passages may vary from slack tide by up to 3 hours. Use current tables in *Tide and Current Tables*, Vol. 5, for slack current times and flow speeds.
➤ Weather and sea conditions can change quickly on the Strait of Georgia side of Valdes Island.
➤ High levels of boat traffic in Gabriola Passage and in the Silva Bay area.
➤ Respect First Nations land (marked IR on charts). Do not disturb these lands or archeological sites.
➤ Sensitive habitat and endangered plant species in area—tread softly.
➤ This is a very dry area—no fires.
➤ This is also a proposed marine protected area. Do not use soap anywhere it might end up in the marine environment.

Getting there/launching: The safest way to get to Wakes Cove Provincial Park is by ferry from Nanaimo to Gabriola Island. Once on Gabriola Island follow South Road to the southeast edge of the island. Turn right onto Coast Road, 400 m (0.2 mi) past the Drumbeg Park sign, then make a quick right onto Stalker Road. (All turns are well marked with signs.)

This will take you to Drumbeg Park, where you can launch. Wakes Cove Provincial Park is on Valdes Island across Gabriola Passage from Drumbeg Park.

Other launch sites:

➤ The Brickyard (Gabriola Island): Off South Road near the intersection of Fernie Road and South Road.

➤ Boat ramp off El Verano Drive (Gabriola Island): El Verano Drive is also off South Road near the intersection with Fernie Road, but it is about 0.5 km/0.3 mi east of the Brickyard.

➤ Boat ramp at Cedar-by-the-Sea, just south of Nanaimo: Consult a map for the turnoff from the Island Highway onto Cedar Road and the route to Cedar-by-the-Sea. The launch is located at the bottom of Nelson Road.

Accommodations: There are B&Bs, lodges and resorts on Gabriola Island. Call the Gabriola Chamber of Commerce and Visitor Information Centre at 250-247-9332 or 1-800-284-9332.

Camping:

➤ Wakes Cove Provincial Park (Valdes Island): With the exception of five small privately owned parcels of land, this new park encompasses the entire north end of Valdes Island. At time of writing, a formal management plan for the park had not been completed. The designated camping area will most likely be the cove known locally as Dogfish Bay, which is across from the south end of Kendrick Island. Some areas may be off-limits to humans in order to protect fauna and flora. Current information about provincial parks can be found at the Discover Camping web site, *www.discovercamping.ca*, or by phoning 1-800-689-9025.

➤ Blackberry Point (Valdes Island): This BC Marine Trail campsite is on the west coast of Valdes Island. You can pull your boat up on the sandy beach.

➤ Pirates Cove Marine Provincial Park (De Courcy Island): Pirates Cove is located at the southeastern end of De Courcy Island. Reservations are not accepted here. The walk-in campsite is available on a first-come, first-served basis. See *www.discovercamping.ca* for more information or call the BC Parks Discover Camping line at 1-800-689-9025.

➤ Descanso Bay Regional Park (Gabriola Island): This Regional District of Nanaimo campground is on Gabriola Island on Taylor Bay Road, 1 km

Rocks at Wakes Cove

(0.6 mi) from the ferry terminal. For reservations call 250-729-1213. You may need to book at least a month in advance, so call ahead for more information.

➤ Page's Resort and Marina (Gabriola Island): From the ferry terminal drive about 20 minutes along North or South Road. Turn on Coast Road and follow it to the sea. For reservations call 250-247-8931 or contact *www.pagesresort.com*.

Travel notes (Gary)

We had visited Wakes Cove before when paddling the Flat Top Islands, but only viewed it from the water. At that time it was private property, so we didn't do any exploring on land. As soon as we heard it had been designated a provincial park, Paul and I decided to revisit this area and see what it would be like as a camping and hiking destination.

Our previous trip to the Flat Top Islands was on a windy day. We travelled through Gabriola Passage to get there, timing our arrival just a little bit before slack current so we rode a mild flood east through the narrows. Once through we travelled south in the sheltered waters between Kendrick Island and Valdes. We then headed into the Strait of Georgia and battled a nor'wester to Silva Bay. Breakwater Island and a few others gave us something to hide behind and kept the seas relatively calm. The wind died as we reached Silva Bay. We had thought it would push us back to Gabriola Passage, but no such luck. The passage was flowing west at full ebb on our trip back, and it was nerve-racking at times to travel through shallow whirlpools the size of my kayak. The current was only running at 3.5 knots according to the tide and current book, but it was wild compared to much faster water we've been in. (It's often not the speed, but the amount of confused water that can make a trip scary or dangerous.) In other words, this wasn't as fun an outing as it could have been.

Back to the present...Today there were going to be six of us visiting Wakes Cove: Paul and I, our wives Imelda and Teesh, and our friends Dave and Celia. We gathered at Drumbeg Park at around 10 a.m. By the time we were in the water and raring to go it was an hour before slack current. According to the *Canadian Tide and Currrent Tables*, high tide would be at 14:15, but it estimated slack current for Gabriola Passage to be at 11:35—quite a difference! We could see the flooding tidal stream as we paddled out of Drumbeg Park's small cove. We didn't have to worry about anyone getting sucked into the narrows because it was flowing east.

View of Kendrick and Breakwater islands from proposed camping area.

We crossed the tidal stream with little effort and met a group of kayakers exiting the narrows moments later. They said the flow was quite mild, so we decided to paddle through the narrows against the current and explore Wakes Cove itself before heading to the proposed camping spot across from the south end of Kendrick Island.

A back eddy along the Valdes shore put a smile on our faces until we reached the tiny finger of rock off Cordero Point that caused the back eddy. We went from a free ride up the shoreline to a rude shove out into the current. With a quick push on the rudder pedal and a few hard paddle strokes we returned to shore and easy paddling for the remaining short distance to the cove.

There is good anchorage inside Wakes Cove, as well as protection for larger boats. Much of the shore is privately owned. We got a laugh from an official-looking sign on a large dock indicating it was home of the Gin Yacht Club. On the right, just before we reached the head of the cove, there is a public landing spot. At low tide you may have to carry your kayak a ways, but at a medium to high tide there's a good beach to pull up on. On our way out of the cove we saw a very large dead jellyfish, one of the biggest I've seen in these parts.

Our trip out and back through the narrows was uneventful as there was a fairly slack current. We headed south past Kendrick Island to the cove that's proposed for the park camping area. There is a sandy beach here, but we landed on the smooth rock beach since the bank and woods looked more inviting. I walked along the shore to the sandy beach, enjoying the round tide pools in the rock. There were many deer hoofprints in the sand, but no sign of the creek that the chart shows here.

After backtracking along the beach I joined Paul and Teesh in the woods, which are quite open and free of underbrush due to the sheep that have grazed here over the years. An old road wound between the trees, and two eagle feathers were lying on the ground a distance apart.

This spot will make a great camping area. There's room for many tents without losing privacy. The landing is good at any tide, and the waters are protected by the reef on the south end of Kendrick Island and by an unnamed small point to the southeast. The only drawback is that you won't be able to watch the sunset unless you walk to the small meadow on top of the hill.

I hiked up, looking for the stream that shows on the chart, and found an old open well less than 1 m (about 5 ft) square. This was the driest summer in 28 years, yet the well was full almost to ground level. Curiously, it didn't appear to be fed by a stream, nor was the ground around it wet, so I assumed it had been dug by members of Brother XII's Mandieh Settlement. I looked for an old house site near the well, but could find nothing. Most of the Mandieh buildings didn't have foundations, which might be why there wasn't any sign of a house. I knew that Brother XII built his last House of Mystery somewhere nearby. This was a temple with concrete vaults in the floor where he is reported to have stored millions of dollars worth of gold. The sheltered cove inside Kendrick Island, known locally as Dogfish Bay, was Brother XII's harbour of choice. Trails and eventually a road went across the island to the cliffs on the west side. All supplies and materials were carried across these trails.

Brother XII

Brother XII (a.k.a. Edward Arthur Wilson) created the Aquarius Foundation, a worldwide cult movement with its headquarters at Cedar-by-the-Sea, Valdes Island and De Courcy Island. People would join and give their money, which XII often converted to gold $20 pieces. In 1928 there were roughly 8,000 members contributing regularly. Many joined and donated their life savings.

False prophet, doomed cult of gold, sex and black magic—some thought this charismatic leader with his pale piercing eyes was so evil that the devil named a holiday in hell after him. Pierre Berton has been quoted as saying his religion was "downright evil." Three books have been written about Brother XII, and of the three, John Oliphant's *Brother Twelve: The Incredible Story of Canada's False Prophet* (1991) provides the most in-depth coverage of the story.

While his wife lived in nearby Cedar, Brother XII housed his mistress, Myrtle Baumgartner, on Valdes. Myrtle was pregnant with what Brother XII prophesied was a Christ child, the reincarnation of Horus, who would become a world leader by 1975. Myrtle miscarried twice and eventually lost her sanity. Meanwhile, XII's followers built cabins, a meeting centre and a warehouse on the Valdes property, described as "parklike, with grassy open spaces and great groves of cedar, maple and madrona [arbutus]." This became Brother XII's Mandieh Settlement, later renamed the Brothers' Centre as a result of bad press after disgruntled followers unsuccessfully accused XII of embezzlement.

When the law finally closed in on Brother XII, he fled with his mistress of the day, a whip-wielding Madame Zee de Valdes. It's estimated that they escaped with $400,000 in gold. In a court case, the Valdes property was awarded to Mary Connally, a millionaire who was one of the foundation's largest contributors, but who also worked like a slave on Valdes Island to prove herself worthy.

Rumours have persisted that buried treasure was left behind. Over the years the buildings have been ransacked, wells have been dynamited and holes have been dug all over the Valdes Island property by treasure seekers. When I first arrived in this area I met several people who had brief run-ins with Brother XII. Surprisingly, most spoke with high regard for the early days of the cult at Cedar-by-the-Sea. All mentioned XII's piercing eyes, with irises so pale that they were almost white.

Who would have thought that one day this property would become Wakes Cove Provincial Park?

Back in the kayaks we headed through the small gap between Kendrick's reef and Valdes Island, aiming for the south tip of Breakwater Island. This busy boating channel is known to get a little bumpy. Fortunately it's a short crossing, like all the others in the area, and takes less than 10 minutes.

As we approached Breakwater Island we joined several large sea lions that were on the prowl for lunch. They didn't seem to be diving very deep, so we got quite a show as we paddled between them. We kept a good distance away and they showed little interest in us.

Seals in Flats Tops

Although the strait was bumpy, we chose to head up that side of Breakwater on our way to the tombolo between Saturnina and Bath islands. It's not a true tombolo—a spit joining an island to the mainland or another island—as the gravel bar doesn't connect the two islands, but it does connect Saturnina Island to an islet. Tombolo or not, this is one of the prettiest places to have lunch in the area. On a clear day the view of the mainland mountains is magnificent.

After lunch we threaded our way through the amazing rock formations of the Flat Tops to Carlos Island. There were at least four other groups of kayakers in the Flat Tops this day, one of which was at Carlos. We had a short stroll around the island and exchanged Chinese fruits with the other kayakers.

On the way back to Drumbeg we paddled through Silva Bay, looking at the various boats and exchanging a few words with people on board. The trip back was all too short. We had paddled only about 12 km (7.5 mi), but wanted to save our energy for the Gabriola Cycle and Kayak festival's salmon BBQ supper and concert by Valdy.

The paddling in this area is some of the best that the Gulf Islands can offer when the weather co-operates. Dave noted that we saw more wildlife in half a day here than we did in four days going around Meares Island. On our short paddle we had seen sea lions, many seals with pups, an otter and lots of bird life. We may have been at sea level, but, as Valdy said later that night, we were high on water!

Local History

Although the Spanish, Russian, British and Americans had been visiting Vancouver Island's west coast as part of the fur trade since the 1770s, the inside waters went largely unexplored until 1792, when the Nootka Sound Controversy brought Spain and Britain to the verge of war over trading rights to, and possession of, the outer coast. In 1788 Captain John Meares set up a trading post in Nootka Sound. The next year, while in China, Meares sent trading vessels to the sound. The Spanish seized the ships and destroyed his village. Meares returned to England and stirred up public and political opinion against Spain. Betting that Spain's ally, France, would be too busy with the French Revolution to help, the British threatened war. The Spanish agreed to the Nootka Sound Convention on October 28, 1790, avoiding a war with Britain.

Captain George Vancouver arrived here in 1792 to explore the coast from latitudes 30°N to 60°N and to meet with a Spanish delegation to reach an agreement over details of the Convention. Vancouver reached Cape Flattery on April 29, 1792, and headed up the Straits of Fuca as they were then known, commemorating Juan de Fuca, who had explored about 160 km (100 mi) up this waterway 200 years earlier. (Although Fuca's claims have been doubted in the past, some experts are now asserting that he did in fact make this journey.) After a month exploring and mapping the Puget Sound area, Captain Vancouver travelled north to meet with the Spanish captains Valdes and Galiano on June 22, 1792, off the coast of Point Grey, the present location of Vancouver. The two Spanish captains were also surveying the local waterways, circumnavigating Vancouver Island from the north (clockwise) while Vancouver was sailing in the opposite direction. The Spanish gave Vancouver copies of the charts they made. This friendly act probably went a long way to preserve the Spanish names that dot our coastline.

George Vancouver named the body of water between Vancouver Island and the mainland the "Gulf of Georgia," not after himself but to honour King George III, or so the story goes. Naturally the islands in the strait became known as the Gulf Islands. The name Gulf of Georgia stuck until 1865, when Captain George Richards, the area's first hydrographer, renamed it Strait of Georgia to reflect its true nature.

Dibuxante Point and Cordero Point on Valdes Island's north end were named to honour the Spanish mapmaker who sailed with Valdes and Galiano. Cordero was the name of the mapmaker and Dibuxante means "mapmaker" in Spanish.

In the late 1800s and early 1900s Valdes Island was much more populated than it is today. In 1885 settlers built a school for 18 pupils, and in 1910 they formed a school district. However, the depression hit Valdes hard and the school was forced to close in 1936 because most residents had moved off the island. There was reportedly a processing plant for bottom fish located in Dogfish Bay, and this may have helped support the population that remained on the island.

Captain William Flewett owned most of the northern end of Valdes Island and the De Courcy Group of Islands in 1889. His home was a two-room log cabin high up on the cliffs near Dibuxante Point. He raised sheep on the islands but was plagued by rustlers. His 162-hectare (400-acre) property was sold to Brother XII in 1928 for $13,000.

Wakes Bay is named after Captain Baldwin Arden Wake, who settled there in the 1870s. Captain Wake rowed across Gabriola Passage each day to teach school. He was killed in a boating accident on his way back from Nanaimo in 1880. His son, also named Baldwin, stayed on Valdes Island and worked as a telegraph operator until his death in 1906. His wife Amelia stayed on and also worked as a telegraph operator until her death in 1946. She kept sheep, which were allowed free range on the island. In 1928 Brother XII had a fence built and sent Amelia a note saying, "If you don't keep your sheep out, I can be a bad neighbour too."

The First Nations also have a long history on Valdes, but today the island is almost deserted.

Northern Gabriola Island

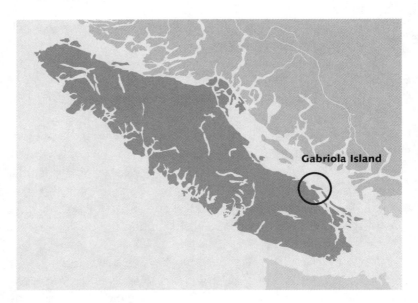

Gabriola, one of the larger Gulf Islands, is known for its temperate climate and abundant marine life. Malaspina Galleries, a dramatic rock overhang shaped like a giant cresting wave, is an impressive natural attraction. The island possesses a wealth of interesting nooks to explore and is large enough that you can usually find sheltered paddling on one side of it or the other.

On the northwest corner of the island, in Gabriola Sands Provincial Park, lie the Twin Beaches: Taylor Bay and Pilot Bay. The beaches form a peninsula and are an attractive place to set out for a day's kayaking adventure. It's an easy paddle from Pilot Bay to Malaspina Galleries or over to Entrance Island, where there is a picturesque lighthouse. Entrance Island is also home to a colony of about 80 seals. Pilot Bay itself is an excellent swimming spot, sheltered by surrounding tall trees. The tide travels over a fair length of sand that nicely heats the water for late afternoon and evening swimming.

Descanso Bay is another recommended launch site for interesting paddling. You can either head north to Malaspina Galleries or paddle south and follow the cliffs in Northumberland Channel. There is an abundance of marine life to view along here as you paddle by at low tide. The current in Northumberland Channel isn't strong for the first few kilometres, but it will give you a boost if you're going with it.

Difficulty levels:
- ➤ Pilot Bay to Malaspina Galleries: Novice to intermediate
- ➤ Pilot Bay to Entrance Island: Novice to intermediate (depending on weather forecast)
- ➤ Descanso Bay area: Novice to intermediate
- ➤ Northumberland Channel and False Narrows: Intermediate to advanced

Approximate travel times:
- ➤ Exploring Malaspina Galleries: Half day
- ➤ Entrance Island area (circumnavigating): Half day or longer
- ➤ Descanso Bay and Malaspina Galleries area: Half day
- ➤ Descanso Bay to False Narrows: Full day

Approximate distances:
- ➤ Pilot Bay to Orlebar Point: 2.8 km (1.7 mi) one way
- ➤ Orlebar Point to Entrance Island: 2 km (1.2 mi) round trip
- ➤ Pilot Bay to Malaspina Galleries: 6 km (3.75 mi) round trip
- ➤ Descanso Bay Regional Park to Malaspina Galleries: 2 km (1.2 mi) round trip
- ➤ Exploring Descanso Bay: 2 to 3 km (1.2 to 1.9 mi)
- ➤ Descanso Bay to Malaspina Galleries: 4 km (2.5 mi) round trip
- ➤ Descanso Bay to False Narrows: 9 km (5.6 mi) one way

Glaciations and thousands of years of wind and water erosion have created unique shapes in the sandstone.

CHS charts:
> 3443—Thetis Island to Nanaimo including Gabriola
> 3458—Western half of Gabriola and Nanaimo Harbour (includes Malaspina Galleries but not Flat Top Islands)

Tidal reference port: Point Atkinson

Weather and sea conditions reference:
> Entrance Island (We strongly recommend checking weather conditions and forecast before paddling this area)
> Strait of Georgia

Prevailing winds: Northwest or southeast; winds can be strong in the Strait of Georgia and pick up quickly in the Entrance Island area.

Warnings:
> Check weather forecast for Strait of Georgia and wind/sea report from Entrance Island.
> Ship and ferry traffic in this area creates large wakes.
> Winds can come up quickly around Entrance Island and the seas can become rough just as quickly.
> There is a strong current and a lack of landing places in some parts of Northumberland Channel.
> Northumberland Channel is a shipping lane; stay close to the cliffs out of the way of larger boats.
> Beware of strong currents—up to 9.5 knots—in Dodd Narrows and currents half that strong in False Narrows.

Getting there: The ferry to Gabriola leaves from the BC Ferries terminal on Front Street in downtown Nanaimo behind Harbour Park Mall. Ferries run every hour.

Recommended launch sites:
> **Descanso Bay Regional Park campground**: This offers the most sheltered and shortest route to the galleries. The campground is located on Taylor Bay Road 1 km (0.6 mi) from the ferry terminal.
> **Pilot Bay**: This sandy beach launching site is in Gabriola Sands Provincial Park. There is a parking area just off Ricardo Road only metres from the beach. If you want to minimize your carrying distance, it's best to launch or exit from Pilot Bay at a medium to high tide. Pilot Bay is

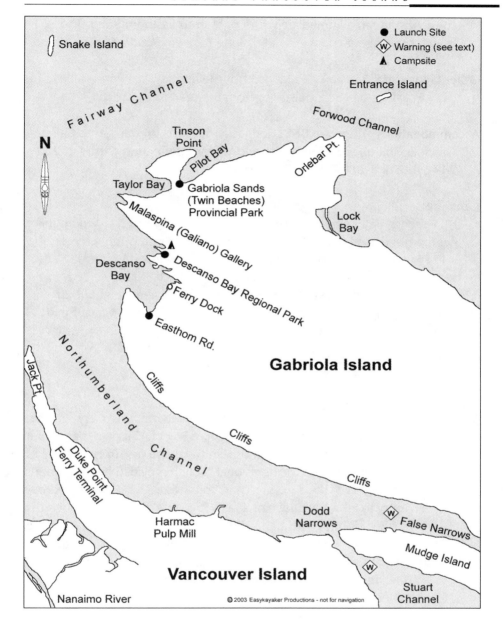

more exposed to prevailing winds than the launch sites in the Descanso Bay area.

➤ **Easthom Road**: On the south shore of Descanso Bay, this is another good launch site, located just south of the ferry terminal. When you come off the ferry, immediately turn right onto Easthom Road. The launch site is about half a kilometre along Easthom Road and easy to find.

Other launch site: You can also launch from Taylor Bay, but you will have to carry kayaks a significant distance from the road to the beach.

Accommodations: There are B&Bs, lodges and resorts on the island. Call the Gabriola Chamber of Commerce and Visitor Information Centre at 250-247-9332 or 1-888-284-9332.

Camping:
➤ Descanso Bay Regional Park: This Regional District of Nanaimo public campground is on Taylor Bay Road, 1 km (0.6 mi) from the ferry terminal. For reservations call 250-729-1213. You may need to book at least a month in advance, so call ahead for more information.
➤ Page's Resort and Marina: From the ferry terminal drive about 20 minutes along either North Road or South Road. Turn on Coast Road and follow it to the sea. For reservations call 250-247-8931 or contact *www.pagesresort.com*.

Travel notes (Paul)

The kayaking conditions were near perfect as Gary, Imelda, Celia, Kitty and I launched from Pilot Bay on Gabriola Island. Our goal: to visit Malaspina Galleries. It was the first truly hot day of summer, and with the occasional cooling provided by stray clouds passing over the sun, the conditions were idyllic. We timed our entry to take advantage of a fairly high tide, paddling through the sheltered bay north and then west around Tinson Point to Malaspina Point and Malaspina Galleries. Sounds of giggling skipped across the water as we approached the gallery. Several teenage girls were swimming at the northwest end while two older boys were diving from the sandstone overhang.

After enjoying some of the natural art of the gallery, we paddled south by southeast toward Descanso Bay along a fairly high wall of sandstone that dropped into the water. Both the direction of the wall, from northwest to southeast, and the striations along it kindled some thoughts from a decades-old geology class.

Malaspina Galleries

Malaspina Galleries—also known as Galiano Gallery, Galiano Galleries and Malaspina Gallery—were formed by wind and salt spray eroding the sandstone over the past millennia. This unique rock formation drew the attention of the Spanish explorers Dionisio Alcala-Galiano and Cayetano Valdes in 1792 when they first entered Fairway Channel and Nanaimo Harbour in their sailing schooners, the *Sutil* and the *Mexicana*.

They named the Galleries after Alejandro Malaspina, a captain in the Spanish Navy, who made Valdes a captain when he was a mere 25 years old. (Alcala-Galiano and Valdes also gave Gabriola its name, derived from the Spanish word for "seagull.") The Galleries were etched into history when they were drawn by the expeditions' artist and mapmaker, Jose Cardero. A famous portrayal of Malaspina Galleries by Fernando Brambila now hangs in the Museo Naval, Madrid.

It's best to view the Galleries at a medium to higher tide as the rock formations are just above water level. The gallery, which can also be accessed on foot from the end of Malaspina Road, is a popular spot for both locals and tourists.

The southern Gulf Islands are part of the Nanaimo Group, which formed 65 to 90 million years ago in the Cretaceous Period. Most of the sandstone seen along this area of the coast is in the Nanaimo Group. In the last 80,000 years three glaciers left their marks on the landscape and sedimentary rocks of the Gulf Islands and Vancouver Island. The rocks and ice at the bottom of a glacier had probably scoured the grooves and striations along the length of the rock wall we were now paddling beside.

Glaciations and thousands of years of wind and water erosion have also created dozens of unique shapes in the sandstone. The object represented by each formation is certainly subject to the viewer's imagination and interpretation. We saw a duck's body, a serpent's head, and many others. Toward the end of the same rock wall was a beautifully shaped rock standing alone. I thought the formation looked like a dwarf with a huge floppy hat and a particularly large nose. All of us agreed that these rock formations were even more interesting than the ones at Malaspina Galleries.

This exposed reef made for a great lunch stop.

After admiring the sandstone sculptures we beached on an exposed reef. I thought we were just stopping for a quick water break, but then Kitty brought out an incredible picnic lunch. Soon we were feasting on locally caught crab legs, marinated vegetables, a strawberry-watermelon drink and chocolate chip cookies.

The meal ended as the tide submerged our Kitty-created haven. We began to paddle back toward Tinson Point through the reflection of sky, wispy clouds and sun that was spread across the calm sea like a painting spread across a canvas.

Back at Tinson Point we decided to paddle 3.5 km (2.2. mi) to the Entrance Island lighthouse. We felt safe paddling to Entrance even though we knew that conditions in this area change quickly—the shelter of Orlebar Point was just a short paddle away, and as we cleared the point, the panoramic view of Gabriola Island and the Strait of Georgia gave us a chance to see incoming inclement weather before it struck. After reaching

Entrance Island I paddled counterclockwise with Celia while Gary, Imelda and Kitty toured clockwise.

When Celia and I reached the northwest side of the island we found Gary, Imelda, and Kitty talking to the lighthouse keeper and the assistant keeper, who were wading in the water along a shelf protruding from the island. A couple of metres away their dog was perched on a rock with only its paws immersed in the salty sea.

Entrance Island Lighthouse

The Entrance Island Lighthouse was originally completed on June 8, 1875. Its construction was plagued by a number of problems including the drowning of three men and the contractor absconding with the building funds. The current buildings, constructed in the 1980s, are a stark contrast to the conglomerate rock they sit on and are visible from quite a distance.

We bobbed for a while in the light waves from passing ferries and dipped our hands in the ocean. The water temperature was 21 degrees Celsius according to the lighthouse keeper. The small waves that passed under our hulls pounded the rocky shoreline with unexpected force.

Seals and their pups poked their heads out of the water only metres from our kayaks. The pups, which are able to swim hours after birth, were numerous, and the seals came surprisingly close to our boats. Occasionally one would lift itself high out of the water to view us. They proved to be very camera shy, much to Gary's frustration.

We could have stayed rocking in the waves for hours, chatting, admiring the lighthouse, watching the ferries pass and the seals coming up for air, but it was time to paddle on. After completing our leisurely circumnavigation of Entrance Island we headed across Forwood Channel toward Orlebar Point, a favourite local scuba diving spot. Imelda and I have both dived at this location. A rock wall inhabited by a rich variety of sea life drops away from the point.

We paddled slowly along the shoreline toward Pilot Bay. The warm summer day had brought loads of people to the small beaches tucked between the rock outcroppings. Laughter occasionally emanated from house decks and beach-goers, rippling across the summer waters.

Imelda and I pulled our craft onto the beach at Pilot Bay. Then Imelda, dressed in shorts and a top, threw herself into the water with a shriek at the sudden cold. Moments later Kitty joined her for a soothing dip. We loaded our kayaks onto Gary's trailer and headed for the ferry. With a few minutes to spare, Gary, Imelda and I had a refreshing glass of beer at the pub next to the ferry. We reminisced about our day's paddling and resolved to come back before summer's end to paddle Gabriola's Flat Top Islands.

Travel notes (Gary)

We didn't make it back to paddle the Flat Tops that summer, but I did return with about a hundred other kayakers to participate in Gabriola Cycle and Kayak's 14th annual kayak and biking festival at Descanso Bay Regional Park.

Dave and Celia arrived in the early afternoon to join me for a paddle and the evening's festivities. We enjoyed exploring all the nooks and crannies of Descanso Bay, Malaspina Galleries and points in between. Although we ventured into the entrance to Northumberland Channel, the weather was iffy so we decided to turn back to paddle the more sheltered areas and examine the wonderful rock formations that seemed to be everywhere we looked.

The sweet sound of stringed instruments greeted us as we neared the campground. Mandolirium had found a secluded piece of beach and was rehearsing for the concert that night. The group's bluegrass/folk music was delightful, and we added a little extra percussion as we lightly drummed on our kayaks while watching from a few metres offshore.

After the salmon BBQ and a slide show presented by Peter and Ana of Gabriola Cycle and Kayak, Mandolirium climbed onto the stage (the back of a flatdeck truck) to perform. As darkness fell, Valdy, one of my favourite folk artists, began his set. It was an incredible show.

The next morning, after several hundred blueberry pancakes were consumed at breakfast, Peter had fleets of kayaks waiting. Guided groups left every half hour for a two-hour paddle. I joined the 10:30 a.m. group of 14 for a paddle down Northumberland Channel.

I chose the right trip—we started our paddle south assisted by an ebbing tide, turned just after the low tide and headed back north assisted by the current from a flooding tide. A couple of years earlier I had paddled from Cedar-by-the-Sea, portaged across Link Island and then continued on the water through False Narrows and along the Northumberland Channel shore, but I had stopped midway to Descanso Bay. That southern portion of the Gabriola shore wasn't very interesting, but the rock formations (known locally as the Gabriola Cliffs) along the 3 km (1.9 mi) from Descanso Bay to my stopping place on the previous trip are wonderful.

Denman and Hornby Islands

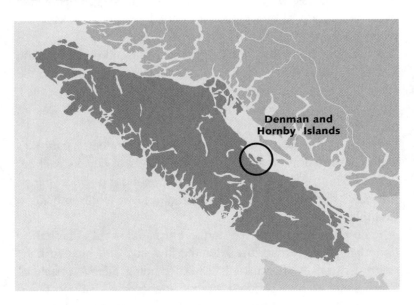

Denman and Hornby Islands

Along with beaches, hiking trails and abundant wildlife, there are plenty of artisans on both Hornby and Denman islands. The two neighbouring islands boast the highest number of artists per capita in Canada and are famous for their potters.

Hornby is called the jewel of the Gulf Islands. Its attractions are white sand beaches, diverse forests—from arbutus and oak groves on the south shores to coastal rain forest inland—and abundant sea life.

Denman Village is Denman Island's "downtown." It's an interesting collection of shops, two community halls, a library, a school and the post office. The art gallery and museum have a collection of works by island artists as well as displays on local history.

Cycling is a good way to explore the islands as most roads are paved. You can rent bikes on Hornby at Off Road Bicycle Shop next to the Co-op, the island's general store.

CHS chart: 3527—Baynes Sound

Tidal reference port: Point Atkinson

Weather and sea conditions reference:
- ➤ Chrome Island
- ➤ Strait of Georgia

Prevailing winds: Northwest or southeast

Getting there: The Island Highway turnoff for the Denman–Hornby ferry terminal at Buckley Bay is well marked about 3 to 4 km (2 to 2.5 mi) north of Fanny Bay. Take the turnoff and drive straight down to the water. Ferries leave about every hour and the trip across to Denman Island takes 10 minutes. To reach Hornby Island, drive across Denman Island and take another 10-minute ferry ride from Gravelly Bay to Shingle Spit.

Accommodations: There are resorts and B&Bs on Denman and resorts on Hornby. For information call the Denman/Hornby Tourist Services at 250-335-1642.
Note: Difficulty levels, approximate travel times, distances, location-specific warnings, launch sites and camping information are listed under specific paddling areas.

Hornby Island

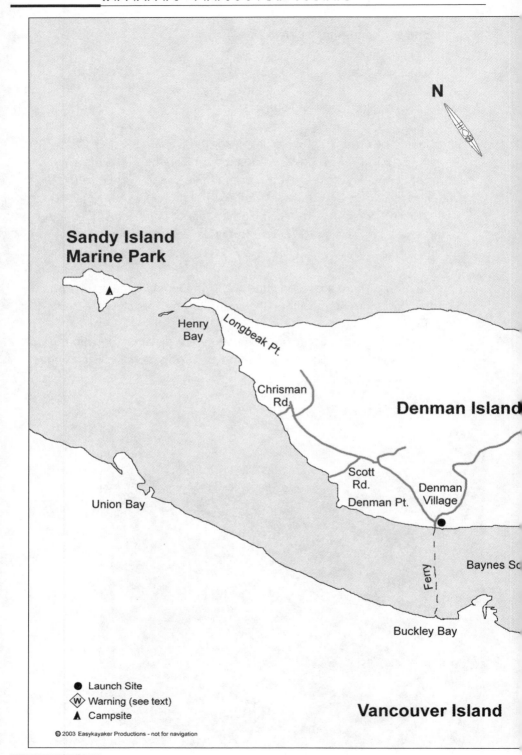

**Sandy Island
Marine Park**

N

Henry
Bay

Longbeak Pt.

Chrisman
Rd.

Denman Island

Scott
Rd.

Denman Pt.

Denman
Village

Union Bay

Ferry

Baynes Sc

Buckley Bay

● Launch Site
Ⓦ Warning (see text)
▲ Campsite

© 2003 Easykayaker Productions - not for navigation

Vancouver Island

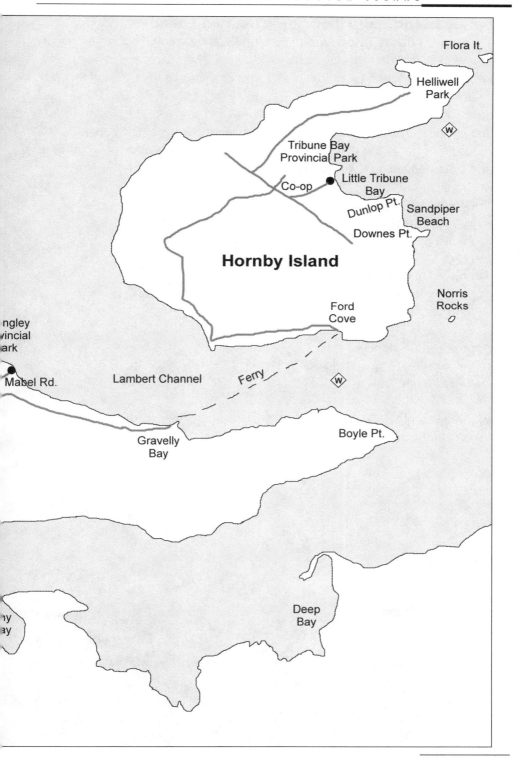

Flora It.

Helliwell
Park

Ⓦ

Tribune Bay
Provincial Park

Co-op Little Tribune
Bay

Dunlop Pt. Sandpiper
Beach

Downes Pt.

Hornby Island

Ford
Cove

Norris
Rocks

ngley
vincial
ark

Mabel Rd. Lambert Channel Ferry Ⓦ

Gravelly
Bay

Boyle Pt.

Deep
Bay

ny
ay

Sandy Island and Fillongley (Denman Island)

Denman's Sandy Island Marine Provincial Park is home to a large population of birds and butterflies. The park includes the Seal Islets and Sandy Island, which is also referred to as Tree Island. You can walk to the island at low tide year-round.

In Fillongley Provincial Park, hiking trails wind through old-growth forests and provide spectacular views of snow-capped mountains. The park is on the east side of the island and features some of the largest stands of Douglas fir and cedar remaining in the region.

Difficulty levels:
➤ Denman ferry dock to Sandy Island: Novice
➤ Fillongley Park area: Novice

Approximate travel times:
➤ Denman ferry dock to Sandy Island: Full day to multiple day
➤ Fillongley Park area: Half day or longer

Approximate distances:
➤ Denman ferry dock to Sandy Island: 10 km (6.3 mi) one way
➤ Fillongley Park to Gravelly Bay: 6.5 km (4.1 mi) one way

Warning: Lambert Channel between Hornby and Denman islands is subject to combined wind and current.

Beach at Fillongley Provincial Park

Recommended launch sites:

➤ **Boat ramp at the Denman ferry dock** (Vancouver Island side): You can drive almost to the water's edge, the beach is gravel and there is lots of long-term parking.

➤ **Fillongley Provincial Park** (Denman Island): From the ferry terminal take Denman Road east across the island. Turn left onto Swan Road and right onto Beadnell Road.

➤ **Mabel Road:** A short road just southeast of the Fillongley Park border on Denman Island.

Other launch sites:

➤ **Union Bay** (Vancouver Island): Approximately 16 km (10 mi) north of Fanny Bay on Highway 19A.

➤ **Scott and Chrisman Roads:** The trails to these two launch sites are long and steep. From the Denman ferry terminal, head west on Northwest Road. You will reach Scott Road first, and a little farther west is Chrisman Road.

Camping:

➤ Fillongley Provincial Park: You can reserve campsites on-line. There are only 10 campsites. When we were there, five were available on a first-come basis while the other five could be reserved. The campsites are small, but the beach area and old-growth forest trails make up for this. For reservations call Discover Camping at 1-800-689-9025 or visit the BC Parks web site at *www.discovercamping.ca*.

➤ Sandy Island Marine Provincial Park: Campsites are walk-in only. No reservations are available. For more information visit the BC Parks web site at *www.discovercamping.ca*.

Travel notes (Gary)

I've gazed at Sandy Island many times over the years as I've passed by on the Island Highway, but this was to be our first trip there. Paul had been suggesting for a couple of years that we pay it a visit. I'd assumed, because it was so close to Comox, that it would be too tame a trip and not that scenic. Boy was I wrong.

Our plan was to launch next to the Denman ferry dock, catch the flood tide and paddle along the northwest side of Denman to Sandy Island. While waiting for the tide to turn we toured the area and visited Abraxas Books & Gifts in Denman Village. When

Close to Comox, Sandy Island is surprisingly beautiful.

we launched around 4:30 p.m. the ferry was about to leave, so we paddled under the ferry wharf, startling a few pigeons into flight, and started happily off on a new journey. One ferry worker called down with friendly concern to ask if we had the appropriate safety gear. I replied in the affirmative and patted my VHF and GPS, neither of which we really needed for such a sheltered easy paddle. The real safety gear—our PFDs, sprayskirts, pumps, whistles, paddlefloats, charts and spare paddles—were all visible on the kayak decks.

The first quarter of our trip took us past a succession of farmed oyster beds in shallow, calm water. The nice thing about our chosen route was that we would be able to land on the shore at any time if necessary. It's an accessible beach all the way to Longbeak Point. After we rounded Denman Point we were paddling into a headwind and slightly choppy seas. The coastline was one cove after another. There were a few houses and farms, but most of the area appeared to be in its natural forested state. Across Baynes Sound on Vancouver Island, the mountains behind Union Bay showed the last traces of snow, even though it was almost mid-July. The scenery in all directions was beautiful.

The wind stiffened and we hugged the shore to hide from it. The occasional rock made us pay attention to the water in front of us, but we also spent a lot of time looking down through the crystal-clear water, which gave us a great view of the bottom. We skimmed over several reefs off the points of land that we passed.

As we approached Henry Bay and Longbeak Point at Denman's northern tip, the wind hit us full force. Water conditions were fine, though that's a relative term. The wind was strong, but our rudders stayed up and, except for spray on our sunglasses, the waves weren't large enough to get us wet.

That final stretch across from Henry Bay to Sandy Island seemed to take forever. The wind slowed us to a crawl, but we finally made it to the island, a place of incredible beauty. There were five other kayaks there plus a group of 40 or more sea cadets from Comox. We had not expected to find sea cadets, but they were very polite and entertaining to watch from a distance.

The 10-km (6.3-mi) trip is a nice easy distance for most paddlers, yet long enough that you feel you've gotten some exercise. All along the shoreline we had been watching bald eagles and an assortment of other marine birds, including what I think were Bonaparte's gulls near Denman's northern end. A small seal swam around just off Sandy Island as we looked for the ideal campsite. Paul chose a level site on the sand near some driftwood furniture. I tucked up into the bush near the base of a Douglas fir with a trunk over 1.2 m (4 ft) in diameter. The front of my tent stuck out onto the beach and my small tarp served as a doormat and sitting area free of sand.

Campsite on Sandy Island

The cadets quieted down about 9:30 p.m., though the campsite is so huge that we couldn't hear them much anyway. The camp area was sheltered from the wind, but it appeared from our view of the water that the wind died down around dusk. I drifted off to sleep listening to the gentle lapping of waves on the shore and wondering if the cadets would wake us with a trumpet reveille at 6 a.m.

Instead of a trumpet, it was the cry of an eagle that blasted me awake just after 5 a.m. Eagles can be heard a long way, especially on calm mornings, and this one was only 15 m (50 ft) above my head. By 5:30 I had listened to many more eagle cries, a dispute between the eagle and a flock of crows over my tent, and a visit from a second eagle. I decided I might as well go for a walk and take a few pictures in the morning light. Of course my first picture was of the eagle overhead. His body was in the shade, but his white head shone brilliantly in the morning sun.

Paul and I had breakfast about 7 a.m., then broke camp, packed up our boats and joined our neighbouring kayakers for a visit. The tide was rising and if we visited long enough our boats would almost launch themselves by the time we were ready to leave.

When we did paddle off, the wind had come up again, but it was in our favour. We crossed over to Longbeak Point and drifted by an eagle sitting atop a tall post stuck into the sand. Later we saw a hawk sitting on a low rock at the water's edge. It was slightly smaller than a red-tailed hawk, but didn't have the chest of a northern goshawk or Cooper's hawk. It seemed an unusual roosting place for that type of bird.

We didn't realize how far Denman Point extended in the form of a submerged sand bar until too late. We could have turned and paddled out, but thought there might be enough water to clear the sandbar. Oops! We were almost right. It took a little effort to push the boats over the bar, but we did it without any serious scratches.

With the wind at our backs, the 10-km paddle went by quickly. Our time for the return trip was 1 hour and 40 minutes, almost an hour shorter than the trip out. We'd had a minor current in our favour going both directions, but the wind was the real difference.

Back at the launch site next to the Denman ferry dock, we quickly unpacked, loaded our boats back on the Toyota and headed across the island to explore the paddling off Denman's northeast coast. We had been told that Lambert Channel had a bit of current and could also get the wind funnelling through it, but the area between Fillongley Provincial Park and the Gravelly Bay ferry dock was a nice place to paddle. As on the southwest coast, the beach is shallow, allowing you to land if the weather kicks up. The area is also fairly well protected from southerly and westerly winds.

Since we had already been to Gravelly Bay when we caught the ferry to Hornby, we headed to Fillongley, parked at the day-use lot, ate way too much lunch and took off exploring. There are scenic views toward the mainland and Hornby, but houses crowd the park's southern boundary. All in all it's a nice spot and I imagine that both Paul and I will return to this little provincial park with our families within the next few years to do some more camping and kayaking.

Little Tribune Bay and Helliwell Provincial Park (Hornby Island)

Tribune Bay is gorgeous with its wide, long, white sand beach and warm water (map pg 182-183). According to the islands' promotional brochure, Tribune Bay holds some of the warmest swimming water in British Columbia and is known as the Hawaii of BC.

Launching at Hornby's Little Tribune Bay.

The paddle from Little Tribune Bay (the northern half of which is the island's nudist beach) to Tribune Bay and on to Helliwell Park is very scenic. The paddle in the other direction (south) is also a great route and follows a series of sandy beaches.

Helliwell Provincial Park's hiking trails wind through large old-growth trees and along ocean cliffs. Marine bird life and sea lions can often be spotted from the 5-km (3.1-mi) trail. Flora Islet is now part of Helliwell and is a good paddling destination.

Difficulty levels:
➤ Little and Big Tribune Bay area: Novice
➤ Helliwell Park area: Intermediate to advanced

Approximate travel times:
➤ Little and Big Tribune Bay area: Half day
➤ Helliwell Park area: Half day to multiple day

Approx. distances: Little Tribune Bay to Helliwell Park: 5 km (3.1 mi) one way

Warnings:
> ➤ There are no places to land along the shore of Helliwell Park.
> ➤ Qualicum winds (from the southwest) come up quickly and can be dangerous off Helliwell Park bluffs.
> ➤ Use caution or avoid the Helliwell Park area when the winds blow from the south or east.

Getting there/launching: There's a path from the Tribune Bay Provincial Park parking lot to the launching area, but it's too far to carry kayaks comfortably so we headed to Little Tribune Bay Road. This is not shown on most maps, but there is a street sign where it hits Central Road, just south of the Co-op. This narrow dirt road takes you to a great launch site with good parking and lots of sand.

Camping:
> ➤ Bradsdadsland Waterfront Camping: From the ferry follow road onto Shingle Spit and travel a short way north to Bradsdadsland. Call 250-335-0757 for reservations.
> ➤ Hornby Island Resort: Just left of the ferry terminal. This resort has nine campsites and four waterfront cottages. For reservations call 250-335-0136 or e-mail the resort at *hornbyislandresort@hornbyisland.com*.
> ➤ Tribune Bay Campsite: From ferry terminal, follow road to four-way stop beside co-op and continue straight through and that turns into Shields Road. For reservations call 250-335-2359 or visit *www.tribunebay.com*.

Virginia Opossums

During our travels on Hornby Island we didn't see any Virginia opossums. Evidently this non-native marsupial was introduced over 20 years ago and has been a prolific breeder. Opossums eat songbirds and small mammals and get into garbage and compost piles. They are described as cute, cat-sized rats with long tails and sharp teeth. Maybe I'm lacking imagination, but I don't picture a cat-sized critter with a long tail and sharp teeth as cute.

Northern
Vancouver Island

Nuchatlitz and Esperanza Inlets

Nuchatlitz and
Esperanza Inlets

Located on the northwest corner of Nootka Island, the Nuchatlitz area is a paddler's dream come true. Esperanza and Nuchatlitz inlets encompass Nuchatlitz Provincial Park, Catala Island Marine Provincial Park, many unique paddling areas and a host of camping sites. On a typical day, paddlers can enjoy sheltered waters or challenge the wide-open Pacific Ocean. They will see small and large sandy beaches tucked in rock-protected coves, sea otters diving for food, waterfalls cascading into the ocean and may possibly catch a grey whale spouting a mist of water in the distance. This jewel called Nuchatlitz offers a true West Coast wilderness experience.

First Nations people have inhabited the area for centuries, and there are a number of significant archeological features in Nuchatlitz Provincial Park, including burial sites. The 2,135-ha (5,275-acre) park took its name from an ancient First Nations village site.

Southeast of the park is Nuchatlitz Inlet. From the Benson Point camping area you can explore a waterfall nearby or paddle into Mary Basin and Inner Basin. At Louie Bay you can access the Nootka West Coast Trail.

Only 2 km (1.2 mi) northwest of Nuchatlitz Provincial Park is 850-ha (2,100-acre) Catala Island Marine Provincial Park. Catala is considered a kayaker's island because it is difficult for powerboats to land on its shores.

Several of the beaches are steep and covered with polished stone gravel. The island is named after Reverend Magin Catala, a Spanish monk who spent one year in the Nootka area during his 40 years of missionary work on the North American coast.

Difficulty levels:
> Little Espinosa Inlet to Nuchatlitz Provincial Park: Intermediate to advanced
> Nuchatlitz and Nuchatlitz Inlet if arriving by water taxi: Intermediate
> Paddling from Nuchatlitz to Nuchatlitz Inlet: Advanced
> Catala Island: Advanced (see warnings)

Approximate travel time: Full day (if dropped off and picked up by a water taxi) to multiple day

Approximate distances:
Nuchatlitz
> Espinosa Inlet launch site to Garden Point: 12.5 km (7.8 mi) one way
> Garden Point to Nuchatlitz Provincial Park: 5.5 km (3.4 mi) one way
Nuchatlitz Inlet
> Nuchatlitz Provincial Park to Benson Point (Nuchatlitz Inlet): 8 km (5 mi) one way, requires paddling exposed to open ocean conditions
> Benson Point to the head of Inner Basin: 4.25 km (2.7 mi) one way
> Benson Point to Laurie Creek: 3.25 km (2 mi) one way

Nuchatlitz Inlet

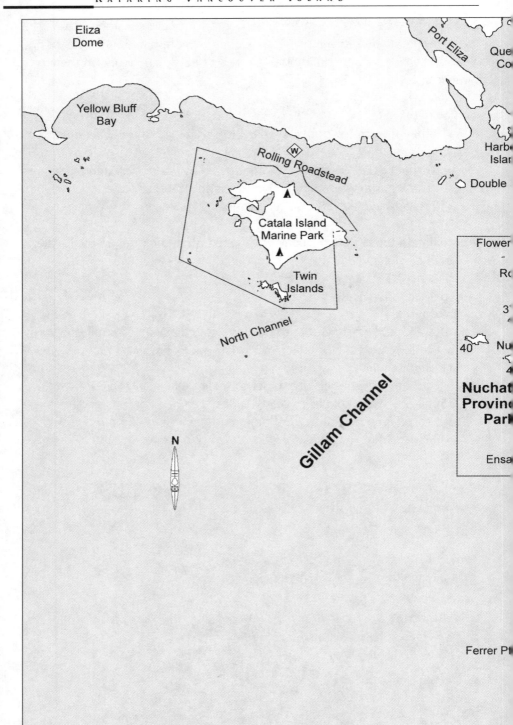

Eliza
Dome

Yellow Bluff
Bay

Port Eliza

Que
Co

Rolling Roadstead

Harb
Islar

Double

Catala Island
Marine Park

Twin
Islands

North Channel

Gillam Channel

N

Flower

R

3

40   Nu

Nuchat
Provin
Par

Ensa

Ferrer P

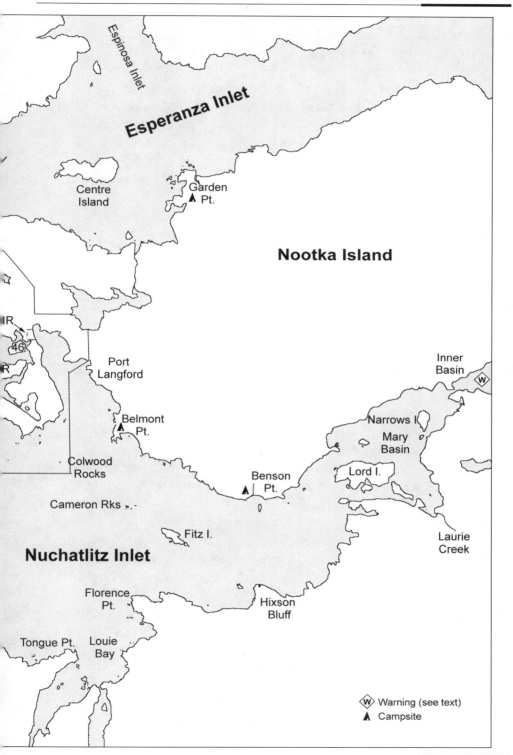

Espinosa Inlet

Esperanza Inlet

Centre
Island

Garden
▲ Pt.

Nootka Island

IR
46

Port
Langford

Inner
Basin

W

Belmont
▲ Pt.

Narrows I.

Mary
Basin

Colwood
Rocks

Benson
▲ Pt.

Lord I.

Cameron Rks

Fitz I.

Laurie
Creek

Nuchatlitz Inlet

Florence
Pt.

Hixson
Bluff

Tongue Pt.

Louie
Bay

W Warning (see text)
▲ Campsite

Catala Island

➤ Head of Little Espinosa Inlet to Catala Island: 19 km (11.8 mi) one way
➤ Catala Island to Yellow Bluff Bay: 4 km (2.5 mi) one way
➤ Nuchatlitz to Catala Island: 2 to 4 km (1.2 to 2.5 mi) depending on where you leave from and arrive
➤ Circumnavigating Catala Island: 7 km (4.3 mi), requires paddling exposed to open ocean conditions

CHS Chart: 3676—Esperanza Inlet

Tidal reference port: Tofino

Weather and sea conditions reference:
➤ Nootka
➤ West Coast Vancouver Island South

Prevailing winds: Strong westerlies or northwesterlies. Winds can blow strong out of Espinosa Inlet.

Warnings:
➤ Much of this area is open to the Pacific Ocean and is subject to quickly changing weather conditions.
➤ Fog can roll in quickly and limit visibility.
➤ First Nations burial sites should not be disturbed. Do not camp on IR land. It is illegal to disturb a burial site or remove First Nations artifacts.
➤ There is a healthy population of black bears in the area, so be bear smart. Some kayakers have been harassed by a bear at several of the area's wilderness campsites. This particular bear was likely "habituated" or conditioned to expect food from humans. We believe the bear has been killed, but you should get updates on current bear problems from the locals in Zeballos.
➤ There are fast-flowing narrows in Nuchatlitz Inlet between Mary Basin and Inner Basin. You can explore the Inner Basin for 30 or 40 minutes during a slack tide period, but you should feel very comfortable with your ability to calculate tides and slack tide before venturing into the Inner Basin. This side trip is not recommended as you may become stuck in the basin until the next tide change if your timing is wrong.
➤ Beaches along the coastline of Catala Island may be steep—this can

cause a kayak to roll in the surf and cause injury.

➤ Catala Island's Rolling Roadstead is very shallow and can be subject to high waves and quickly changing conditions. It is possible to get trapped on this side of Catala Island in stormy conditions.

Emergency contacts: Coast Guard and other boaters monitor channel 16. Many locals also monitor VHF channels 6 and 10. Search and Rescue Emergency can be reached at 1-800-567-5111 or by dialing *311 on your cell phone. Tofino Coast Guard Radio is at 250-726-7716, 250-726-7777 or 250-726-7312. The nearest station for distress calls is the lighthouse at Friendly Cove on Nootka Island, only 45 km (28 mi) from Nuchatlitz. There may be reception problems due to hills between Nuchatlitz and this station.

Getting there: Nuchatlitz and Catala provincial parks are located approximately 18 km (11.2 mi) southwest of Zeballos between Nuchatlitz and Esperanza Inlets.

➤ By road to Zeballos: Zeballos is a seven-hour drive from Victoria, 460 km (285 mi) north of Victoria and about 42 km (26 mi) west of Highway 19 on an active gravel logging road. Follow Highway 19 north 20 km (12.4 mi) north of Woss (about 7 km/4.3 mi south of Nimpkish) and turn west onto Atluck Road. Then take Pinder Road to Zeballos Road. The turnoffs to Zeballos are signed. *Backroad Mapbook: Vancouver Island* is recommended as a navigational aid.

➤ From Zeballos to Nuchatlitz: From Zeballos you can paddle from Little Espinosa Inlet or travel by water taxi to any of the Nuchatlitz area

*Entering
Nuchatlitz*

Zeballos Expeditions' water taxi is a fast and sweat-free way to get to your paddling destination.

destinations except Catala Island. The cost of this service is usually the same for one person or six. You should check to ensure the water taxi is licensed to operate within Nuchatlitz Provincial Park boundaries. At times strong winds can make the trip via kayak to or from Nuchatlitz or Catala Island a real slog. In the event of really poor weather your party can return early by calling the water taxi by VHF radio (channel 16, locals also monitor channels 6 and 10). Dan of Zeballos Expeditions runs a licensed and insured water taxi for this area and also owns a small rental kayak fleet. He will not enter the Rolling Roadstead or do pickups or drop-offs at Catala Island. Contact him by phone at 250-761-4137, by e-mail at *kayak@netcom.ca* or through his web site, *www.zeballoskayaks.com*.

➤ By road to Gold River and then by coastal freighter: Gold River is 89 km (55 mi) west of Campbell River on Highway 28. The MV *Uchuck III*—a passenger and freight vessel that services Nootka Sound, Esperanza Inlet and Kyuquot Sound—departs from Gold River and drops kayakers in Nuchatlitz Provincial Park or near Catala and Rosa islands. The boat is operated by Nootka Sound Service Ltd. in Gold River. You will need to make reservations in advance for you and your kayak. Phone 250-283-2515 or reserve via the web site, *http://www.mvuchuck.com/*.

Recommended launch site: From Zeballos drive 8 km (5 mi) along the road to Fair Harbour to the bridge crossing Little Espinosa Inlet. Launch on the north side of the bridge.

Accommodations: There are motels and B&Bs in Zeballos. Call the Visitor Information Centre at 250-761-4070

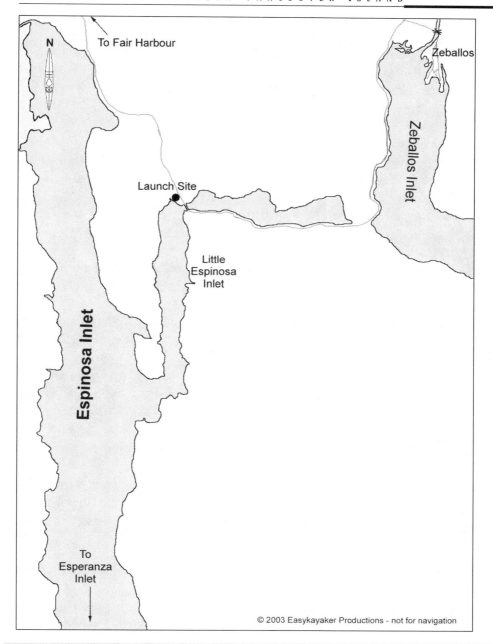

© 2003 Easykayaker Productions - not for navigation

Camping:
Zeballos area camping
➤ Cevallos campground: This is a town-owned public site in Zeballos. Contact 250-761-4229.

➤ Resolution Campsite: A BC Forest Service campsite located 3 km

(1.9 mi) out of town, on the opposite side of Zeballos Inlet from Zeballos. There are no services and you may need 4-wheel-drive to negotiate the rough road.

➤ Zeballos RV Campground: Offers full hookups. Call 250-761-4229 for information.

Nuchatlitz area camping

➤ Garden Point (Esperanza Inlet): This campsite has an outhouse, a lightly sloped beach, panoramic mountain views and nearby old-growth trees.

➤ Queens Cove (Port Eliza area): There is a gravel beach and camping spot in Queens Cove near the mouth of Park Creek in Birthday Channel.

➤ Nuchatlitz Provincial Park: There are various non-designated camping locations on islands and islets in the park. Several of the larger islets in the area have beaches with camping sites available.

➤ Rosa Island: This island in Nuchatlitz Provincial Park has a small protected cove and beach/forest area for a small number of tents.

➤ Catala Island: There is room for several tents facing the Pacific Ocean opposite Twin Islands, but this site can get quite windy. There is also camping near the sandy spit on the Rolling Roadstead side of the island.

➤ Belmont Point (Nuchatlitz Inlet): There is camping in the mouth of the inlet at Belmont Point, which is about midway between Nuchatlitz Provincial Park and Benson Point.

➤ Benson Point (Nuchatlitz Inlet): We're told that this is an excellent campsite. The Nanaimo Paddlers group camped on the more sheltered side of the point, and one of the members, Francine, described the beach as a "soft incline" and very beautiful. The windward side of the point had heavier surf. She spent many days camped at Benson Point with her group and made various day trips from here.

Travel notes (Paul)

The many reefs and islets make it difficult to enter Nuchatlitz Provincial Park in a powerboat, and consequently the park is ideal for kayakers. The waters in and around the park are both protected and open. The tide pools, plentiful beaches, natural beauty of the land and serene coves are drawing more and more people here.

Dan O'Connor, co-owner of Zeballos Expeditions, whisked Gary and me out to the marine park in his covered transport boat in early July. We had visited the south side of Nootka Island a few years earlier, but as we headed out from Zeballos, Dan must have read our minds as he said that Nuchatlitz was nothing like what we saw in Nootka Sound. He described it as much more beautiful and gentle. We had an inkling that the park must be special because every kayaking guide's face lit up when we mentioned Nuchatlitz.

We arrived at Nuchatlitz in idyllic conditions. The provincial park and Nuchatlitz Inlet generally experience less stormy weather than the south end of Nootka Island around Friendly Cove and Bligh Island. There was very little ocean swell in Esperanza Inlet though it is open to the Pacific Ocean. The islets in the park were surrounded by calm waters and sea otters were diving near a submerged sand dune.

We landed on an islet designated 33 on CHS chart 3676. A First Nations burial site is located nearby. The Nuu-chah-nulth people were often buried in cedar-planked boxes. Some of the sites are in caves. If you do encounter a burial site, please do not remove bones or artifacts or disturb the site in any way. It's important to respect the rights and feelings of indigenous people of the West Coast. Treat their graves as you would your own grandparents' burial sites.

Many kayakers who camp on Catala Island circumnavigate the island, exploring sea caves and coastline. I read one sailor's account of venturing into a sea cave that was nearly 31 m (100 ft) deep with stalactites on the ceiling. (See this story at *http://agunther.home.donobi.net/log.vi.4.html.*) The shoreline facing the Rolling Roadstead is a wonderful place to investigate

First Nations village site

when the winds and the surf are negligible.

On your way to or from Catala Island you may wish to make a side trip up Birthday Channel. Across from the village of Queens Cove is the old log dump at Port Eliza. Old but sometimes active logging roads run from here past Eliza Dome and all the way to Rugged Point. Remains of the old cannery are still visible by Saddle Point.

Gary and I have only seen Catala Island in the distance, but we did get a chance to talk to Francine, who was part of a group of 15 or 16 people from the Nanaimo Paddlers, a canoe and kayak club, who journeyed to Catala Island a few days after we visited Nuchatlitz. They launched from the head of Little Espinosa Inlet around 8:00 a.m. and arrived at Catala Island around lunchtime. They encountered little wind on this leg of the trip and obviously paddled the more than 19 km (12+ mi) distance in excellent time.

On their first day the Nanaimo group kayaked along the outside of Catala Island to spectacular Yellow Bluff Bay on Vancouver Island. On the return trip the winds had increased dramatically, making it too difficult to follow the earlier route, so they ended up paddling east along Vancouver Island and crossing the Rolling Roadstead in the lee of Catala Island. However, even this crossing to the island marine park was difficult. Francine described one or two moments of the return trip as heart-stopping. Several waves had washed over her kayak, including one or two near shoulder height. Her group passed the sandy spit and stayed in the lee of the island until they finally fought their way back against the wind on the open ocean side of the island.

We have not been to Nuchatlitz Inlet, but we've heard about its rugged beauty. There are beautiful waterfalls at Laurie Creek, just southeast of Lord Island, and in Louie Bay.

The waterfall at the end of a cove in Louie Bay is accessible through tall grasses, and a hike from Louie Bay to the start of the Nootka Island West Coast Trail takes approximately 30 minutes. This hike is fairly rough and can become muddy during rains. The Nootka Island West Coast Trail is a four- to six-day hike to Friendly Cove. Some kayakers paddle to Louie Bay, have their boats picked up by water taxi and then hike the trail, which leads you through tidal zones, across reefs and under sea caves. Many hikers relax for a day at Crawfish Falls.

Zeballos: A town whose streets were truly paved with gold

In the 1977 version of *Logging Road Travel*, Volume 2, Alec and Taffy Merriman describe Zeballos as the new gateway to the West Coast. Canfor and Tahsis logging companies had pushed the road through to Zeballos only nine years earlier, in 1968. In those days you drove to Gold River, then to Tahsis and finally by what the book describes as a "grueling gravel road" to Zeballos. As I recall, it took about seven hours from Nanaimo.

When the Carrot Highway (Highway 19—so named for the statue at the Port Hardy end of the road) was finally completed in 1979, the route to Zeballos changed to follow the existing logging roads from Nimpkish. Provincial forests minister Ray Williston called this "the rawest piece of road some people with us have been over in all their lives." The trip is now only about four to five hours from Nanaimo and the gravel road is far better than what it once was.

Besides being the gateway to Nuchatlitz, Catala Island, Esperanza and Espinosa inlets, Kyuquot Sound, Rugged Point, Bunsby Islands and South Brooks, Zeballos is also a place worth visiting in its own right. The town-owned campsite on the edge of Zeballos River is a nice place to camp, the nature walks are enjoyable and you can walk from one end of town to the other in just a few minutes. There's a small grocery store, a café, restaurant and even a pub. There are also bears occasionally wandering through town and the campsite.

Captain Malaspina named this inlet in Nootka Sound after one of his lieutenants, Ciriaco Cevallos, in the 1780s, and over the years the name became anglicized to Zeballos. Trace gold was found as early as 1907, but it wasn't until the mid-1920s that gold mining started. In 1929 two tons of hand-dug ore started the Zeballos gold rush.

As late as 1938 the CPR coastal boats only went as far as the California Packing Corporation cannery. Located just past Tahsis Narrows, this cannery became known by its initials and still shows on charts and maps as Ceepeecee. People would travel on the CPR boat to Ceepeecee, cover the remaining 18 km (11.2 mi) by small boat and then walk the final leg to their claims. Ore was brought out in 23-kg (50-lb) pack loads, usually two trips per day for the average worker. Those with packhorses did better, but not by much.

In 1938 there were 28 registered gold mines. Two of the biggest were the Privateer and the Spud Valley mines. Some of the others were the Britannia, Man of War, King Midas, Golden Gate, North Star, White Star, Zeballos Gold Peak and Central Zeballos. Assays ran as rich as 45 ounces per ton and according to one mining man (quoted by T.W. Paterson and Garnet Basque in their book on Vancouver Island ghost towns), the Tacoma smelter staff said it was "the richest ore and most extensively impregnated with free gold that they had ever received." Due to the high unemployment of the Depression the rush brought many gold seekers, and by October 1938 over 3,000 claims had been staked.

Warren Cullins grew up in Zeballos. His father, James Cullins, founded and ran the town's newspaper, *The Zeballos Miner*, from 1938 to 1944. In his history of Zeballos, Warren remembers the Goat Ranch, which was built about a mile from town with the support of the mine operators. It provided music, relaxation and women for the miners to prevent their leaving Zeballos to seek similar entertainment elsewhere. Warren writes that as a boy, he and a friend went to see the goats only to be told by the woman in charge, "Sorry, children, we have no goats here."

In 1938 it rained 98 inches in a matter of weeks, and the December 12, 1938, *Zeballos Miner* reported, "The heavy rain of the past few days threatened serious consequences to the place known as the Goat Ranch. Situated about a mile from town at a low point where the river floods, it was half under water when the occupants were rescued by boats rushed by truck from the beach. Occupants of the Goat Ranch awakened when their beds began to float."

The main street of Zeballos was known as Rotten Row due to the deep mud. The river would often flood during the spring, and in March 1940 Rotten Row was under five feet of water in places. To combat the mud, waste from the mines was used to gravel the roads. Later, locals realized that the early sorting methods hadn't been too efficient and there was a gold rush to dig up Zeballos's roads.

In the town's heyday, the population of Zeballos swelled to 1,500 and there were many hotels, restaurants, stores, a bank, school, hospital, newspaper and even a library. Between 1938 and 1943 more than $13 million worth of gold was shipped out of this town, but by 1948, when the Privateer was the last mine to close, the population dove to 35 people.

The town was finally connected to the outside world by telephone in 1965, and in 1970, when the road opened and Tahsis Logging moved from Fair Harbour to Zeballos, this ghost town came alive once more. The current population is about 250 people.

For more information about Zeballos's mining history, read *Ghost Towns and Mining Camps of Vancouver Island*, by T.W. Paterson and Garnet Basque. Another book of interest to Zeballos history buffs is *Zeballos: Its Gold, Its People, Yesterday and Today*, by Warren and Laura Cullins.

Kyuquot Sound (Rugged Point)

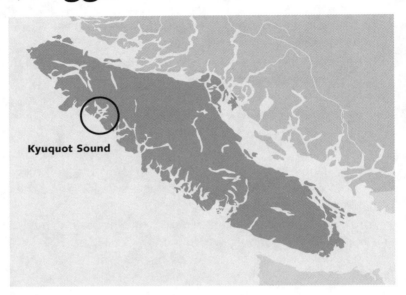

Kyuquot Sound

Situated on the rugged northwest coast of Vancouver Island, Kyuquot Sound lies midway between Nootka Island and Brooks Peninsula. The only road accesses to the sound are at Fair Harbour and the mouth of the Artlish River, both on its eastern shore.

Rugged Point Marine Provincial Park, a remote, 308-hectare (760-acre) wilderness area, is approximately 33 km (20.5 mi) west of the town of Zeballos (see page 197). Located on the eastern shore of Kyuquot Channel, Rugged Point is home to spellbinding scenery and some of the most magnificent stretches of beach on the West Coast. One of the most popular trips in this area is from Fair Harbour to Rugged Point, though it's a long paddle, especially if you have a headwind and are pushing a loaded boat.

Instead of driving to Fair Harbour, an appealing alternative mode of travel to this remote area is the MV *Uchuck III*. This 41-m (136-ft) former World War II minesweeper sails from Gold River to Kyuquot every Thursday morning. If you have the time, and assuming the weather is decent, it makes for a great extended trip. You can stay at a B&B in Kyuquot, a fishing village of about 300, for a night or two, explore that area, then paddle over to Rugged Point to mellow out on the beach for a few days before returning to Kyuquot.

Difficulty Levels:
> ➤ Fair Harbour to Rugged Point: Intermediate
> ➤ Kyuquot to Rugged Point: Intermediate to advanced

Approximate travel times:
> ➤ Fair Harbour to Rugged Point: Multiple day (can be a day trip by water taxi)
> ➤ Kyuquot to Rugged Point: Full day to multiple day

Approximate distances:
> ➤ Fair Harbour to Rugged Point: 18 km (11.2 mi) one way (Can be shortened by a few kilometres if you portage the neck of Markale Peninsula.)
> ➤ Kyuquot to Rugged Point: 12 km (7.5 mi) one way if the waters are calm enough to travel the southwest side of Union Island; the trip is 20 km (12.4 mi) one way if you travel the more protected route north around Union Island
> ➤ Exploring McLean Cove: 3 km (1.9 mi) round trip from Rugged Point's beach on the Kyuquot Inlet side (requires high tide)
> ➤ Rugged Point crossing to Union Island: 2 km (1.2 mi) one way

CHS chart: 3682—Kyuquot Sound

West side of Rugged Point. One of the area's magnificent stretches of white sand beach.

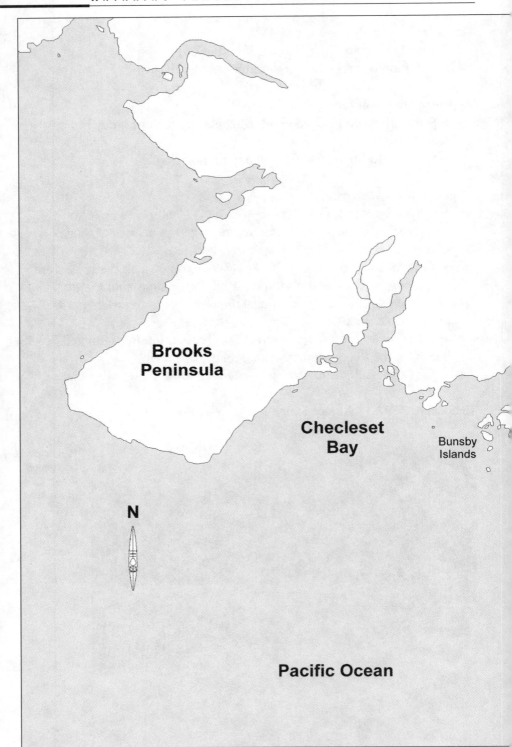

Brooks
Peninsula

Checleset
Bay

Bunsby
Islands

N

Pacific Ocean

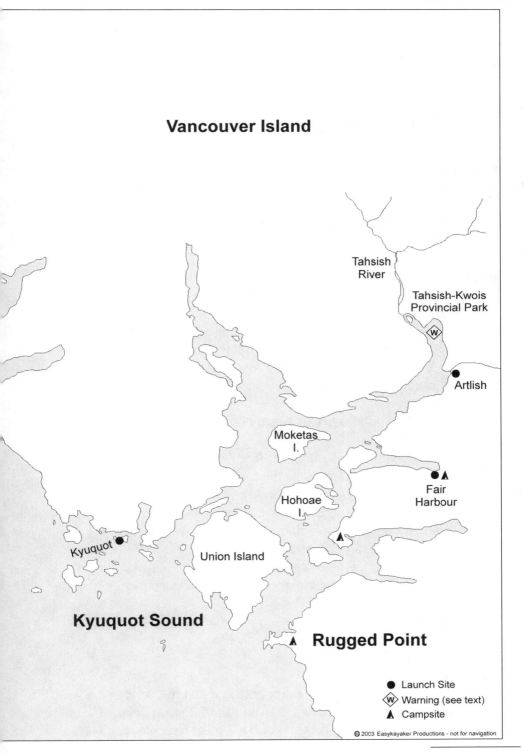

Vancouver Island

Tahsish River

Tahsish-Kwois Provincial Park

Artlish

Moketas I.

Fair Harbour

Hohoae I.

Kyuquot

Union Island

Kyuquot Sound

Rugged Point

● Launch Site
Ⓦ Warning (see text)
▲ Campsite

© 2003 Easykayaker Productions - not for navigation

Tidal reference port: Tofino

Weather and sea conditions reference:
➤ Solander Island (western tip of Brooks Peninsula)
➤ Nootka
➤ South Brooks (ocean buoy)
➤ West Coast Vancouver Island North

Prevailing winds:
➤ Winds usually rise in the afternoon and are westerlies or southwesterlies.
➤ On summer days kayakers may face a headwind first thing in the morning when paddling out of Fair Harbour.

Warnings:
➤ Weather and sea conditions change quickly, especially outside Kyuquot Sound.
➤ You may need insect repellant at camping areas, including Fair Harbour. Rugged Point's Pacific Ocean side seems to be bug benign (there are few biting bugs here relative to inland areas).
➤ Fog can roll in quickly and limit visibility, even in August (known locally as Fogust).
➤ Respect First Nations land (marked IR on charts) and do not disturb archeological sites.
➤ There is a healthy population of black bears and wolves. Do not leave food in your boats and do leave the hatch covers off when beached. Even empty hatches can smell of food and tempt a bear to rip them open, and a curious bear could damage your kayak. We strongly advise you to use BC Parks' bear caches or rig a pulley and rope to hang your food high in a tree a good distance from your camp.
➤ The flatlands at the mouth of the Tahsis River flood quickly when it rains. This is also an ecological reserve, so do not camp here.

Emergency contacts: The village of Kyuquot monitors channel 14; Coast Guard and other boaters monitor channel 16.

Getting there:
➤ Drive from Zeballos to Fair Harbour (about 33 km/20.5 mi on a good 2-wheel-drive gravel road) and then paddle to Rugged Point. (The *Backroad Mapbook: Vancouver Island* is a great resource for travelling

Voyager water taxi. Water taxis offer kayakers safe access to some remote paddling areas and will relocate paddlers every few days.

to these off-the-beaten-track launch sites.)

➤ Take the MV *Uchuck III* from Gold River to Kyuquot Village and then paddle to Rugged Point. The ship leaves Gold River Thursday morning and arrives in Kyuquot around 5 p.m. the same day, then departs for Gold River Friday morning.

➤ Leo Jack offers a water taxi service from Fair Harbour or the mouth of the Artlish River to Rugged Point. Contact him through his web site, *www.kyuquotwatertaxi.com* or phone 250-332-5301. If you catch the water taxi at the Artlish River it adds a bit of extra water travel, but cuts down the time you spend on logging roads considerably.

Recommended launch site: Follow the signs from Zeballos to Fair Harbour. The road ends at Fair Harbour and a recreational campsite where you can launch.

Other launch site: An alternate site is at the mouth of the Artlish River. From Highway 19 take the turnoff for Zeballos (Atluck Road) and travel about 9 km (5.6 mi) until the road forks. On the left is Pinder Main, which leads to Zeballos, and on the right Atluck Road carries on (the fork is signed for Zeballos and Artlish). About 11 km (6.8 mi) after that fork, a turnoff to Artlish road is on the left. Follow Artlish Road to Tahsis Inlet (off Kyuquot Sound), a journey of about 20 km (12.4 mi) that may require 4-wheel-drive.

Accommodations:
- ➤ Several B&Bs: Call Zeballos Tourist Information at 250-761-4070
- ➤ Houpsitas Motel in Kyuquot: Call 1-888-817-8716 for reservations

Camping:

➤ Rugged Point Marine Provincial Park: Camping is in undefined sites in the woods or at the beach on the Pacific Ocean side of the point. There is one BC Parks outhouse, a covered cooking shelter and a four-compartment bear-proof food cache on the Kyuquot Channel side. Several streams and creeks provide fresh water on the Pacific Ocean side. Fires are discouraged but currently permitted below the high tide line. All garbage must be packed out.

➤ Amai Inlet: There is an unimproved recreational site in a cove at the northwest section of Amai Inlet (near Whiteley Island).

➤ Markale Point: It is possible to camp en route to Rugged Point at a beach a short way south of Markale Point.

➤ Hohoae Island: There are some small, protected, sandy beaches on this island that could be used for camping in a pinch. Part of Hohoae and neighbouring Copp Island are included in Dixie Cove Marine Provincial Park.

➤ Fair Harbour Recreational Site: This campground is very busy because Kyuquot Sound is a popular sport-fishing area.

Zeballos camping

➤ Cevallos campground: This is a town-owned public site in Zeballos. Contact 250-761-4229.

➤ Resolution Campsite: A BC Forest Service campsite located 3 km (1.9 mi) out of town, on the opposite side of Zeballos Inlet from Zeballos. There are no services and you may need 4-wheel-drive to negotiate the rough road.

➤ Zeballos RV Campground: Offers full hookups. Call 250-761-4229 for information.

Travel notes (Gary)

Although I had flown into Kyuquot in the mid-1970s, I completely missed Rugged Point. It might have had something to do with the weather. The thick cloud ceiling was less than 30 m (100 ft) and from my seat I had a good view of the altimeter. I think the highest we reached was 23 m (75 ft) above sea level as I gazed at beaches and tree trunks through the window. At least we weren't hitting downdrafts. At Kyuquot we picked up enough

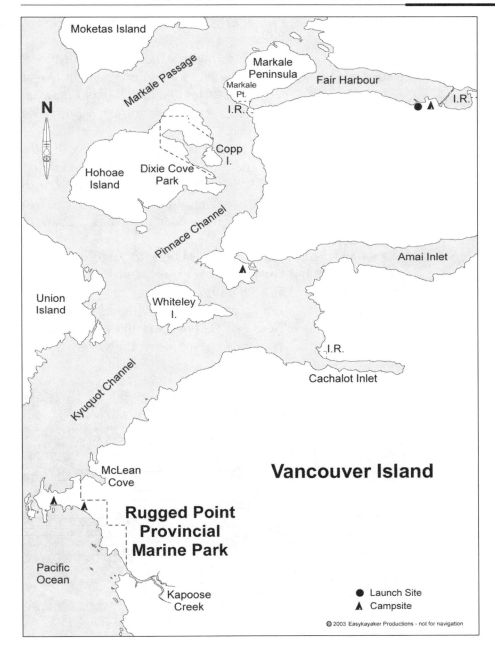

passengers to fill the plane to its full capacity of six. The problem was, we were all guys and some of us were really big! We must have taxied a couple of miles, trying to break the suction in order to take off. It was a calm day and we were in open ocean before we hit a swell large enough to make us airborne. It was almost as exciting as kayaking.

Rugged Point first came to my attention thanks to Michael Blades' book, *Day of Two Sunsets*. Soon after reading it I went out and bought CHS chart 3682 for Kyuquot Sound. I drew up plans to paddle there the next summer, but as often happens, life and other trips got in the way.

It seemed like Rugged Point was calling—every few months someone would tell me about his or her experiences along this beautiful coastline. The Spring 2000 issue of *Beautiful British Columbia* teased me with wonderful photos of the area. Two more summers passed. If this book hadn't acted as a catalyst I might not have arrived there yet.

Paul and I travelled from Fair Harbour to Rugged Point by water taxi, which is one of the easier ways to make the trip. Leo Jack was to pick us up with his boat, *Voyager*, at 1:30 p.m., but we arrived at the meeting place about two hours early, which gave us time to explore Fair Harbour and the portage across Markale Peninsula. We made good time as the water was like glass.

Rugged Point east side

The narrow neck of land that joins the Markale Peninsula to Vancouver Island is like a large sand bar. When you approach from Fair Harbour you will find a portage trail on the far left of this strip of land. It takes only a minute or two to walk to the other side, where you can relaunch your kayak from a nice pebble beach into Pinnace Channel. Many years ago there was a small First Nations settlement on the neck of land, and it is now designated an Indian Reserve (IR). The Kyuquot/Checklesaht First Nation welcomes day-use visitors, but if you want to camp overnight on the sand bar you should contact them at 1-888-817-8716. There is an orchard poking out above the dense bush that has overgrown this neck of land. We had a quick lunch here and then paddled back to meet Leo and the *Voyager*. On the way we saw an eagle's nest in a lone tree at the water's edge.

Leo was able to bring his flat-bottomed boat right in to shore, which made it easy to place the kayaks onboard. As the kayaks have to be placed on top of his boat, it's best to leave them unloaded so they aren't too heavy to lift. A loaded kayak can slip and drop, damaging its hull. Leo commented that he has even seen a kayak split open.

It took about 25 minutes to get to Rugged Point, where Leo pulled up to a beach on the Kyuquot Channel side of the point. After we unloaded, he headed off to move some other kayakers from South Brooks Peninsula to the Bunsby Islands. I'm becoming more and more sold on the idea of water taxis. They give kayakers safe access to some wonderful remote spots, and you can get picked up every few days and moved to a new location. For those without the stamina or open ocean kayaking skills, this method of travel opens up a variety of new paddling locations. It also gives you more time at your destination as you don't need to spend two to four days paddling there and back. Another advantage is it helps take occupant load and ecological impact off the paddling/camping areas closer to civilization.

After Leo left we decided to explore by foot and then by kayak. The park was deserted except for a small group of campers on a fishing trip two coves over. We hiked the short trail that starts by the cooking shelter and runs over to the Pacific Ocean side of the park. The trail is quite flat, and part of it is a boardwalk.

The beaches along the Pacific are magnificent wide expanses

The beaches along the Kyuquot Channel side of Rugged Point are wonderful to explore but beware of rapidly changing sea conditions.

of driftwood-littered white sand. They extend for several kilometres and at higher tides are separated by headlands. There are good trails over the headlands—large floats hanging from ropes mark the trailheads. If we were staying here any length of time I would want to camp on these beaches. Plenty of sand above the high tide line provides hundreds of possible campsites, and there is abundant driftwood to rig good tarp-covered wind shelters.

In *Day of Two Sunsets*, Michael Blades describes landing in the shelter of Kapoose Creek. The day we arrived one could have landed anywhere on the Pacific side of Rugged Point, as the seas were flat. The problem is that you might have to wait a week before launching again as sea conditions can change rapidly on this side. That's why kayakers are advised to land on the Kyuquot Channel side and leave their kayaks there, even though this means hauling tent and clothes across to the Pacific side to camp. If it is calm, as it was when we were there, you could paddle around, drop off your gear and then paddle back.

After hiking the beaches, taking lots of photos, walking the headland trails, checking out the camping areas and visiting the outhouse, we had a snack and paddled out into the blue expanse around Rugged Point. We had hoped to be able to pass inside the islands at the point. It was fun exploring the passageway but the tide was too low for us to get through. We did go outside the islands and around the point, but there were some dark squalls visible out to sea so we reversed direction and went to investigate McLean Cove and the coast in that direction.

Leo picked us up about 7 p.m. Counting our paddle in Fair Harbour, we had done about 15 km (9.3 mi) of paddling that day. We were sad to be leaving so soon—in hindsight I wish we had spent the night and paddled back on our own the next day—but I'm sure we'll be back for a much longer visit.

Marble River Canyon

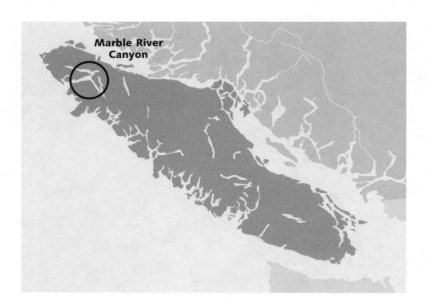

Marble River Canyon, though part of a West Coast waterway, is on the east side of Vancouver Island. Off Rupert Inlet near Quatsino and Coal Harbour, about 22 km (14 mi) from Port Hardy as the crow flies, the canyon is a treasure of rock caves and still waters. Fortunately the canyon, the rest of Marble River, most of Varney Bay and all of Quatsino Narrows make up Marble River Canyon Provincial Park. This 1,512-hectare (3,736-acre) park protects eagle nesting habitat, a steelhead fishery and an extensive waterfowl habitat. According to BC Parks, outdoor enthusiasts visit the park for rafting, whitewater kayaking, hiking and camping. The river is also considered to be one of the best steelhead fishing locations on Vancouver Island.

Across from the launch site at the end of Varney Main (a logging road) stand the buildings of the decommissioned Utah Copper Mine (a.k.a. Island Copper Mine). The open pit mine shows on the chart and extends 314 m (1,030 ft) below sea level. During the 1970s and 1980s this copper molybdenum mine, owned by BHP Copper, employed about 600 people. It shut down in 1995. Vancouver Island has a garbage disposal problem and this very deep hole was being considered as a solution in the late 1990s. It could hold all of Vancouver Island's garbage for the next 40 years or longer. This idea didn't make everyone happy, though, and soon the "friends of the big hole" put a stop to the plan.

While the mine was operating, BHP had a permit to dump tailings in Rupert Inlet. This silted up the inlet and it took two years for the water to clear once dumping stopped. Fortunately, marine life is now rapidly returning to Rupert Inlet. Other than the mine buildings, some logging and the Newfie Dock, little sign of human activity remains in the area.

Difficulty levels:
> ➤ Coal Harbour to Marble River Canyon: Intermediate to advanced (due to length of trip)
> ➤ Varney Main (Newfie Dock) to Marble River Canyon: Intermediate

Approximate travel times:
> ➤ Coal Harbour to Marble River Canyon: Full day
> ➤ Varney Main (Newfie Dock) to Marble River Canyon: Full day

Marble River Canyon. To avoid a lengthy portage you must enter the canyon near high tide.

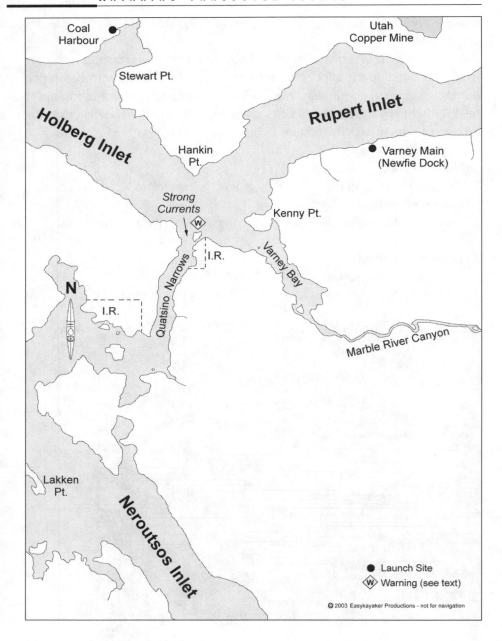

Approximate distances:
- ➤ Coal Harbour to Marble River Canyon: 22 km (13.7 mi) round trip
- ➤ Varney Main (Newfie Dock) to Marble River Canyon: 17 km (10.5 mi) round trip

CHS chart: 3679

Tidal reference port: Winter Harbour

Current reference: Quatsino Narrows

Weather and sea conditions reference:
- ➤ Quatsino Sound
- ➤ Queen Charlotte Strait

Prevailing winds: Winds usually rise from about 2 p.m. till 6 p.m. Winds blow in either direction along the length of the inlets.

Warnings:
- ➤ Quatsino Narrows has currents up to 8.5 knots. These affect nearby waters.
- ➤ Marble River can turn into a raging torrent during a heavy rain.
- ➤ The area between Coal Harbour and Quatsino Narrows usually gets quite windy starting around 2 p.m. and lasting until about 6 or 7 p.m.
- ➤ Boat traffic occurs in and near narrows.
- ➤ Fog can roll in quickly and limit visibility.
- ➤ The small Indian Reserve area in the narrows is culturally significant. You should not land here.
- ➤ The head of Varney Bay is a waterfowl habitat.
- ➤ There is a healthy population of black bears—be bear smart.
- ➤ There is also a healthy population of cougars.

Getting there:
- ➤ Coal Harbour is 16 km (10 mi) from Port Hardy along a paved and well-marked road.
- ➤ You can get to Varney Main via logging roads from Highway 19 or from the Port Alice Road. Turn off Highway 19 onto a road known as Rupert Main about 100 m (330 ft) north of the road to Port Alice. When Rupert Main hits Rupert Inlet, turn left. About 1 km (0.6 mi) farther turn right onto Varney Main and follow it to the end. If Rupert Main is closed due to active logging, use the Port Alice Road. Drive about 10 km (6.3 mi) along it till you reach Port Hardy Main. Turn right onto Port Hardy Main and follow it for about 6 km (3.75 mi), then turn left when you get to Varney Main.

Recommended launch sites:

➤ **Coal Harbour boat ramp**: Follow Coal Harbour Road until you reach the water.

➤ **Rupert Inlet**: The launch site at the end of Varney Main (see directions under "Getting there") is a big flat gravel area. At high tide you can launch from the beach, but at low tide you will need to carry your boats down the gangway to the float (Newfie Dock).

Other launch site: The Rupert Inlet recreational campsite is at the head of Rupert Inlet, at the end of Rupert Main.

Accommodations: Motels and numerous B&Bs. The Port Hardy Visitor Information Centre run by the Chamber of Commerce is open year-round. Phone 250-949-7622, e-mail *phcc@island.net* or visit the web site at *www.ph-chamber.bc.ca*.

Camping:

➤ Quatse River Campground: From Port Hardy, follow Highway 19 south to Coal Harbour Road and turn right, following the signs. For reservations phone 250-949-2395.

➤ Sunny Sanctuary Campground: About 3 km (1.9 mi) south of Port Hardy on Highway 19 turn left at the "Big Logger." For reservations phone 250-949-8111.

Newfie Dock. At low tide you need to carry kayaks to this float at the end of Varney Main.

➤ Recreational sites on Rupert Inlet and Alice Lake: The Alice Lake site is just over halfway (14 km/8.7 mi) from Highway 19 to Port Alice on the Port Alice road. It's at the top end of Marble River. The Rupert Inlet sites are at the head of Rupert Inlet. One is where Rupert Main ends at Rupert Inlet, and the other is where Varney Main intersects with Port Hardy Main.

➤ Marble River Provincial Park: The park has a developed campground with 33 vehicle/tent campsites. Access is at the east end of the park just off the Port Alice Road. There's a boat launch and a beach for swimming in the lake. A hiking trail from the campground follows the south bank, providing access to Marble River.

Travel notes (Gary)

I had never heard of Marble River Canyon until the day I received an e-mail from David in Port Alice, responding to our Easykayaker web site. When I asked him about interesting paddling in his area, David told me about Marble River Canyon and e-mailed two photos of the rock caves and still waters of the area. It certainly looked appealing and different from the usual paddling we do. Soon after that I met Kip, who lives around the corner from Marble River in the tiny village of Quatsino. After looking at his photos of the canyon, I knew Marble River was a trip I wanted to make.

If travelling on logging roads keep an eye out for signs of active logging

Eleven months later, Paul and I headed north to check out different North Island paddling areas. Our visit to Marble River ended up being the last day of the trip, and after the paddle we planned to drive home. This would make for a very long day, so in spite of local outfitters' advice that we paddle to the canyon from Coal Harbour, we decided to shorten the trip by launching at the end of Varney Main. (This involved travelling on a portion of an active logging road—something we found out later we weren't supposed to be doing.)

Paddling into Marble River requires a high tide unless you are prepared to carry your kayak a long distance. This means paddling against a flooding current going there and, most likely, against an ebb on the way back. This was another good reason for choosing Varney Main (on Rupert Inlet) instead of Coal Harbour (on Holberg Inlet) as our launch site. Rupert Inlet is only about 10 km (6.3 mi) long. Holberg Inlet is about 30 km (18.6 mi) long. The currents are stronger in Holberg Inlet because there is almost three times the volume of water to move. Both inlets are quite deep and they both drain through Quatsino Narrows, which has tidal flows up to 8.5 knots.

As we were preparing to launch, about three hours before high tide, I looked down at the tidal flats just east of us and saw a doe and her two fawns having a salty snack on the aquatic plants there.

When we started off, paddling against a minor current, we noticed that the seaweed near shore was pointed the way we were going. By moving closer to shore we were able to catch helpful back eddies most of the way to Varney Bay. As we rounded the last point into the bay we could see and feel Quatsino Narrows quite well.

Entering Varney Bay

Varney Bay is peaceful and serene, or so it seemed when we were there. It's also very shallow. On the left most of the way up its 3-km (1.9-mi) length is the old Varney Homestead. Both the Varneys have passed on, but we hear they were characters. Mrs. Varney was a self-designated fisheries officer—God help you if you fished in her bay without permission—while Mr. Varney was known for always wearing jodhpurs. They were just two of the eccentrics who populated remote areas of the coast and make British Columbia's history so interesting.

Varney Bay is about 0.75 km (0.5 mi) wide at its head, and

Marble River is on the far right side. As we approached the river a bald eagle flew over us with a small fish in its talons. A moment later Paul recognized the excited call of a hungry baby eagle and we soon spotted the nest.

A small island at the mouth of the river splits it into two channels. The flooding tide was pushing us up the river, but there seemed to be more flow up the right channel. We chose to enter via the larger channel on the left side of the island, and as we neared the top of the island we saw that we had made the correct choice—there was not enough water in the right-hand channel and we would have run aground.

A short distance farther we hit the first gravel bar. This is in the wide spot just before Marble River Canyon. The tide was too low to paddle over the bar, and it was still two hours until high tide, which would only be a 3-m (9.8-ft) tide. We could wait half an hour or get out and walk the boats. We chose to walk. The small rocks are quite round and partially covered with aquatic plants, which made them slippery and made walking difficult, but the kayaks travelled easily. Fortunately both boats had bowlines.

Partway through the light rapids running over the bar, we reached a sandy shore that was covered with deer tracks of many sizes. It was reassuring to see no bear tracks. Just past this small sandy beach the water deepened and we were able to paddle again. Once in the canyon the water became very deep and there was no feeling of a current.

The rock formations in the canyon are incredible. There are many caves with pillars and much is covered with delicate maidenhair ferns. The canyon walls are tall, and except for the occasional birdcall it is very quiet as you paddle along. We were impressed by the untouched wildness of the area.

All too soon the canyon walls widened and we hit the next set of shallows. We would need another 46 cm (18 in) of higher tide to paddle upstream, so we got out, tied our kayaks to a log and continued up the river on foot. We talked of portaging, but it was already lunchtime and we still had to drive home that night. We had our lunch sitting by the edge of the rapids, enjoying the river's beauty and the lack of biting bugs. The saltwater environment is great for avoiding mosquitoes, black flies and no-see-ums, but freshwater environments usually aren't so benign. We also kept one eye peeled for bear.

The high canyon walls create a unique and serene paddling experi-ence.

After lunch we headed slowly back through the canyon, savouring every moment. As we drifted downriver the only sound was the clicking of our camera shutters. We were both deep in concentration, trying to photograph a rock formation, when a huge splash erupted in the water next to Paul. In the deep still-ness of the canyon this gave us both a start. Had a bear just done a belly flop from the canyon wall? We had a few moments of wild imagining, but then realized a seal had joined us. Because we were drifting it didn't know what to make of us until it had an all-too-close look. We didn't see the seal surface, but it saw Paul from only about a metre away and dove as fast as it could. Fortunately neither of us dropped our cameras.

By the time we exited the canyon the tide was high enough that we cleared the first gravel bar. It was also high enough for us to take the narrower channel around the island at the river's mouth. The gap through the weeds wasn't very wide and reminded us of the channel on Quadra Island between Village Bay Lake and Main Lake.

It was about 1:30 p.m., but the 2 o'clock winds were already starting to blow. High tide would be at 2:20 p.m.; the narrows would go slack at 3:10 and then start to ebb. However, the times of slack tide and slack current can differ by quite a bit, and we expected that the current would still be flooding up Rupert Inlet even after 3:10. Sure enough, as we rounded the point out of Varney Bay we picked up the current still flooding in from Quatsino Narrows and rode it back up Rupert Inlet. As well, we got a push from the wind.

We made good time most of the way back, but for the last 15 minutes the current turned against us and the water became rougher as the wind and current were travelling in opposite directions. Fortunately Rupert Inlet is small enough that waves seldom build very high, although I'm sure that it can get windy here. Back at the launch site the tide was high enough that we could use the beach for landing.

Paul deep in Marble River Canyon.

On the way back to the highway we saw a little bear cub bound off the logging road and quickly disappear in the bush. I'm sure Mom wasn't far away. It looked like a cute teddy bear. It's funny how as kids we cuddle these likenesses and then become so afraid of them when they and we grow up.

Quadra Island

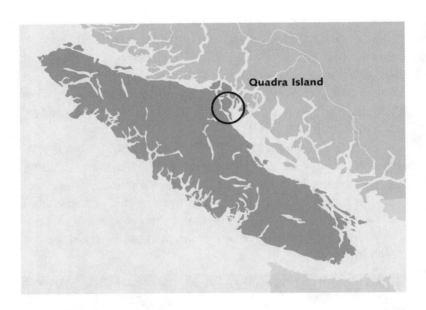

When you look at a map of Vancouver Island, you quickly notice that the Strait of Georgia, the large liquid expanse between mainland British Columbia and Vancouver Island, ends at Quadra Island. Quadra and the many surrounding islands are known as the Discovery Islands. At the north end of this group lies Johnstone Strait.

Quadra is an island worth exploring. It boasts excellent hiking trails, interesting stores and some incredible accommodations. There are some wonderful sheltered paddling places for those wanting self-guided expeditions, and trips of a lifetime for those who take a guided tour around Quadra's uninhabited north end.

The island is 27,600 ha (68,200 acres) and has a full-time population of around 3,800 residents. It was named after the 18th-century explorer Don Juan Francisco de la Bodega y Quadra, who was a Spanish naval officer and close friend of Captain George Vancouver. (The latter originally named Vancouver Island "the Island of Vancouver and Quadra," as this is where the two naval explorers met.) Until 1903, Quadra Island and two adjacent islands were known as the Valdez Islands, but were renamed to avoid confusion with Valdes Island, near Ladysmith.

CHS chart: 3539—Quadra Island, Maurelle Island and Campbell River

Tidal reference ports:

➤ Campbell River (for Granite Bay, Small Inlet, Kanish Bay and Gowlland Harbour), *Canadian Tide and Current Tables*, Vol. 6

➤ Point Atkinson for southeast side (Heriot Bay, Hyacinthe Bay, Open Bay, Rebecca Spit, Breton Islands and Village Bay), *Canadian Tide and Current Tables*, Vol. 5

Currents: Strong currents affect over 75 percent of Quadra's shoreline, yet this island is a paddler's paradise. As tides rise in the Pacific, currents flood and flow in around both ends of Vancouver Island. The Discovery Islands are affected each day by tidal flows from both the Strait of Georgia and Johnstone Strait, which create interesting and sometimes deadly situations. All outside waters surrounding Quadra Island, except Sutil Channel and the southern half of Hoskyn Channel, should be attempted only by experienced paddlers or those in guided trips.

➤ Sutil Channel (between Quadra Island and Cortes Island) floods north and ebbs south. Currents reach 2 knots and the area can have large wind-generated waves. Tide predictions can be found in *Canadian Tide and Current Tables*, Vol. 5.

➤ Discovery Passage (between Vancouver Island and Quadra Island) floods south and ebbs north. Flows reach up to 4 knots north of

Rebecca Spit

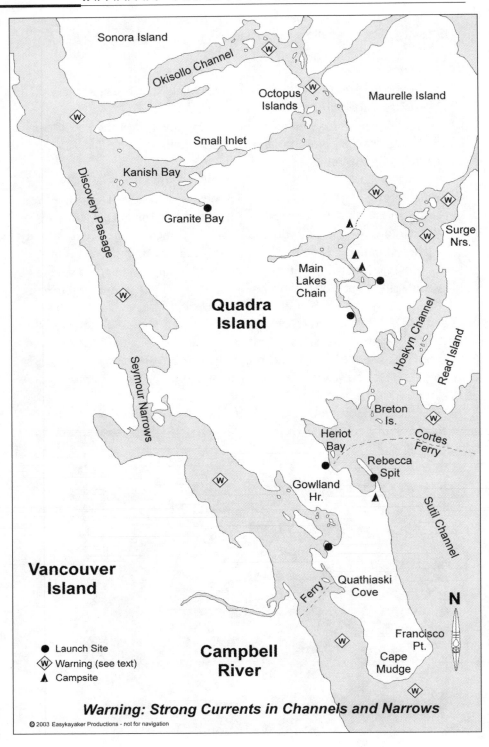

Sonora Island

Okisollo Channel

Octopus Islands

Maurelle Island

Small Inlet

Kanish Bay

Discovery Passage

Granite Bay

Surge Nrs.

Main Lakes Chain

Quadra Island

Hoskyn Channel

Read Island

Seymour Narrows

Breton Is.

Heriot Bay

Cortes Ferry

Rebecca Spit

Gowlland Hr.

Sutil Channel

Vancouver Island

Quathiaski Cove

Ferry

N

● Launch Site
Ⓦ Warning (see text)
▲ Campsite

Campbell River

Francisco Pt.

Cape Mudge

Warning: Strong Currents in Channels and Narrows

© 2003 Easykayaker Productions - not for navigation

Seymour Narrows. Currents below Seymour Narrows reach 8 knots. Seymour Narrows' currents flow up to 16 knots. Current predictions can be found in *Canadian Tide and Current Tables*, Vol. 6.

➤ Hoskyn Channel (between Quadra Island and Read Island) floods south and ebbs north with flows up to 2 knots. At the north end of Hoskyn Channel, Beazley Narrows' (Surge Narrows) currents reach 11.5 knots. Current predictions can be found in *Canadian Tide and Current Tables*, Vol. 6.

➤ Okisollo Channel (between Quadra Island and Sonora Island) floods southeast and ebbs northwest with flows up to 2 knots for much of the channel. Flows increase dramatically north of the Octopus Islands and are influenced by Hole-in-the-Wall. Lower and Upper Rapids, where Okisollo Channel is restricted at the northeast corner of Quadra, have currents that reach 11 knots. Current predictions can be found in *Canadian Tide and Current Tables*, Vol. 6.

Weather and sea conditions reference: Cape Mudge

Prevailing winds: Southeast or northwest depending on the type of weather system.

Warnings:

➤ Very strong currents in most channels surrounding Quadra Island and at Cape Mudge—see cautions on chart. Whirlpools and rapids in and near the narrows mentioned above (see "Currents"). Current flows can reach 16 knots.

➤ Heriot Bay, Hyacinthe Bay, Open Bay and Sutil Channel are exposed to southeast winds and wind-waves.

Getting there: Quadra Island is a 3-km (1.9-mi) ferry ride from Campbell River, 270 km (168 mi) north of Victoria and 160 km (100 mi) north of Nanaimo.

Accommodations: Lodges, resorts and B&Bs. Call the Campbell River visitor information centre at 866-830-1113 or go to *www.quadraisland.ca*.

Camping:

➤ We Wai Kai Campsite: This waterfront campground on the south end of Drew Harbour, near Rebecca Spit, is one of the best-run camp-

We Wai Kai campground. One of the best-run campgrounds we have visited.

grounds we have visited. For reservations phone 250-285-3111.

➤ Heriot Bay Inn & Marina: This resort is 8 km (5 mi) from Quathiaski Cove ferry terminal on West Road and is located next to the Heriot Bay ferry terminal. It offers cottages overlooking Heriot Bay, B&B units, RV and tent sites, and full hookups. Call 250-285-3322 for reservations and information.

➤ Main Lakes Chain Provincial Park: There are user-defined wooded campsites in at least six locations within the park boundaries. Most camping areas can support many tents, but there are outhouses in only a few areas. The park is north of Heriot Bay on Cramer Road.

Note: Information on launch sites and area-specific warnings are given under paddling areas.

Gowlland Harbour

We ran out of time and didn't get to paddle Gowlland Harbour, but we have been told by many people that exploring its eight islets and shoreline makes for a very nice day paddle.

Difficulty levels:

➤ Gowlland Harbour: Novice

➤ Outside Gowlland Harbour in Discovery Passage: Advanced

Approximate distances:

➤ Gowlland Harbour is 4.5 km (2.8 mi) long and 1 km (0.6 mi) wide at the widest point.

➤ There are over 14 km (8.7 mi) of shoreline to explore.

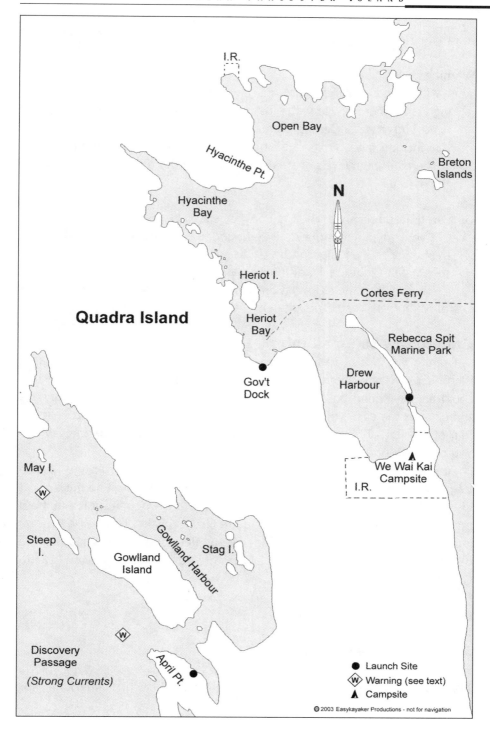

I.R.

Open Bay

Hyacinthe Pt.

Breton Islands

Hyacinthe Bay

N

Heriot I.

Cortes Ferry

Quadra Island

Heriot Bay

Rebecca Spit Marine Park

Drew Harbour

Gov't Dock

We Wai Kai Campsite

I.R.

May I.

W

Steep I.

Gowlland Island

Gowlland Harbour

Stag I.

W

Discovery Passage

(Strong Currents)

April Pt.

● Launch Site
Ⓦ Warning (see text)
▲ Campsite

© 2003 Easykayaker Productions - not for navigation

Approximate travel time: Half day or longer

Warnings:
> ➤ Although Gowlland Harbour is sheltered and away from the fast-moving water, there is wild water just outside it in Discovery Passage. April Point Lodge (see "Getting there/launching") has kayaking guidelines that include safety limits outlining where you should not venture.
> ➤ There are high levels of small boat traffic in the southern portion of the harbour.

Getting there/launching: There do not appear to be any public launch sites, but you can launch from April Point Lodge for a fee or rent kayaks from the Lodge and paddle from its docks. To reach April Point from the ferry terminal at Quathiaski Cove, take Harper Road to the shopping area and turn left at the stop sign onto Pidcock Road. Follow Pidcock Road to April Point Road. The lodge is at the end of April Point Road.

Granite Bay to Small Inlet

Granite Bay is a peaceful paradise near the northwest corner of Quadra Island. Granite Bay opens into the much larger Kanish Bay, where a kayaker could happily spend hours exploring the Chained Islands. If you follow the shoreline to the east, you will pass an eagle's nest on an island and hear the roar of a waterfall hidden away in the forest. There are a few beaches where you can pull up to stretch your legs and admire the scenery.

At the head of Small Inlet there is a short 800-m (about 0.5-mi) hike to Waiatt Bay on the eastern side of Quadra Island. From here you get a great view of the Octopus Islands. A second trail forks to the right a short way from the Small Inlet beachhead and takes you to Newton Lake. This trail is approximately 1.6 km (1 mi) long and fairly steep. Newton Lake is reputed to be beautiful, and a great swimming hole. Another trail connects Newton Lake to Granite Bay.

Difficulty level: Novice to intermediate

Approximate travel time: Full day

Approximate distance: Granite Bay to Small Inlet: 13 km (8.1 mi) round trip

Getting there: Take the road from the ferry up the hill and past the shopping

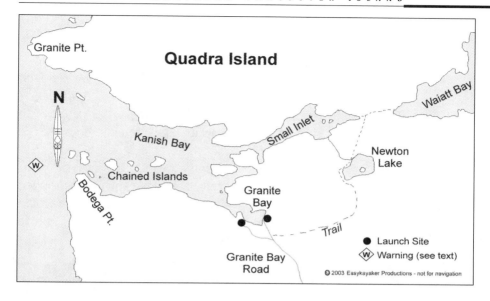

plaza. Turn left on West Road (by the RCMP station) and follow it to the junction of West Road and Cramer Road. (Some maps may show Cramer as Hyacinthe Road.) From the junction travel approximately 9.8 km (6.1 mi) along Cramer, Hyacinthe and Village Bay roads to Granite Bay Road.

Recommended launch site: From the Village Bay Road turnoff, follow Granite Bay Road for 11 km (6.8 mi) to Granite Bay. Park along the edge of the road.

Other launch site: Shortly before the main launch site, a side road on the right leads to a parking lot, small wharf and launch site. The road down to the parking lot is seriously rutted and potholed and not recommended for cars.

Travel notes (Paul)

The journey by truck to Granite Bay set the mood for an extraordinary day of paddling. Our first adventure with sea life came on Hyacinthe Road, where we encountered a misguided young seagull sitting by the side of a straight stretch of road in the centre of Quadra Island. As our truck approached, the gull started flying at eye level just a few metres ahead. Normally a gull would have flown up and away, but this bird flew like the Spruce Goose (and looked like Howard Hughes' aircraft too), gliding past the standing forest. Maybe it had been a porpoise in a previous life and was flying at the bow of our vehicle. As we slowed, it also slowed in order to stay just a few metres ahead of us. We even stopped and started again, but so did the seagull. (Note: Our Easykayaker policy is to avoid disturbing wildlife.) I managed to snap a picture just before the gull launched itself over the treetops in a sudden change of performance.

Granite Bay Road winds through a forest of Douglas fir, hemlock, alder and other species of trees. At times the forest dropped away from the shoulder of the road on a steep incline. We would be reminded by day's end that the forests of Quadra Island hide numerous stories about mining and logging.

Mouth of Small Inlet

After launching, Celia, Dave, Gary and I decided to explore Small Inlet first, and leave the Chained Islands and Kanish Bay for later if time and energy allowed. The inlet is protected from winds, with only minor tidal currents. We set off toward Small Inlet Provincial Park, enjoying the sunny, late August day.

The chart shows that you can duck behind a fairly large island if you keep right after exiting Granite Bay. We tried this, but the tide was too low to get through. However, we did get to see some extra coastline.

Celia was the first to notice the large number of jellyfish at the entrance to the inlet—dozens of them. Dave, Gary and I looked through the green depths and saw that there were thousands of them. By the time we had paddled another 100 m (330 ft) or so into Small Inlet we had changed our estimate to hundreds of thousands and finally millions.

These were moon jellyfish, which are between 7 and 15 cm (3 and 6 in) in diameter. They sting their prey with tentacles to cap-ture and feed on them. The stinging sensation is caused by a protein mole-cule. Apparently, meat tenderizer neu-tralizes the pain because it breaks down the protein molecule. When I paddled over the moon jellyfish "belling" their way in the mild current I decided it might not be a good time to practise rolling or edging. I later discovered that moon jellyfish have such short tentacles their sting is ineffective on people. However, I didn't want to discover the effect of swimming with thousands of them.

Just beyond a small bay on the south side of the inlet, an eagle's nest sits on a wind-torn tree that pokes above the forest. We idly paddled past it without seeing any birds of prey. A kilometre farther and southwest of two islands we could hear a noisy waterfall; we stopped on an iron-stained pebble beach to investigate, but the lack of trail and visibility dis-couraged exploring.

Head of Small Inlet

A short paddle later we landed at the end of the inlet and enjoyed lunch by the entrance to the Waiatt Bay trail. Nearby a fleet of kayaks was pulled up on the beach, and soon Liam Edwards of Geophilia Adventures emerged from the trail with a group on a four-day Spirit of the West trip from Heriot Bay to Small Inlet. It turned out that Liam is one of Granite Bay's 16 residents and is a great source of local history and paddling knowledge.

In the 19th century, Granite Bay served as a base of operations for logging. Using an old CPR steam engine, the Hastings Company developed railway logging in BC at Granite Bay. According to the Campbell River Museum, "At peak operations in the 1890s, the Hastings outfit employed up to 200 men. A small settlement sprang up around their beach camp and log dump, including a store/post office, school, hotel, brothel, and a government dock where the Union steamships called to deliver passengers, mail, and supplies. About six ranches were established along the company's mainline."

Union steamship circa 1890

After an enjoyable chat with Liam we decided to hike to Waiatt Bay. Unfortunately I could not do the longer hike to Newton Lake because of a torn cartilage in my knee.

After a short climb we walked into a unique area of forest floor. Gary, an amateur naturalist, found an albino deer fern frond right on the edge of the trail. At Waiatt Bay, large swaths of sword ferns populated the underbrush. Occasionally the sun would penetrate the forest canopy, revealing thousands of spores floating in the air, thick as ocean algae during a summer bloom. Fern spores are produced through asexual reproduction and form on the underside of leaves in clusters of spore cases called sporangia. When the cases dry out they break open and release the spores into the wind.

Licorice ferns were flourishing on deciduous tree trunks and a few delicate-looking maidenhair ferns grew nearby. The area appeared ideal for ferns—moist and largely shaded with a rich soil containing lots of organic matter. It was a great example of a rainforest environment.

Waiatt Bay is also a moorage for sailboats. Several small row-boats and Zodiacs were on the beach.

By the time we returned to Small Inlet my knee was throbbing, so paddling seemed like a great thing to do. After leaving the inlet we explored some of the coastline in Kanish Bay. As we paddled into Granite Bay, we tried to visualize the thriving community that once populated these shores.

We unloaded our equipment, secured the boats on top of the vehicles and headed for the Lucky Jim Mine. After leaving Granite Bay, travel 4.3 km (2.7 mi) back the way you came to a turnoff on the left side of the road—it's almost a straight exit from Granite Bay Road when it turns 90 degrees to the right and starts up a hill. Drive 0.3 km (0.2 mi) to a wide point in the road and park where two old dirt roads begin on the left. The dirt road on the right leads to the mine. If you take the wrong one, it will dead-end before you go too far. The walk to the mine only takes a minute or two. **Watch out for open mine shafts!**

The Lucky Jim gold and copper mine operated from 1903 to 1910. At its peak it removed over 1,100 tonnes of ore a month. Gary and I found a huge iron fly-wheel that likely pumped water from the mines. Many of the shafts we inspected were open, with old wooden ladders leading down into them. In the shaft just behind the fly-wheel we counted at least 30 rungs. The shafts were lined with concrete and appeared to drop vertically for 30 or more feet before presumably moving horizontally along a tunnel. Some shafts are closed, but the wooden covers are decaying. Please don't let children play in this area.

Old machinery at Lucky Jim Mine site

On the way out (or in) look for the original log bunkhouses of the mineworkers. The forest is slowly consuming them and they are hard to see.

Breton Islands from Rebecca Spit. A paddle to the Breton Islands requires a calm day, as winds and currents can make the passage difficult.

Breton Islands

Five small islands/islets make up the Bretons. Their pleasant beaches provide great picnic spots (map pg 233). Nearby, just east of Open Bay, several more islands/islets offer their shorelines for exploring. Paddlers who desire a longer trip can travel north from the Bretons to explore Village Bay. Several of our friends have paddled over to the Breton Islands and enjoyed it as a day trip. We started off in that direction, but were driven back by high winds and a forecast that said things would get worse.

Difficulty level: Intermediate

Approximate travel times:
> ➤ Half to full day
> ➤ Unless the wind and current are against you, the paddle along the shoreline from Heriot Bay to the Breton Islands should take about 60 to 90 minutes. If going directly it should take about 30 to 40 minutes.

Approximate distances (one way):
> ➤ Rebecca Spit launch site to Breton Islands: 3 km (1.9 mi)
> ➤ Heriot Bay launch site to Breton Islands: 3 km (1.9 mi)
> ➤ Crossing from the tip of Rebecca Spit to Breton Islands: 2 km (1.2 mi)
> ➤ Following the shoreline from Heriot Bay to Breton Islands: 7.5 km (4.6 mi)
> ➤ We Wai Kai Campsite to Breton Islands: 4 km (2.5 mi)

Warnings:
> ➤ Check your weather forecast before heading off to the Breton Islands.

Both Hyacinthe and Open bays are exposed to southeasters.

➤ Watch for boat and ferry traffic.

➤ The current has little effect between Heriot Bay and the Breton Islands. However, just past the Bretons, Sutil Channel floods north at 2 knots and meets Hoskyn Channel, which floods south at 2 knots. These two intersecting flows can create turbulence near the southern tip of Read Island.

Getting there/launching:

➤ **Rebecca Spit**: There is an easy-to-find boat launch in Rebecca Spit Marine Provincial Park, which is on Rebecca Spit Road (turn east off Heriot Bay Road about 2 km/1.2 mi south of Heriot Bay). From the launch site paddle to the tip of Rebecca Spit and cross over to the Breton Islands.

➤ **Heriot Bay**: There is a boat ramp next to the public dock on Antler Road. From this launch site, one option is to cross to the tip of Rebecca Spit and then paddle over to the islands. A longer, but much more interesting paddle is to follow the shoreline from Heriot Bay to Hyacinthe Bay and then to Open Bay. On this route there aren't any real crossings and you paddle by many interesting sandy beaches and rugged headlands.

➤ **We Wai Kai Campsite**: Located on Rebecca Spit Road, this launch site at the head of Drew Harbour is for guests only. You can access a fairly level beach from most shoreline campsites. Follow the shore of Rebecca Spit and cross over to the Breton Islands.

Drew Harbour's calm waters are great for beginning kayakers.

Rebecca Spit and Drew Harbour

Rebecca Spit Marine Provincial Park is a beautiful spot for both hiking and paddling (map pg 233). Surrounded by sandy beaches, this 2-km-long (1.2-mi) spit is well worth exploring. Several trails wind through trees and other plant life. The spit forms and protects Drew Harbour, a picturesque and usually calm body of water that is a great place for swimming and for beginner kayakers to practise.

On the east side of Rebecca Spit is Sutil Channel and an incredible view of the rugged mainland mountains. Kayakers can paddle south along the shoreline for 10 km (6.3 mi). There is a sandy/gravel beach to land on the entire way.

We Wai Kai Campsite is located at the head of Drew Harbour adjacent to Rebecca Spit and is a great place to stay when visiting this area.

Difficulty levels:
➤ Drew Harbour: Novice
➤ Sutil Channel side: Intermediate if windy

Approximate travel times:
➤ Circumnavigating Drew Harbour and Heriot Bay: Half day
➤ Exploring the shoreline along Sutil Channel: Half to full day (depending on how far you go)

Approximate distances (one way):
➤ Circumnavigating Drew Harbour and Heriot Bay: 7 km (4.3 mi)
➤ The head of Drew Harbour to Heriot Bay: 2.5 km (1.5 mi)
➤ Rebecca Spit boat ramp to Francisco Point: 12.5 km (7.8 mi)

Warnings:
➤ Check your weather forecast before heading into Sutil Channel. It is exposed to southeasters. Fortunately you never have to venture far from a sandy beach during this trip.
➤ Watch for boat and ferry traffic in Heriot Bay and at the tip of Rebecca Spit.
➤ Sutil Channel floods north and ebbs south at currents up to 2 knots.

Getting there/launching:
➤ Rebecca Spit: Near the main parking area there is an unimproved boat ramp on the Drew Harbour side. Kayaks can also be carried from the parking area to the Sutil Channel side and launched from the beach.

➤ Heriot Bay: From this launch site you can cross over to the tip of Rebecca Spit or head into Drew Harbour.

➤ We Wai Kai Campsite: This launch site at the head of Drew Harbour is for guests only.

Travel notes (Paul)

My grandfather's sister, Great-Aunt Mary Grey, and her husband Gordon Clandening were the original owners of Rebecca Spit. Their property was always open to their friends and the public. In 1959 an American company offered to buy the property, but a development on the spit would likely have limited the public's access at best. Gordon and Mary Clandening wanted to ensure full public access to this exquisite point of land, so they donated it to the provincial government in June 1959. I attended the celebration as an eight-year-old. An old home movie captures some of the events—my lively grandmother, Madge Grey, singing and dancing; children climbing the greased pole and playing in the field; and adults picnicking under the shelter of the trees.

Main Lakes Chain

Main Lakes Chain Provincial Park features a series of lakes connected by natural and artificial channels. Created in 1996, the park is made up of over 3,000 ha (7,413 acres) of land and 466 ha (1,150 acres) of fresh water, and is billed as the largest freshwater waterway in the Gulf Islands. Many paddlers consider it a "must do."

The paddle starts near the south end of Village Bay Lake. You paddle the length of that lake, then through a long narrow canal that's full of plant life

One of the Main Lake islands. Many of these islands are privately owned.

243

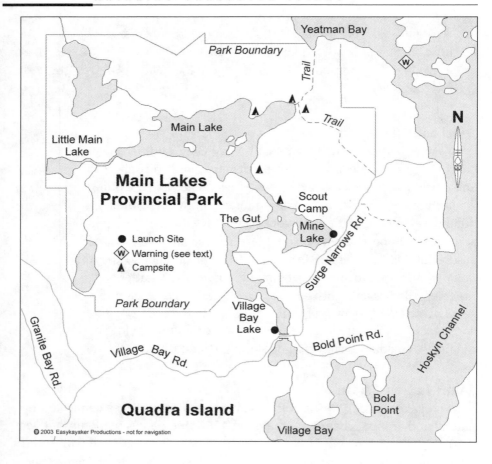

and into the lower part of Main Lake (also known as Mine Lake). Main Lake narrows and then widens into a large body of water. If the salmon aren't spawning or hatching you can go from the west end of Main Lake into Little Main Lake. The spawning channel is well marked and can be avoided.

There are several trails along the lakes' shores. From the northeast corner of Main Lake, a trail leads to Yeatman Beach and the road to Surge Narrows. The 1.2-km (0.7-mi) trail to Yeatman is mostly downhill, and visiting the beach is worth the hike.

Unfortunately, the compass rose on CHS chart 3539 completely covers the Main Lakes Chain. However Kirby Stevens of Coastal Waters Recreation produces a map that covers this area and Hornby and Denman Islands. We found Kirby's map quite useful as it shows launch sites and camping areas along with points of interest.

Difficulty level: Novice

Approximate travel time: Full day to multiple day

Approximate distances (one way):
➤ Village Bay Lake launch to Yeatman trailhead campsite: 6.4 km (4 mi)
➤ Village Bay Lake launch to far end of Little Main Lake: 7 km (4.3 mi)

Warnings:
➤ There is no fire protection available. Use only BC Parks fire enclosures or do not have a fire.
➤ Some of the islands within the park are privately owned. The east end of Little Main Lake is also privately owned. Scouts have a camp on Mine Lake.

Getting there: The Village Bay Lake launch site is approximately 16 km (10 mi) from Heriot Bay. Follow Hyacinthe Bay Road 6.3 km (3.9 mi) past the Granite Bay Road junction. Hyacinthe Bay Road becomes Village Bay Road at the Granite Bay junction.

Recommended launch site: Launch from either side of the Village Bay Road bridge near the south end of Village Bay Lake.

Other launch site: An alternative launch site is the Mine Lake picnic area on Surge Narrows Road (east end of Mine Lake). Continue over the bridge past the Village Bay Lake launch site. The road forks and becomes Surge Narrows Road on the left and Bold Point Road on the right. The launch site is on the left side of Surge Narrows Road about 2.4 km (1.5 mi) past the fork. Mine Lake and the launch site are close to the road. If you continue farther on this road it becomes steep and rough, suitable for 4-wheel-drive only.

Travel notes (Gary)

No tides! Clean boats at the end of the day! A freshwater paddle—what a change for us. In all the years we've kayaked, our only freshwater paddles have been practice sessions in Nanaimo's Westwood Lake and Ladysmith's swimming pool. I've asked myself a few times why we paddle the briny deep, ignoring freshwater lakes. Maybe it's because saltwater paddling offers an incredible diversity of shores, marine life and viewscapes, while the tides and currents make salt water alive and wild. Well, it was time for something different.

We had had near perfect weather for our Small Inlet paddle, but today seemed to promise wind. Some Quadra Island kayak companies had told us the Main Lakes Chain was a trip they saved for windy days when conditions were unfavourable for sea kayaking. It looked like we had planned right.

John at Spirit of the West had told us we could launch from either side of the Village Bay Road bridge—we would recognize it by the many aluminum skiffs nearby. I expected to see about 10 skiffs and was amazed to see somewhere between 40 and 60. These are the principal means of transportation to reach the multitude of cabins on Village Bay Lake.

Beaver lodge along Village Bay Lake shoreline

A sign on a tree near the launch site stated that 10 horsepower was maximum motor size allowed on the lakes, though I later found out from BC Parks staff that this rule doesn't apply to people whose land ownership predates the park's creation.

Dave and Celia launched their kayaks on the south side of the bridge while Paul and I embarked on the north. Parking was plentiful. There was even an outhouse, but it had seen better days— the door was gone, as was the toilet seat, and the hole was full of garbage.

Dave and Celia paddled under the bridge and joined us as we headed up Village Bay Lake. This lake is not part of the park and is dotted with summer cottages. One of the expanses of uninhabited shoreline contained a beaver lodge. There were a few freshly chewed sticks, which indicated that the lodge was active. I've canoed and even swum side by side with beaver, but today we weren't lucky enough to see one. (I have an affinity for beavers. A few years ago a beaver wandered several kilometres overland to build his home in a pond next to my house. We were enthused to have our own resident beaver and would go out almost every evening at dusk to watch him. He only lasted a few months, however, before the pond's low water levels drove him away.)

As we paddled Village Bay Lake, we met a few of the people who summer there. One fellow told us that the water level drops almost a metre between winter and late summer. Another family we chatted with was renting for a week or so, and of course we started thinking how wonderful it would be to come back with our families and rent a cabin so that we could swim, kayak and explore for a week.

Village Bay Lake is about 2 km (1.2 mi) long and quite narrow. As we neared the north end we passed the last cabin. The provincial park starts near here, but there are no signs to indicate that fact. There were no signs anywhere in the park, except for one marking the salmon-spawning channel into Little Main Lake. Someone seems to have a vendetta against BC Parks signage; parks staff told me that signs are torn down soon after they're posted.

Just before the end of Village Bay Lake, a shallow channel on the right side connects it to the smaller portion of Main Lake. This channel is known locally as "The Gut," and most people we've talked to say it is one of the highlights of paddling the Chain. Village Bay Lake was dammed in 1894 to raise the water level, and this channel was dug out for shipping logs from the other lakes. During the summer it's about a foot deep and full of bulrushes except for a waterway so narrow that we had to proceed in single file.

Once in the lower portion of Main Lake (a.k.a. Mine Lake) we turned north and paddled toward the narrows that separates it from the major portion of Main Lake. We stopped to explore the

Entering "The Gut," a narrow man-made channel connecting Village Bay Lake to Mine Lake.

camping area at the south end of the narrows. Like most of the campsites it had a sandy/gravel beach that was alive with very small frogs. There were many areas for tenting in the woods, and a trail ran along the shore up the lake's narrows.

Back in the kayaks we passed through the narrow section. As the lake opened up we came to the next campsite. A family was well-entrenched there and we visited with them for a few minutes. They told us it was their second holiday here, and both times there were no mosquitoes. The absence of mosquitoes had impressed us too. Their son had caught a trout just before we arrived, and he brought out what would be that night's dinner to show us. This spot was my favourite of the camping areas we saw.

Little Main Lake was calling to us, but instead the group opted to explore the camping areas and trails located at Main Lake's northeast corner. We found lots of camping sites and BC Parks' latest innovation in toilets: one-piece, green, molded plastic units with no roof, no door, and walls that are shoulder-height when sitting. They're round, quite odourless and can be relocated by one worker when the hole becomes too full. The seat would be a little damp on a rainy day, but the design made sense.

After a great lunch we headed out to explore one more camping area on a point of land about 50 m (165 ft) west of our lunch spot. Then we heard a haunting call that echoed off nearby shores and islands. Dave started imitating the calls. Soon every loon in the area swam toward him. It was comical to watch this large flock approach. We weren't sure if he had insulted them or not.

We paddled between the islands, cutting swaths through thousands of dead insects that Paul speculated had reached the end of their life cycle. The islands are within the park boundaries but privately owned. Evidently this ownership predated Main Lakes becoming a park, which happened in 1996.

After returning south through the narrows and exploring most of Mine Lake, we headed back to Village Bay Lake and the Heriot Bay Pub. It had been a nice day of paddling, and even though we were there during the height of summer holidays, the campsites were virtually deserted. After 20 years of canoeing, I'd subconsciously given up freshwater paddling for sea kayaking, but this trip brought back positive freshwater paddling memories for all of us and we vowed to visit the Main Lakes Chain again soon.

Cortes Island

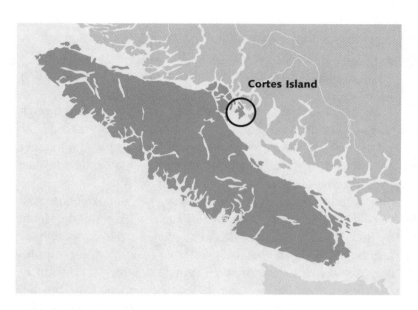

Cortes Island, situated at the north end of the Strait of Georgia and the south end of Johnstone Strait, is part of the Discovery Islands group. Along with Quadra and Redonda islands, Cortes is an entry point to Desolation Sound. It is also home of the Klahoose First Nation. Mitlenatch Island Nature Provincial Park, south of Cortes, has the largest seabird colony in the Strait of Georgia, while at the north end of Cortes, narrow channels between islands and deep fjords with steep cliffs make for interesting travels. Southern Cortes and Mitlenatch are in Vancouver Island's rain shadow and don't get much precipitation, so it's not surprising that most of the island's 900 residents choose to live in the south.

CHS chart: 3538—Desolation Sound and Sutil Channel

Tidal reference port: Point Atkinson (add about 30 minutes for Von Donop Inlet area)

Weather and sea conditions reference:
- ➤ Johnstone Strait
- ➤ Cape Mudge
- ➤ Sentry Shoal

Prevailing winds: Southeast or northwest depending on the type of weather system

Warnings:
- ➤ There are black bears and wolves in some areas.
- ➤ Beware of tidal currents.
- ➤ Tidal rapids of up to 8 knots at the entrances to saltwater lagoons in Von Donop Inlet, Carrington Bay, Mansons Landing and Squirrel Cove.
- ➤ The southern half of Cortes Island is exposed to the Strait of Georgia—sea conditions can change quickly and waves can build over a long distance.
- ➤ Oysters are Cortes Island's number one industry; no human waste at or below the tide line.
- ➤ South Marina Reef and Sutil Point Reef are pupping areas for seals.
- ➤ Three Islets, Little Rock, Central Rock and North Powell Islets (east of Twin Islands in Desolation Sound) are all signed as oystercatcher habitat and are not to be disturbed by humans.
- ➤ Respect First Nations land (marked I.R. on charts). Do not disturb these lands or archeological sites.

Getting there: To reach Cortes Island you must take two ferry trips and a drive across Quadra Island. A 12-minute ferry ride from Campbell River

On one of the two ferries you must take to get to Cortes Island.

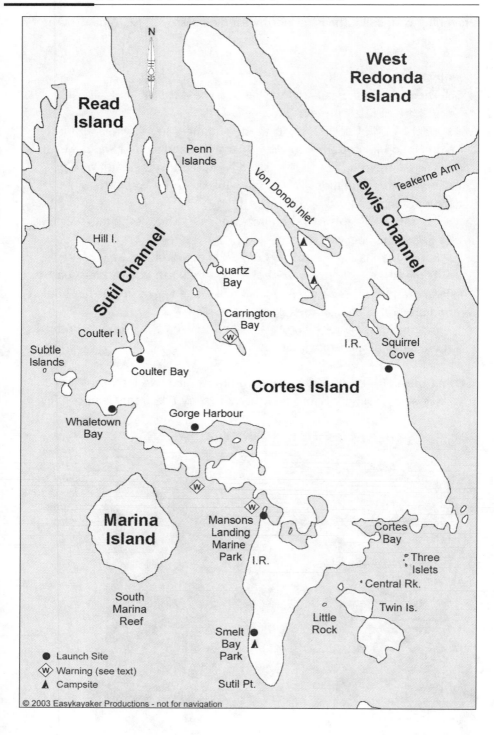

N

Read Island

West Redonda Island

Penn Islands

Von Donop Inlet

Teakerne Arm

Lewis Channel

Hill I.

Sutil Channel

Quartz Bay

Carrington Bay

Coulter I.

I.R.

Squirrel Cove

Subtle Islands

Coulter Bay

Cortes Island

Whaletown Bay

Gorge Harbour

Marina Island

Mansons Landing Marine Park

I.R.

Cortes Bay

Three Islets

Central Rk.

South Marina Reef

Little Rock

Twin Is.

Smelt Bay Park

Sutil Pt.

● Launch Site
W Warning (see text)
▲ Campsite

© 2003 Easykayaker Productions - not for navigation

brings you to Quathiaski Cove on Quadra Island. Drive to Heriot Bay (follow the road signs) on the east side of Quadra where you will catch the second ferry, a 45-minute crossing to Whaletown Bay on Cortes Island. Island maps are usually available at the Campbell River ferry terminal.

Accommodations: There is a lodge, resorts, motel and B&Bs on Cortes. Phone visitor information at 250-285-2724.

Camping: Smelt Bay Provincial Park (23 campsites) is on Sutil Point Road, 15 km (9.3 mi) south of the Whaletown ferry terminal. Follow Harbour Road from the ferry terminal to Carrington Bay Road, where you will turn right. Turn left on Whaletown Road and follow it past the end of Gorge Harbour, then turn right onto Gorge Harbour Road. Turn right onto Seaford Road and follow it to Sutil Point Road. Turn left and follow south to the park.
Note: Difficulty levels, approximate travel times, distances, location-specific warnings, launch sites and camping information are listed under specific paddling areas.

Squirrel Cove

On the east side of Cortes facing Desolation Sound and Lewis Channel is Squirrel Cove, often described as one of the most picturesque anchorages for boaters on BC's West Coast. The Klahoose First Nations village is about 0.75

Squirrel Cove Trail begins at the tip on the cove's most westerly finger.

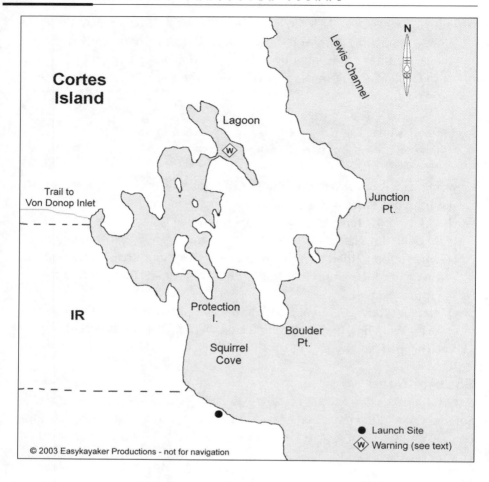

km (0.5 mi) west of the dock. The community of Squirrel Cove has a well-stocked general store, which includes a liquor section and a walk-in cooler filled with fruits and vegetables. A restaurant and craft store are also close by. The craft store has a good selection of books by Gilean Douglas, Cortes's beloved author, who died in 1993. You can read her account of life on Cortes Island in *The Protected Place*.

Squirrel Cove offers fairly protected paddling and a good day trip. At the northern end of the cove, past two islets, is a saltwater lagoon. At low tide a waterfall runs over rocks at the entrance, while at high tides the sea floods rapidly in and then ebbs out of the lagoon at speeds estimated as high as 10 knots. There is also a trail that cuts across the island to the head of Von Donop Inlet. You will find the trailhead at the end of the most westerly finger of water/mud in Squirrel Cove.

Difficulty level: Novice to intermediate

Approximate travel time: Half day or longer

Approximate distance: Boat ramp to the tip of Protection Island: 1 km (0.6 mi)

Warnings:

➤ Many boaters anchor in the area north of Protection Island. Most boaters enter via the channel on the northwest side of Protection, so you may prefer to paddle in through the southeast one.

➤ If you want to hike to Von Donop Inlet, check your tides carefully or you could have quite a carry across a mud flat.

➤ The rapids can flow at up to 10 knots into the lagoon. If you want to try running this, you're going to shoot through fast and experience some eddies and countercurrents before dipping your paddle into a calm surface.

➤ The slack period in the passage between Squirrel Cove and the lagoon only lasts about 5 to 10 minutes. You can get trapped here for hours.

Getting there/launching: Follow Harbour Road from the ferry terminal to Carrington Bay Road. Turn right and follow Carrington Bay to its junction with Whaletown Road. Turn left on Whaletown and follow it to Gorge Harbour Road, where you will turn left and continue on to Squirrel Cove. Launch from the boat ramp between the craft shop and restaurant. There is no launch fee for kayakers.

Camping: Some kayakers and canoeists enter the lagoon and camp in a grassy meadow on the eastern shore.

Mansons Landing, Smelt Bay Provincial Park and Gorge Harbour

Mansons Landing is located on a narrow peninsula of land between Sutil Channel and Mansons Lagoon. It is also part of Mansons Landing Provincial Park (47 ha/116 acres). From the government dock it is an easy paddle to Smelt Bay Provincial Park. Along the way there are some inviting white sand beaches where you can stop and swim. South of the dock there is a large boulder (about 2.5 m/8 ft wide) with a very faded petroglyph of a fish.

Heading north from Mansons Landing to Gorge Harbour will take you past a few small islets and steep slopes where arbutus trees grow out of crags in

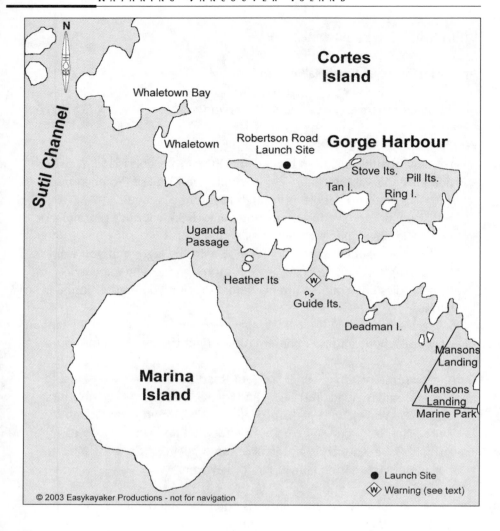

the rock. There is an amazing variety of colours, shapes and textures along the shoreline.

Keep an eye out for pictographs on the high cliffs leading into Gorge Harbour. Although a number of homes line the rocky shorelines of the Gorge, this enclosed harbour provides a perfect half-day paddle around low-lying islets or past several designer homes cleverly situated amongst trees, in small coves or atop rocky points.

Difficulty levels:

➤ Mansons Landing area: Novice
➤ Entrance to Mansons Lagoon: Novice to intermediate

> Gorge Harbour: Novice
> Entrance to Gorge Harbour: Novice to intermediate

Approximate travel times:
> Mansons Landing area: Half day or longer
> Gorge Harbour: Half day or longer
> Mansons Landing and Gorge Harbour: Full day

Approximate distances:
> Mansons Landing government dock to petroglyph: 1.5 km (0.9 mi) one way
> Mansons Landing government dock to Smelt Bay Provincial Park: 4 km (2.5 mi) one way
> Mansons Landing government dock to mouth of Gorge Harbour: 3 km (1.9 mi) one way
> Exploring Gorge Harbour: 8+ km (5+ mi)

Warnings:
> There is a strong tidal current, up to 4 knots, in Gorge Harbour entrance.
> The current can be strong at the mouth of Mansons Lagoon.

Recommended launch sites:
> **Government dock at Mansons Landing**: Follow Harbour Road from the ferry terminal to Carrington Bay Road. Turn right on Carrington and left onto Whaletown Road. Continue past Gorge Harbour to Gorge Harbour Road. Turn right. At Seaford Road turn right and follow it past Hague Lake to Sutil Point Road. Turn right or north and follow to Mansons Landing. A trail next to the dock leads to the beach.
> **Robertson Road beach at Gorge Harbour**: Follow Harbour Road from the ferry terminal to Carrington Bay Road. Turn right and then left onto Whaletown Road. Look for the sign for Robertson Road on your right. There is a beach access next to the dock.

Other launch sites:
> Mansons Landing boat ramp: This ramp leads into the lagoon and is best used during a high tide near slack as there is only a narrow canal meandering toward the mouth of the lagoon at low tide. It could be hard for a weak paddler to enter or exit the lagoon if the water is running with any strength.

➤ Smelt Bay Provincial Park: This park is near the south end of Sutil Point Road. See directions under "Camping" on page 253.

➤ There is a trail from the BC Ferries terminal parking lot on the north side of Whaletown Bay. This short trail is very easy to find. It is a little steep, but has a nice beach.

Mansons Landing

Travel notes (Paul)

Gary's friend Karl met us at the ferry in Whaletown, and we followed him in our vehicles as he drove along Whaletown Road to his house. After introductions and a brief visit, Gary, Celia and I went out to tour the southwest portion of the island and decided to take a paddle from Mansons Landing to Gorge Harbour.

Touring Cortes Island in Bullwinkle the Truck

It didn't take long to discover the Cortes Island spirit. We toured the island in Bullwinkle, looking at launch sites, beaches and countryside from the long and winding roads. Everyone we passed—hikers, cars travelling in the opposite direction or just people standing on the roadside—waved at us. When I sat in the Tak Restaurant a small boy came up to me and said, "Hi." He waited patiently while I swallowed my food and then returned his "hi" with a smile. His expression showed that he expected this courtesy.

Whaletown was one of our stops. It's a quaint community of about 140 people consisting of a general store at the head of the government dock, a white mission church and what is perhaps one of Canada's smallest post offices. There is limited parking at the end of the road to Whaletown.

One of our next stops was the Cortes Island museum. It's located in a small village area near the Tak Restaurant (good food!) between Mansons Lagoon and Smelt Bay. Gary and I were impressed with the records and accounts kept here. The museum houses a number of interesting artifacts that reflect both pioneer life and the culture of the Klahoose people. It's definitely worth a visit.

Hague Lake is a popular location for locals and tourists. A sandy beach and warm waters await the summertime visitor a short walk from the parking lot. We had our second freshwater swim in as many days, which left us feeling quite clean—unusual for saltwater-crusted kayakers. A small creek runs from the lake to Mansons Lagoon.

Smelt Bay Provincial Park is off Sutil Point Road. There are 23 campsites here (including overflow camping) and a beautiful gravel beach. It's a great place to stay. At the southern tip of Cortes there is access to a pebble beach that bends around to Sutil Point. The spectacular views are worth the visit.

Unfortunately on this trip we didn't get to visit Mitlenatch Island Nature Provincial Park, referred to as "the Galapagos of the Strait of Georgia." The island is 6 or 7 km (3.75 to 4.5 mi) south of Cortes Island, and you can travel there by boat or charter. The island has a thick groundcover and is the summer home for nearly 4,000 pairs of seabirds. Please stay on the trails and respect the sanctuary.

We parked my truck (known as Bullwinkle because the kayak rack looks like moose horns) at Mansons Landing and launched our three kayaks from a small trail alongside the government dock. We first paddled south under the dock and headed toward the Indian Reserve, trying to find the petroglyph of a fish carved into a large sloping rock. There are long stretches of white sand beach along this section of the shoreline between Cortes and Smelt Bay Provincial Park (especially near the park). It was a sweltering summer day and we paddled along slowly, admiring the scenery and looking at the beds of sand dollars in the clear, green water. We found the boulder with the fish etched into it, but the petroglyph had weathered to the point where only a few lines could be seen. It might have been more clearly visible if the sun had been at a different angle.

Gary investigated the shoreline a bit farther south toward the Indian Reserve while Celia and I bobbed and snoozed in our kayaks. A few minutes later we were paddling back to Mansons

Landing to check out the lagoon. I paddled fairly close to the mouth and found myself being dragged backwards into it with the flood tide. I did a quick power paddle to escape from the current's grip.

The northern shore of Mansons Bay rises steeply. Arbutus trees grow on elevated crags above the waterline, while a forest of Douglas fir and western red cedar, with the occasional maple, crowds the higher elevations. Pines dot the shore. In and above the intertidal zone, large boulders with sharp, squared edges lay in heaps. The rock faces and boulders looked like granite or tonalite, a coarse-grained rock. At the high tide mark, the rock faces at the point near Deadman Island were light green from algae growth. In other places the rock seemed to be stained pearl-pink.

Rest stop in Gorge Harbour. A keen eye can spot pictographs on the cliffs of the Gorge.

About an hour later we arrived at Gorge Harbour. I scanned the walls carefully but had difficulty finding the pictographs. The best time to view them is apparently during a slack high tide. There are stories that Gorge Harbour First Nations ambushed enemies by balancing large rocks on top of the cliffs and releasing them to fall on warriors below.

We experienced little difficulty and very light back eddies. We paddled along the Gorge's shoreline counterclockwise admiring several designer homes cleverly situated amongst trees, in small coves or atop rocky points. We had travelled about 14 or 15 km (8 or 9 mi) by the time we pulled onto the beach at the end of Robertson Road, where we had left Celia's car. Gary stayed with the kayaks while Celia drove me to retrieve Bullwinkle.

We ended the day with a communal dinner at Karl's home, then retired, eager to start our three-day trip to Von Donop–Ha'thayim Marine Provincial Park.

Von Donop–Ha'thayim Marine Provincial Park

Von Donop Inlet, a long narrow finger of water stretching from Sutil Channel more than halfway across Cortes Island, is a great place to get away from it all. The narrow inlet has caves, hiking trails and a beautiful lagoon guarded by a set of reversing rapids. If you kayak from Coulter Bay to the mouth of Von Donop Inlet during a lower tide, you will see some amazing intertidal life clinging to the steep, fjord-like shore.

The inlet was named after Victor Edward John Brenton Von Donop, a midshipman on HMS *Charybdis*, in 1863 and was originally called Von Donop Creek. It's confusing to hear an inlet referred to as a creek, but that's what locals and visitors have called it for years.

There is a trail from the head of the inlet to the head of Squirrel Cove on the east side of the island. Another trail leads from about 1 km (0.6 mi) north of the mouth of the inlet to Robertson and Wiley lakes.

Difficulty levels:
➤ Coulter Bay to Von Donop Inlet: Intermediate
➤ Reversing Rapids: Intermediate to advanced (depending on current)

Approximate travel time: Multiple day

Approximate distances (one way):
➤ From Coulter Bay to the mouth of Von Donop Inlet: 8 km (5 mi)
➤ From the mouth of the inlet to the first campsite and lagoon area: 2 km (1.2 mi)
➤ From the mouth of the inlet to the head of the inlet: 3 km (1.9 mi)
➤ Crossing the mouth of Carrington Bay: 1 km (0.6 mi)

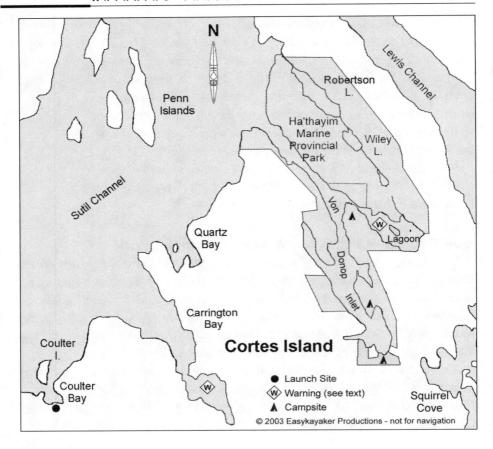

Current:
> ➤ Mild currents flood north and ebb south along this portion of the west coast of Cortes.

> ➤ Mild currents flood into and ebb out of Von Donop Inlet.

> ➤ Strong currents flood into and ebb out of Von Donop's lagoon.

Warnings:
> ➤ There are few places to pull out along the shoreline between Carrington Bay and Von Donop Inlet.

> ➤ Paddling the Reversing Rapids can be risky depending on what the tide is doing.

Getting there/launching: Coulter Bay is the closest launch site for paddling to Von Donop Inlet. Follow Harbour Road from the ferry terminal to Carrington Bay Road. Turn left and then right onto Coulter Bay Road. Follow it to the launch site.

Camping:

➤ Southwest of the lagoon entrance there is a great campsite on a grassy knoll. It has a picnic table.

➤ On the north shore inside the head of the inlet there is a good camping area fairly high above the tide line with a picnic table.

➤ You could camp near the trailhead (to Squirrel Cove) at the head of Von Donop Inlet, but it's not a sunny spot and it has a very muddy beach. There is an outhouse here.

➤ You might be able to squeeze a couple of tents on the small islet in the southwest corner of the lagoon.

➤ There is a large, level grassy campsite on the west side of the lagoon.

Travel notes (Paul)

The drive from Karl's place near Whaletown to Coulter Bay, our launch site, took about 15 minutes. I backed the truck down a short, washed-out boat ramp parallel to a private driveway and stopped short of the mud flat.

We had brought supplies for three days of paddling and two nights of camping. Celia packed her boat in record speed (a skill I've never fully mastered) and helped Gary and me with our final preparations. After I parked the truck in a small parking area opposite the boat ramp, we lifted the loaded boats across the short flats, sinking slightly into the oozing mud, and were soon on our way.

As we passed Coulter Island after paddling out of Coulter Bay, Hill and Penn islands came into full view. There was nary a breeze on the sea and we were lightly rocked by the occasional set of waves from boats cruising past somewhere in the distance. The surface of the channel sparkled like thousands of floating diamonds. If I'd been the Tin Man from the *Wizard of Oz*, I would have been a navigational aid for boaters given the way the sun lit up the water and our kayaks. The effect of the morning sun, the spectacular views of distant islands and mountain peaks, and the extraordinary varied shoreline overwhelmed me. I felt a sense of elation at being part of nature—this elation is what many of us seek in our kayaking journeys.

We soon arrived at Carrington Bay and started crossing to its far shore. At one point Celia yelled out, "Porpoises!" We watched

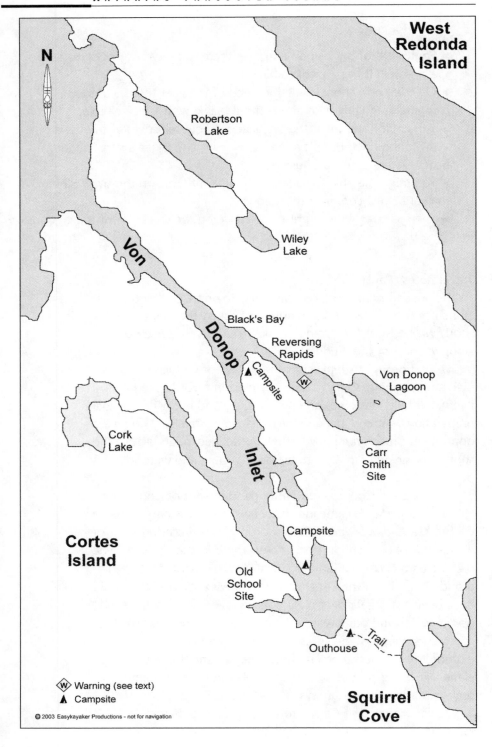

Gary with Penn Islands in the distance

as a small group of Dall's porpoises surfaced and dove again. We lingered in the bay, hoping these sleek mammals would reappear. No sound, not an engine, a voice or even the wash of waves on shore, broke the silence for the next minute or two. Suddenly the porpoises surfaced again, exhaling a mist of water and air. We all heard a sound like a long exhaled breath and a slight splash.

I had my sprayskirt off for quick access to my camera in the dim hope of snapping a picture of this mammal, which can reach speeds of up to 55 km/hour (35 mph) and which often surfaces for only short periods. Though sightings are common, the porpoises are rarely photographed! They had unwittingly set me up for getting wet. Right after we saw these creatures, an odd set of breaking waves about 1 m (3.5 ft) high struck my kayak. Celia and Gary, just 10 m (32 ft) ahead of me, were hardly experiencing a ripple. It was a short moment of unexpected excitement. Why was this set of waves, generated by some distant boat, so narrow? Perhaps they had been clipped on both sides by reefs. The waves smashed across my bow and a small rain of sea water fell into my cockpit.

We soon reached the headland between Carrington and Quartz bays. The tidal current was strong enough to create eddies, but they scarcely shifted our kayaks as we paddled through. The tide was ebbing, so the current was heading south as we went north. Our intention was to reach the mouth of Von

Donop Inlet around low tide and ride the flood tide into the inlet.

The coarse-grained intrusive rock of the shoreline rises steeply from the water to be covered by thick forest along much of this coastline, especially between Carrington Bay and Von Donop Inlet. We were paddling during a reasonably low tide and paused infrequently to examine the multitude of sea life growing in crevices and cracks or on the rock walls. Bright green and white sea lettuce grew in some places. Purple starfish were plentiful and tucked away in the crevices.

Just after noon we beached our boats and consumed our lunches in a small cove inside the mouth of Von Donop Inlet.

The Reversing Rapids at low and high tides

After lunch we started paddling up Von Donop, scanning the east side of the inlet for caves. In her book *Destination Cortez Island*, June Cameron wrote that the First Nations people used the caves close to the inlet's mouth as burial sites.

Two km (1.2 mi) into the inlet we landed on shore below the rapids, known as the "Reversing Rapids," at the entrance to the huge lagoon. It was about 30 minutes after low tide and we stood nearly 1.5 m (5 ft) below the surface of the lagoon. The turbulent water shot over the rocks in a waterfall and emptied into the inlet. A cursory view of the lagoon piqued our curiosity, and we decided to return closer to high tide and poke around.

A few minutes later we were paddling past a low promontory just southwest of the lagoon entrance when I saw a picnic table and a small grassy knoll. "We should check this out," I yelled. Because it was quite a low tide, there was only a small landing spot between some sharp-edged rocks. Gary and Celia waited in their boats while I disembarked (with a slight grinding sound on my hull) and soon found a first-class camping site. We decided to carry on to the head of Von Donop in search of other possible locations.

The head of the inlet looks like an arrowhead—powerboats and sailboats are able to anchor in the tips of the arrowhead, which give them ideal protection against weather—and when we reached it, Gary set off counterclockwise and Celia and I headed clockwise, checking out other potential campsites.

Gary disappeared for a while. It turned out he had kayaked right into the mud flats at the northwest tip of the arrowhead where a stream, with fairly pronounced banks on a low tide, flows into the flats. Gary briefly reconnoitered the property surrounding the flats and noted hundreds of deer tracks and one set of wolf tracks. At one time a small pioneer community containing the Von Donop school, a homestead, and a logging camp was located here. In the mid-1930s there had also been an early oyster lease on the opposite side of the head of this inlet.

Celia had paddled past a bluff and around a high promontory to land on the north shore inside the head of the inlet. She arrived at the same time as a park ranger who was travelling to the various parks, hanging signs that said: "No Fires." He remarked that the place we had discovered earlier and the location she was standing on were the most popular camping spots.

I scouted the south shore of the arrowhead and found the trail to Squirrel Cove. The three of us met up in the southwest corner of the inlet at a small islet covered in tall grasses. It likely was the site of an old kitchen midden.

Satisfied that the first camping spot we saw (halfway up the inlet at the lagoon) was the best, we paddled vigorously back and set up our three tents near or under magnificent large cedars. Mine overlooked the inlet and was cushioned by a bed of moss. After an hour's rest, we decided it was time to uncover the secrets of the lagoon. This turned out to be a small adventure.

We approached the Reversing Rapids approximately 90 minutes before high tide. Though the tide was rising, the water was still draining from the lagoon. I estimated the current we had to paddle against was around 2 to 3 knots. To get through the rapids we had to paddle through two distinct sections: the first 10 m (32 ft) was a slight incline with the roughest deep currents; the second section, about 10 to 20 m (32 to 65 ft), was relatively level with a faster surface current.

Portaging rapids on our trip to Von Donop Inlet

Gary entered first and paddled vigorously against the fast current. A minute later he was positioned at the top of the first part and lightly hung onto a rock on the side for a brief rest. After a few moments he pushed off and easily paddled through the rest of the rapids. I almost duplicated Gary's path and effort. Celia entered the bubbling waters last and kayaked forcefully against the inclined rapids. After a short rest stop wedged against a rock, she made it through the Reversing Rapids with flying colours.

Later we learned that the rapids turned to slack about 15 minutes after we had gone through, but it wouldn't have been as much fun if we had waited. It was quite a treat to paddle over the abundant marine life in the rapids.

The reward for our moment of adventure was a lovely lagoon. Kingfishers chattered from their perches, grasshoppers sang, thrushes and warblers called, and small fish darted under our crafts. We explored the western shoreline of the lagoon. I alighted on a shore opposite the islet and found yet another large, level, grassy campsite behind a log.

The head of the lagoon was once home to Tom Marflett and Carr Smith. They raised chinchilla rabbits for fur and meat, and also used the rabbits to clear stumps. Marflett and Smith would put the rabbits in an enclosed area, and the rabbits would dig under the stumps in the enclosure. Later the pen would be moved to a new place and the stumps would be burned out. There was a trail from Carr Smith's place to Squirrel Cove.

Calm waters inside lagoon, where we found a perfect grassy campsite.

In the late 1940s, five killer whales came into the lagoon and stayed for a length of time. Unfortunately theirs was not a happy ending due to people's attitude toward these creatures at that time—the five were shot by rifle from shore. It's hard to imagine them fitting through the Reversing Rapids, but some fair-sized boats have also made it through this passage.

We paddled around the head of the lagoon and along the east shore but were cut off by a mud flat. By the time we returned to the Reversing Rapids the inlet was flooding into the lagoon. All three of us attacked the currents. We made reasonable headway but eventually were stopped by the current. I turned and crossed to the west side of the rapids while Gary and Celia stayed on the east shore to rest. Gary pushed off, got swung around by the current, crossed over and then paddled up the west shore to where I was stopped.

I had come to a small nook in the rocky, barnacled shoreline and eased my kayak onto a level boulder. Soon afterward Gary arrived and we lifted our boats onto the rocks. Celia, still on the east shore, had become jammed into an alcove, but managed to get out of her boat safely. She tried to pull her kayak through the currents along this shore, but her towline was a bit too short to stretch from the shore to the water. The roar of the rapids was near deafening, but with hand signals we indicated Celia should paddle across to the shore we were on. Later we watched an older couple land on the eastern shore and guide their small Zodiac through the rapids with a line. Just as they made it to the far end of the rapids, both of them fell into the water. They had a hearty laugh and obviously a quick bath before they motored away.

We portaged our kayaks across the rocks, stepping in crevices and on the occasional sharp edge of a rock. I had thin soles on my beach boots and felt every footstep. I would not want to portage fully loaded boats across this area, but it can be done. Finally we launched from small pools into a light current, quite happy to have our adventure over.

Back at our campsite we relaxed for a while and then cooked dinner. Elsa and Imants, a couple from a nearby sailboat, landed at our camp with their cat. They took the curious creature for a walk into the forest and returned about 45 minutes later for a chat. They told us about a hike to Wiley Lake, pointing to an old road on the east shore of Von Donop Inlet that led to the lake.

Their cat sat staring wide-eyed into the forest. An orange-bellied squirrel had inquisitively approached our camp and peeked at us from its foothold on the trunk of a Douglas fir. I'm a cat-lover and enjoyed watching the feline study the squirrel and the unfamiliar settings. It turned out this was a city cat who had lived in the confines of a house in Port Townsend and never been on a sailboat before, let alone out in the wilderness!

After they left Gary, Celia and I watched the sun dip behind the trees. A swath of light ran from the sea beyond the mouth of the inlet onto our campsite. Our location would have been ideal for a First Nations camp, as people could have easily seen a warring tribe entering the mouth of Ha'thayim even at dusk. Though the distance from Coulter Bay to our campsite was only 10 km (6.3 mi), we had actually paddled around 24 km (14.9 mi) during the day and were weary. We headed to bed as the last of the evening light reflected in the wash of a small powerboat cruising by on the far shore.

Time to reflect. View from our campsite.

On both evenings at our camp I could hear the bullfrog sound of nighthawks very clearly. The nighthawk, also known as "bullbat," "mosquito hawk," and a slew of other names, is a summer visitor to Canada, arriving from its winter haunt around late May and staying until late August. Its food consists mostly of insects and it prefers a timbered area for its habitat. It is not a nocturnal bird but hunts in the early morning, the evening or during cloudy weather, returning to its nest soon after dark. I believe we heard it through the early night because the moon was full. A few times during the night Gary could hear its nasal "peent" call. The bullfrog sound it makes comes from the roar of its wings. The nighthawk is an aerial artist, much like a falcon, and is a member of the goatsucker family of birds.

Gary, who was camped farther into the forest than Celia or I, also heard the Reversing Rapids change direction once or twice throughout the night.

I was awakened early the next morning by the call of a loon and was soon sipping my coffee, feasting on the beauty of the inlet and surrounding wilderness. The water was so still and clear that the reflection of one sailboat with blue sail-covers anchored near our campsite seemed like two ships.

Around 8:00 a.m. we decided to walk to the rapids. The trail from camp to the rapids was quite good except for the stretch down the bank. The tide was fairly low when we arrived, which gave us the opportunity to inspect the sea life more closely. We saw several types of anemones, the five-arm leather star and crabs. People have also sighted octopus and other creatures here.

We launched mid-morning and paddled over to say hello to Elsa, Imants and their cat. They were going to hike to Wiley Lake and we asked them to keep track of the time it took.

We paddled the 3.5 km (2.2 mi) back to the head of the inlet, beached our kayaks by the Squirrel Cove trail sign and were soon gallivanting up the hillside to the cove. The trail levelled off after a quick rise and dropped slowly toward the cove. In places the well-trodden footpath weaved amidst a sparse, alder forest. I remarked to Gary that the trail seemed more like a well-groomed route through Stanley Park than a wilderness hike.

The three of us reached a finger of Squirrel Cove that was mostly mud flats at low tide. We crossed the mud and walked along an oyster-laden shore for a few minutes. Across the finger on the western shoreline we could see Marilyn's Salmon Café, where traditional First Nations food is served. It's only open from July until mid-August.

We hiked back to our kayaks and returned to our campsite, arriving just as Elsa and Imants reached Black's Bay (named after early settlers William Reid Black and his wife, who built a log cabin here in 1929 and passed it to their son, William Black, in 1950). Gary paddled over to get the specifics on the trek to Wiley Lake. The sailing couple referred to it as "heaven," which was enough for us. After catching our breath we cruised across to Black's Bay (just a minute or two away) and started our hike.

The logging road is clearly visible from the beach. What we didn't know is that this is private property. We learned this when we were doing our research at the Cortes Archives. There is an official BC Parks trail that starts from the little cove about 1 km (0.6 mi) north of the mouth of Von Donop Inlet. That trail goes along Robertson Lake and then to Wiley Lake.

The trail we took followed the logging road up the hill for 6 or 7 minutes from Black's Bay. Then we turned onto a small flagged trail to the left. It has also been marked with a rock arrow on the ground and the occasional rock pile. The trail initially winds through some thick underbrush and then opens up into a well-spaced forest. We continued hiking along the winding trail, keeping track of the orange and sometimes pink flagging, for another 25 to 30 minutes. As we neared the lake we saw the log float at the lake's edge that Imants had described. With much aplomb Gary and I dove (belly-flopped, really) into the refreshing yet warm lake; Celia made a much more graceful dive. The air temperature was around 30° Celsius, so the lake was the answer to our prayers.

Old logging winch, an essential piece of equipment for early loggers and settlers.

On our way back we discovered, just in from the edge of Black's Bay, a rusted logging winch near the bottom of the logging road. It was a couple of metres into the salal. A newer engine with an aluminum block was lying on the ground below it. I believe that winches like this were one of the handiest pieces of equipment for early loggers and settlers. They used the winches to haul homes and trucks from floats, drag massive old-growth trees from the shoreline forest to the water and lug everything uphill and across the land. It was dangerous work.

We joined Elsa and Imants for a beer in their boat's cabin, then had dinner back at our camp. Finally, I settled into my chair with a novel. A few minutes later the sun sank below the western shore, casting dark shadows across the inlet. A low, reflected light from the sun washed through the inlet mouth and lit our camp enough to read by.

As the evening light disappeared we heard the occasional nighthawk calling from the far shore of the inlet. Then we heard a huge splash near the mouth—sound carried remarkably well across the still water. We speculated that it was either sea lions or porpoises. Then I thought I saw a large gray body break the water, but our only light was the last slivers of dusk and the contrast between the dark sea and the breaking wake from the animal. Gary had grabbed his monocular, but we still couldn't distinguish our twilight creature.

The next morning we packed quickly and launched about 9:00 a.m. since Celia had to catch the 11:50 a.m. ferry from Whaletown. As we approached the mouth of the inlet we saw a splash again, but it was a bit too far away to identify what caused it. I swear that animal did this on purpose to keep us guessing.

We were able to travel close to the coastline much of the way back and managed to keep out of the hot rising sun. We saw Dall's porpoises again near Carrington Bay and enjoyed the sparkling calm waters on our return trip. Two hours after leaving camp we pushed ashore at Coulter Bay, quickly unpacked, tied our kayaks on the truck and returned Celia to her car with half an hour to spare.

Local History

Captains Valdes and Galiano, Spanish explorers, named Cortes Island after Hernán Cortés (1485–1547), the Spanish conquistador who destroyed the Aztec empire of Mexico. Before the Spanish arrived, however, the Klahoose people inhabited Cortes Island. Most of them now live in Squirrel Cove, but originally they occupied a greater territory including both coasts of Cortes Island. Their population suffered from raiding tribes and the smallpox epidemic of 1862. The band is currently negotiating a treaty with the BC government and has been working with the Cortes Ecoforestry Society to obtain tenure over the industrial forestlands of Cortes in order to create a community forest.

A shallow lagoon at the head of Von Donop Inlet was known as Tl'itl'aamin, "a small place that you head towards." Young Klahoose women would shake clam rattles to scare porpoises into the shallows here, where the young men wrestled them onto the beach to prove their manhood.

By the late 1800s, white people were coming to the island. The Dawson Whaling Company set up a plant at Whaletown in 1869. It took 22 hump-back whales between early June and late December—this was considered quite successful. The whales were processed for their blubber and whalebone (baleen). The whaling operation was moved to Hornby Island the next year.

Over the next half-century the island was settled by Old World pioneers who came on coastal steamers to farm and log the land. They built home-steads, planted orchards and drove trails and roads across the island. Some started oyster farms while others were whalers, fishermen or loggers, often taking these jobs to support a family and farm. Their stories are sometimes revealed by island place names or by remnants left on overgrown pieces of the island—an old trail, the rotting timber of a pioneer home or a rusted logging winch.

Mansons Landing was one of the first areas settled on Cortes. Michael Manson ran a trading post around 1886 and swapped supplies for dogfish oil from the First Nations people. He shipped the oil to Nanaimo to be used as a lubricant for machinery in the coal mines. In the late 1800s a diphtheria epi-demic killed five of the six Manson children including a newborn baby. Jane Manson survived the disease just after giving birth in a hospital, then returned to a near-empty home and raised a new family (including two sets of twins).

In the 1930s, Henry Byers owned the land on which Gary, Celia and I camped. Byers logged huge old-growth cedar at the head of Von Donop and on Carr Smith's place (at the head of the lagoon) in 1925 and 1926. These were still the years when individual loggers could make a living. In 1939 five families, including Henry and Ruth Byers, their son Clarence and his wife Etta, and three others, moved to Von Donop, bringing five homes on separate floats chained together and pulled by a tug.

Seven years later there were enough children to open Von Donop School, which operated from 1946 till 1952. Winter conditions made it too difficult to travel to Whaletown (where the old Whaletown School is now an art gallery). Violet Herrewig taught in the log schoolhouse from 1947 until 1950. The school was condemned in June 1950 because it was claimed to be hazardous to life! A new school was floated in but was closed in 1952 due to low enrollment.

Beaver Harbour (Fort Rupert)

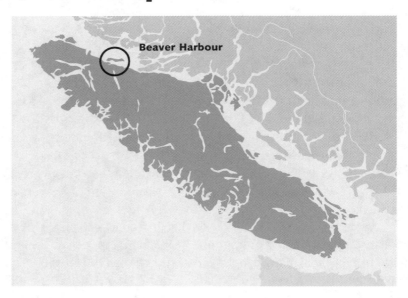

Beaver Harbour

Just east of Port Hardy, Fort Rupert was built by the Hudson's Bay Company on the shores of Beaver Harbour in 1849 after coal was discovered in the area. Mining operations were not successful, and soon the coal miners were relocated to Nanaimo. Today the area hosts a small mixed Native and non-Native community whose roots extend back to the days of the fort.

The area's annual precipitation is 177 cm (70 inches), approximately twice the amount Nanaimo receives. Fortunately for summertime kayakers, most of the rain in the north falls during the winter months.

For those of you who end up here on a day too windy to paddle, the Tex Lyon trail to Dillon Point is a great alternative excursion, a 7-km (4.3-mi) round trip. Because a rock bluff at the start of the trail near the north end of Storey's Beach makes a beach crossing necessary, you should probably do this hike on a falling (ebb) tide. Midway along the trail is Basket Eaters' Cove, named when one family tried to outdo another by claiming, "We harvested so many clams that they ate the bottom out of the baskets before we could get them home." There's a picnic site with tables at the end of the trail at Dillon Point. You can also access both these spots by kayak when the weather co-operates.

Difficulty levels: Beaver Harbour area: Novice to Intermediate

Approximate travel times: Beaver Harbour area: Half day to multiple day

Approximate distances:
- ➤ Storey's Beach to Peel Island: 4.5 km (2.8 mi) round trip
- ➤ Peel Island to Deer Island: 1.25 km (0.8 mi) one way
- ➤ Deer Island to Cattle Islands: 1 km (0.6 mi) one way
- ➤ Storey's Beach to Dillon Point: 8.5 km (5.3 mi) round trip
- ➤ Boat ramp on Hardy Bay to Dillon Point: 11 km (6.8 mi) round trip

CHS chart: 3548—Queen Charlotte Strait (Central portion)

Tidal reference port: Alert Bay

Weather and sea conditions reference:
- ➤ Scarlett Point
- ➤ Herbert Island
- ➤ Pulteney Point
- ➤ Queen Charlotte Strait

Prevailing winds: Northwesterlies and southeasterlies

Paul in Queen Charlotte Strait

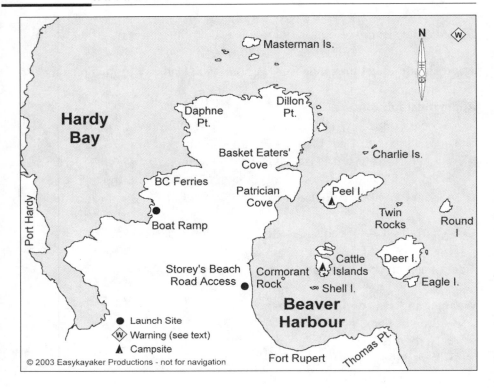

© 2003 Easykayaker Productions - not for navigation

Warnings:

> ➤ Queen Charlotte Strait is subject to storm conditions.

> ➤ Deer and Eagle islands are First Nations land—you will need permission to land on the beaches.

> ➤ There is a healthy population of black bears in the Port Hardy area—be bear smart.

> ➤ There are also a high number of cougars in this area. Some attacks on humans have occurred in outlying areas—children are at greatest risk.

Getting there/launching: Port Hardy is approximately six hours' drive north of Victoria on Highway 19. You'll get to Beaver Harbour by taking the Highway 19 connector just south of Port Hardy toward the airport. Take the connector to Bing Road. Turn left on Beaver Harbour Road and follow it to Scotia Road. Turn right. The recommended beach access is at the corner of Scotia and Storey's Beach Road. You can also launch from the Port Hardy boat ramp, which is on Bear Cove Highway, the road to the ferries. Bear Cove Highway turns off Highway 19 south of Port Hardy.

Paul getting ready at Storey's Beach launch site.

Accommodations: Numerous motels, hotels and B&Bs. The Port Hardy Visitor Information Centre run by the Chamber of Commerce is open year-round. Phone 250-949-7622, e-mail *phcc@island.net* or visit the web site at *www.ph-chamber.bc.ca.*

Camping:

➤ Peel and Cattle islands: There are campsites on these islands in Beaver Harbour.

➤ Quatse River Campground: From Port Hardy, follow Highway 19 south to Coal Harbour Road and turn right, following the signs. For reservations phone 250-949-2395.

➤ Sunny Sanctuary Campground: About 3 km (1.9 mi) south of Port Hardy on Highway 19 turn left at the "Big Logger." For reservations phone 250-949-8111.

Travel notes (Paul)

Gary and I arrived at Storey's Beach Road fairly early in the morning. There were light clouds high above amid teasing slivers of blue sky. We had checked out the launch site the evening before at a reasonably high tide. Now, at low tide, the beach seemed to stretch to Cormorant Rock. We quickly took our boats off the trailer, prepared them for the trip and half-heartedly began the walk to the water's edge. Our only consolation was that the kayaking distance to the nearby islands was reduced, but paddling a Solstice GT is always preferable to carrying it.

When we finally reached the water's edge we paddled to Cormorant Rock—a big rock sitting in 9 to 16 m (30 to 50 ft) of water. It loomed high above the low tide and appeared even taller due to the marine navigation sign rising from a concrete foundation at the top of the rock. Perched on the sign was a bald eagle scanning the harbour intently. We snapped several pictures of it and then paddled north toward the Cattle Islands. Small silver-backed fish (likely smolt salmon) leapt intermittently into the air. The chances of a fish landing on my sprayskirt seemed high.

I was smitten by Beaver Harbour and its islands only minutes into our day's paddling adventure. Perhaps I've developed an intuition after visiting so many Vancouver Island kayaking spots, but I knew today was going to be special.

As we neared the southwest cove on Peel Island we saw a tall fellow stand up and walk down to the rocks. The large pebble beach sloped quickly down to a number of jagged rocks that were partially exposed during the low tide. Pat Kervin of Odyssey Kayaking had told us that his brother and sister-in-law, Mike and Adrienne, were camping in the islands, and we figured we'd found them. With a quick exchange of greetings Mike helped us dry beach our boats, and we joined him and Adrienne on the beach. Adrienne made us cappuccino while Gary brought out his deluxe trail mix with chocolate raisins, smarties (no purple ones!) and other ingredients. We feasted sitting on logs and camp chairs. After an amiable chat Gary and I launched our crafts and headed

Kayaking companions. A curious seal pup and mother kept an eye on us.

clockwise around Peel Island. The forecast had predicted wind from the northwest. It didn't arrive, but we had intended to use this wind for a free ride or at least to avoid battling it head-on.

A colony of seals inhabits Beaver Harbour. Along the north end of Peel Island we sighted several mother seals, each accompanied by a pup. I whistled and called to them while they gingerly followed us. The abundance of seals answered the question why fish leapt as high as a metre above the water. I still hoped a fish or two would land directly on my sprayskirt.

After rounding Peel Island, we caught a glimpse of a ship heading into Beaver Harbour. It had the classic lines of a North Sea trawler, but even from a distance we noticed a kind of shine to it. It looked much cleaner than other large old trawlers we had seen. After a moment it disappeared behind the Cattle Islands. What was it doing in Beaver Harbour?

Gary and I quietly paddled to Twin Rocks to observe two very young bald eagles standing stoically on a large flat rock, infrequently shaking their tail feathers. We stopped at a respectable distance in the midst of a bed of bull kelp to watch the birds. One eagle took flight and left the other standing unperturbed. We bobbed in the kelp, enjoying the behaviour of the young eagle as it watched us and the surrounding waters. Suddenly a seal head popped above the surface between the eagle and us. Unaware of our kayaks only a short distance away, the seal began spying on the eagle. Once or twice the eagle cocked its head like a curious puppy watching or listening to a new sight or sound.

A few minutes later a second seal popped up between our kayaks, saw us and did a panic dive, breaking the spell, so we dipped our paddles and started to kayak across to Deer Island. We travelled along Deer's eastern shore and then south past the outside of Eagle Island. The area by Eagle Island is a great spot to observe marine birds. As well, a humpback whale had spent 90 days in this particular stretch of water the previous summer, and though we knew it was wishful thinking, we hoped to see a humpback, a grey or even a minke whale.

Wishes led to seeing things, real and imagined. Gary saw a dark object floating a few hundred metres away and yelled, "What's that?" I focused my 50-year-old eyes, squinted and replied, "It's a log." Seconds later Gary saw porpoises swimming swiftly about 100 m away. We kayaked in their general direction to try and get a photo, but they were elusive and swift. We saw them twice more that afternoon.

A little disappointed at not viewing a whale of any kind, we paddled vigorously toward the Cattle Islands to explore and look for future camping spots. As we passed between Shell and Cattle islands, the curved outline of the former North Sea trawler came into view. Its dark green hull contrasted perfectly with white cabins and decks. Gary called out, "It's the *Curve of Time*."

The Curve of Time *was once owned by* Greenpeace *and crossed the Atlantic four times under the name* Moby Dick *before being purchased and renamed by Due West Charters.*

We paddled to the ship to greet the two people on deck. The skipper, Jan Bevelander, and a summer deckhand/cook, leaned over the gunwale. I didn't recognize the deckhand immediately when she said, "Hi Paul," and when I was silent a little too long she added, "It's me, Katya." I clued in pretty fast then, recognizing a colleague who teaches primary French immersion in Nanaimo.

They invited us on board for coffee and muffins, and we entered a spacious galley decorated with panelled walls, bookcases, paintings, and a huge dining table. The inside of the ship was as immaculate as the exterior. Jan owns the *Curve of Time* and operates it as a kayaking mothership for his company, Due West Charters. It has sleeping accommodations for 16 people including crew. Its unusual name comes from a classic BC coast book, *The Curve of Time*, by M. Wylie Blanchet. In the book Blanchet remembers the summers she spent sailing and camping with her five children along British Columbia's coast in the 1920s and 1930s. They followed the routes of early European visitors to the coast and encountered tides, fogs, storms, bears and cougars.

Jan's *Curve of Time* has a history of its own. The ship was built in 1959 and worked as a commercial fishing boat until 1984, when it was bought by Greenpeace and renamed *Moby Dick*. Under this new identity it crossed the Atlantic four times and campaigned in Europe before it was purchased by Due West in 1997.

Gary and I returned to our kayaks and set off to continue our investigation of the Cattle Islands. We found a nice little beach on the west side of the largest of the three islands and landed there to check out the camping area. The island is fairly flat and we were impressed as soon as we stepped from the beach to the woods. There was almost no underbrush and the trees were huge for these parts. The forest floor was deeply littered with bark and needles, making it very soft underfoot. Visitors could set up many tents here without being on top of each other.

Beach on west side of the largest of the three Cattle Islands

From the Cattle Islands we paddled near Shell Island. I had heard a First Nations story that identified this island as the burial place of Haklath, a ritual slave-killer. Mean-spirited Haklath would cut off the heads of slaves and leave their corpses on the beach in front of the village to rot. This angered many of his own people and eventually they killed him. Unwilling to leave his headless body on their beach, they moved him to Shell Island. Some local First Nations people will not set foot on this island even today.

All good things must end, and we reluctantly returned to our launch site on Storey's Beach Road. The tide was high so we were able to paddle our boats almost to the truck and load them on quickly—minutes later we were driving to Port Hardy, where Gary met with Debbie from North Island Kayaks while I completed some research in the downtown museum.

Local History

Native people first arrived at Beaver Harbour about 6,000 years ago, drawn by an abundance of food, a moderate climate and close proximity to the West Coast by way of Quatsino Sound, which placed them in the middle of an east-west corridor for trade. The resulting healthy economy helped shape the Kwakiutl people, who for thousands of years developed complex systems of art, warfare, and social organization.

Today the Kwakiutl are recognized for their remarkable building and artistic skills. They carved cedar canoes up to 21 m (70 ft) in length that were capable of carrying 50 people. The same cedar was used to build longhouses that each housed several families. The wood was so versatile that it could be fashioned into pots, spoons, bowls, baskets, mats and clothing. The inner bark of the cedar was used to create waterproof hats and capes—necessities for the North Island's inclement weather and for Kwakiutl voyages in their ocean-going canoes.

Food was plentiful in the sea, along the shoreline and on land. The abundance of clams must have been evident to the Europeans when they arrived on the shores of Beaver Harbour in the mid-19th century—they were greeted by a mountain of clamshells that was 3 km (2 mi) long, 0.8 km (0.5 mi) wide and 15 m (50 ft) high.

As more and more steamships arrived on the west coast of North America, the need for an accessible coal supply grew. It took nearly nine months for a ship to travel from the British Isles to Vancouver Island, and it was impractical for ships to transport coal for their return voyages. Coal was discovered near Beaver Harbour in 1835, and the Hudson's Bay Company (HBC) built Fort Rupert there in 1849 when it sent men up to mine the coal.

A village of 3,000 Kwakiutl sprang up on the beach near the fort as the Natives gathered to trade furs and salted or smoked salmon for other goods. The Kwakiutl were also often employed to clear land and chop firewood in exchange for seven to nine sticks of tobacco a day.

The few whites at the fort were wary of the numbers of Natives surrounding them, and tensions escalated when three HBC deserters (they had jumped ship in hopes of reaching the California goldfields) were murdered, likely by a warrior group from the Nahwitty First Nation. The murders caused a major panic amongst the Europeans, especially when the Nahwitty taunted the occupants of the fort by climbing up the walls and jeering from the top.

The Nahwitty had thought the deserters were like runaway slaves and that murder was a socially acceptable course of action. In later negotiations the Nahwitty chief offered to pay compensation for their deaths, a common method of handling disputes. Instead, British marines were sent in to shell and burn the Native village. However, the Nahwitty had already deserted it.

About ten months later a gunboat with 60 marines stormed a rebuilt village upcoast from Fort Rupert and destroyed it. The Nahwitty gave in after the destruction of their second village and presented the British with three bodies claimed to be the murderers.

Little coal was ever found in the Fort Rupert area, and tensions grew between European managers and employees as well as between Natives and non-Natives. The immigrant Scottish miners initially worked building living quarters within the fort and sinking pits in search of coal seams. The Scots were a proud group and resented the menial chores they were assigned. Finally, poor mining conditions, the attractive gold strike in California (where men earned three times the regular wages), the isolation of Fort Rupert, resentment and imposed fines lead to a strike. Two men, Andrew Muir and John McGregor, were shackled and thrown into the fort's bastion for refusing to work.

Eventually Dr. John Helmcken arrived to mediate. Helmcken had been appointed magistrate for the newly formed Crown Colony of Vancouver Island, and the colony's governor, Richard Blanshard, hoped Helmcken could restore order at the fort. The dispute was never settled, however, and ended when the two men slipped out of Beaver Harbour and made their way to Oregon. When a better grade and greater quantity of coal was discovered in Nanaimo the HBC quickly transferred its mining operation there.

The influx of Europeans over the next decades decimated the Kwakiutl population from a high of 20,000 in 1836 to 1,088 people in 1927. Smallpox in particular ravaged these proud people.

Epilogue

Gary and I have paddled dozens of trips around Vancouver Island from Victoria to Port Hardy. Each time we've discovered something special—whether it's an unusual call from a night hawk or a magical moment of stillness during an evening paddle. And there are so many more paddling trips and places around Vancouver Island to discover and enjoy!

One winter's day about four years ago I stood next to the Fort Rupert Band's longhouse and gazed over the water at the white beaches and small islands of Beaver Harbour, wondering what it would be like to paddle there. That thought soon led to the question of *when* I would get an opportunity to paddle this incredibly beautiful area. Writing this book has given Paul and me the reason and motivation to visit this and so many other wonderful areas around Vancouver Island. We are often asked which are our favourites—they all are, especially when the sun is shinning and winds are calm.

Happy Paddling!
Gary Backlund
Paul Grey

Further reading

Backroad Mapbook, Volume II: Vancouver Island, Mussio Ventures Ltd., 1997

British Columbia road & recreational atlas, Phototype Composing Ltd., 2001

Blades, Michael. *Day of Two Sunsets, Paddling Adventures on Canada's West Coast,* Orca Book Publishers, 1993

BC Marine Parks Guide, OP Publishing Ltd., 1999

British Columbia Approved Accommodation 2002 Guide, OP Publishing, 2002

Cameron, June. *Destination Cortez Island: A sailor's life along the BC coast,* Heritage House Publishing Co., 1999

Douglass, Don. *Exploring Vancouver Island's West Coast, a Cruising Guide,* Fine Edge Productions, 1994

Nicholson, George. *Vancouver Island's West Coast, 1762- 1962,* Morriss Printing Co., 1962

Government of Canada, Ministry of Fisheries and Oceans, *Sailing Directions: British Columbia Coast (South Portion) 2003*

Grey, Paul & Backlund, Gary. *Easykayaker, a guide to laid-back Vancouver Island Paddling,* Greyswan Publications, 2001

Lyons, C.P. *Trees, Shrubs & Flowers to Know in British Columbia & Washington,* Lone Pine, 1995

Jones, Elaine. *The Northern Gulf Islands Explorer: The Outdoor Guide,* Whitecap Books, 1991

Meares Island, Protecting a Natural Paradise, Friends of Clayoquot Sound and Western Canada Wilderness Committee, 1985

Kayak Routes of the Pacific NorthWest Coast, edited by Peter McGee, Greystone Books, 1998

Oliphant, John. *Brother Twelve: the Incredible Story of Canada's False Prophet,* McClelland & Stewart, 1991

Paterson, T.W. & Basque, Garnet. *Ghost Towns and Mining Camps of Vancouver Island,* Sunfire Publications Ltd., 1989

Pojar, Jim & MacKinnon, Andy. *Plants of Coastal British Columbia including Washington, Oregon & Alaska,* Lone Pine, 1994

Scott, R. Bruce. *Bamfield Years: Recollections,* Sono Nis Press, 1986

Scott, R. Bruce, Illustrated by Scott, Susan M. *People of the Southwest Coast of Vancouver Island,* Morriss Printing Co. 1974

Streetly, Joanna. *Paddling through Time,* Raincoast Books, 2000

Snowden, Mary Ann. *Island Paddling,* Orca Book Publishers, 1997

Tofino Insider's Guide 5th edition, 2001

Wave~Length Paddling Magazine, edited by Alan Wilson, issues from April 1997 to August 2002

Wolferstan, Bill. *Cruising guide to the Gulf Islands and Vancouver Island from Sooke to Courtenay,* Interpress Publications, 1976

Yorath, C.J & Nasmith, H.W. *The Geology of Southern Vancouver Island,* Orca Book Publishers, 1995

Additional Reading from Harbour Publishing

The Beachcomber's Guide to Seashore Life in the Pacific Northwest
by J. Duane Sept
5.5" x 8.5" • 240 pages, 500 colour photos • 1-55017-204-2 • $21.95
274 of the most common animals and plants found along the saltwater
shores of the Pacific Northwest are described in this book. Illustrating each
entry is a colour photo of the species in its natural habitat.

Coastal Villages by Liv Kennedy
9" x 12" • 176 pages, photos throughout • 1-55017-057-0 • $42.95
Fascinating local history and more than 300 photographs, from archival photos to lush contemporary images of BC's picturesque coastal villages.

Exploring the BC Coast by Car by Diane Eaton and Alison Eaton
5.5" x 8.5" • 400 pages, 150 photos, 50 maps • 1-55017-178-X • $22.95
This indispensable book shows how you can use BC's world-class ferry and
coastal road system to reach the coast's most spectacular places in the comfort of your family car.

Paddling The Sunshine Coast by Dorothy and Bodhi Drope
5.5" x 8.5" • 192 pages, 40 photos, illustrations and maps •
1-55017-164-X • $17.95
This book will introduce both new and experienced sea kayakers to the
matchless paddling opportunities of the Sunshine Coast, from Howe Sound
in the south to Desolation Sound in the north, including Sechelt Inlet, the
islands of Georgia Strait and Jervis Inlet.

Jedediah Days: One Woman's Island Paradise by Mary Palmer
6" x 9" • 224 pages, 100 photos • 1-55017-184-4 • $26.95
For 45 years, Mary Palmer was owner of Jedediah Island, a picturesque 640-
acre jewel in British Columbia's Strait of Georgia. This book is her story, a
wonderful tapestry of life on the island between 1949 and 1994.

Pacific Reef and Shore: A Photo Guide to Northwest Marine Life
by Rick M. Harbo
5.5" x 8.5" • 80 pages, 300 colour photos • 1-55017-304-9 • $9.95
A brilliant full-colour field guide to the marine life of coastal British
Columbia, Alaska, Washington, Oregon and northern California is perfect
for divers, boaters, beachwalkers and snorkellers. The successor to Harbo's
1980 bestseller Tidepool and Reef.

Pacific Seaweeds: A Guide to Common Seaweeds of the West Coast
by Louis Druehl
5.5" x 8.5" • 192 pages, 80 colour photos, illustrations • 1-55017-240-9 • $24.95
The authoritative guide to over 100 common species of seaweed. Includes interesting facts, scientific information and tasty recipes.

Salt Spring by Charles Kahn
6" x 9" • 344 pages, 150 photos • 1-155017-262-X • $24.95
Chronicles the island's rich history through some 150 years of settlement by many diverse groups. This is the engaging and thoroughly researched story of all these special people, and the very special palce they called home.

Shells and Shellfish of the Pacific Northwest by Rick M. Harbo
5.5" x 8.5" • 272 pages, 350 colour photos • 1-55017-146-1 • $24.95
This easy-to-follow, full-colour guide introduces more than 250 species of mollusks found along the beaches and shallow waters of the Pacific Northwest.

Visions of the Wild by Maria Coffey and Dag Goering
8" x 9.5" • 182 pages, colour photos • 1-155017-264-6 • $36.95
Brimming with breathtaking colour photographs and compelling journal entries from all stages of their three-month kayaking journey, this book is at once an inspiring chronicle of an adventure of a lifetime, and a beautiful book of photographs that rejoices in the untamed spirit of Canada's West Coast.

Where to See Wildlife on Vancouver Island by Kim Goldberg
5.5" x 8.5" • 174 pages, 100 colour photos • 1-55017-160-7 • $20.95
Info-packed and user-friendly, this guide introducess the 50 best wildlife viewing hot spots on Vancouver Island, from the busy Victoria waterfront to Nanaimo's Buttertubs Marsh to "Gator Gardens" in Alert Bay.

Whales of the West Coast by David A.E. Spalding
6" x 9" • 256 pages, 100 photos • 1-55017-199-2 • $18.95
Huge, powerful, intelligent and beautiful, whales have fascinated human beings for millennia. From the better-known orcas, greys and humpbacks to porpoises, blue whales and sperm whales.

Whelks to Whales: Coastal Marine Life of the Pacific Northwest
by Rick M. Harbo
5.5" x 8.5" • 248 pages, 500 colour photos • 1-55017-183-6 • $24.95
This full-colour field guide to the marine life of coastal British Columbia, Alaska, Washington, Oregon and northern California is perfect for divers, boaters, beachwalkers and snorkellers.